Praise for *Warriors for Liberty*

"*Warriors for Liberty* is a multifaceted gem that sparkles with both the individual story of the remarkable, formerly enslaved William Dollarson and the collective story of resistance to slavery in antebellum Michigan. It illuminates Dollarson's extraordinary fight against American slavery, which began with his own escape from enslavement, continued as he built a life for himself and his family, and intensified when war came and the elderly man risked his own life and family's security to join the military destruction of slavery by serving as Union Army cook. Moreover, *Warriors for Liberty* roots Dollarson's story of conviction and resistance in a rich antebellum history of abolitionism and free Black activism in Michigan."

Chandra Manning is professor of history, Georgetown University, winner of the Avery O. Craven Prize from the Organization of American Historians for the most original book on the Civil War years, and expert on slavery and emancipation

"A marvelous saga of courage, *Warriors for Liberty* recalls to life the story of William Dollarson, a self-emancipated Black Virginian who rose to become the leader of Detroit's Black community before risking his life by serving in slaveholding Maryland or near Confederate lines while on the staff of General Alpheus S. Williams. Exhaustively researched and extremely well-written."

Douglas R. Egerton, author of *Thunder At the Gates: The Black Civil War Regiments That Redeemed America*, professor of history, LeMoyne College

"*Warriors for Liberty* shines a light on the stories of Black Michiganders during the Civil War—stories of immense bravery, heroism, and patriotism that have long been unsung. A valuable resource for researchers, educators, and Michigan history enthusiasts, it is also engaging and inspirational, a chance to glimpse the diverse lives of soldiers, officers, abolitionists, and countless everyday people who risked everything for freedom."

 Amy Elliot Bragg, Director of Education & Communications, Historic Elmwood Foundation, and author of *Hidden History of Detroit*

"Well written and very impressive. Citing sources is very important for historians, and the MCWA has done an excellent job here."

 Bryan Cheeseboro of the National Park Service is a historian/Park Ranger for the Civil War Defenses of Washington, DC. He is also a reenactor with the 54th Massachusetts Volunteer Infantry, and a social media leader at the Civil War Historian's Page on Facebook

"A most compelling story of Black Michiganders, who came from a range of backgrounds to fight for the Union to end the horrific practice of slavery. In *Warriors for Liberty*, we learn how Blacks who were free and escaped slaves, who volunteered and were drafted, filled the decimated ranks of Michigan and other states to become fierce fighters for freedom, with some 40,000 total perishing in the two years they fought. The book's research reveals how racial hatred reigned in both the Union and the Confederacy with Black folks fighting this evil on the battlefields of the South and streets of Detroit. It invites us to hear the voices of those soldiers, to understand their plight, and to stand with Black people today and for their ancestors."

 Steve Spreitzer is Co-Director of the Michigan Roundtable for Just Communities

"*Warriors for Liberty* uncovers the story of Michigan's African Americans during the Civil War. Beginning with the pre-war struggles for freedom, the volume explores the fight to get into the fight, and the ultimate wartime contributions of units like the 102nd U.S. Colored Troops. Homefront issues are covered also, including the

1863 Detroit riot and the role of African American women. Readers will find important excerpts from hard-to-find contemporaneous sources. A key source for investigating this important chapter in our state's history."

Roy E. Finkenbine is professor of history and co-chair, History Department, University of Detroit Mercy. He teaches courses in African American history, modern Africa, slave resistance, the Civil War era, and the Underground Railroad, and serves as Director of the Black Abolitionist Archive

"Fascinating and powerful."

Kimberly L. Simmons is recipient of the 2022 Michigan Humanities Champion of the Year award, Executive Director of the Detroit River Project, and a longtime advocate for telling the important histories of America

WARRIORS *for* LIBERTY

Publications of the
Michigan Civil War Association

Heart in Tatters: Eunice Hunt Tripler and the Civil War
His Sword a Scalpel: General Charles Stuart Tripler, MD, USA
Warriors for Liberty: William Dollarson & Michigan's Civil War African Americans

WARRIORS *for* LIBERTY

WILLIAM DOLLARSON &
MICHIGAN'S CIVIL WAR
AFRICAN AMERICANS

MICHIGAN CIVIL WAR ASSOCIATION

MISSION POINT PRESS

Copyright © 2024 by Michigan Civil War Association

All world rights reserved.

No part of this book may be reproduced, stored in a retrieval system, or transmitted in any form or by any means electronic, mechanical, photocopying, recording or otherwise, without the prior consent of the publisher.

Readers are encouraged to go to MissionPointPress.com to contact the author or to find information on how to buy this book in bulk at a discounted rate.

Published by Mission Point Press
2554 Chandler Rd.
Traverse City, MI 49696
(231) 421-9513
MissionPointPress.com

ISBN: 978-1-961302-78-5
Library of Congress Control Number: 2024911925

Printed in the United States of America

1st Michigan Colored Infantry. Painting by Stewart Ashlee (1929-2000). Courtesy Laura Rose Ashlee and Dean L. Anderson. Photography by Dave Thompson.

Third in a series

※ ※ ※

Proceeds from this volume benefit the Michigan Civil War Association in preserving and sharing Michigan's role during the American Civil War.

At the time of this publication, the MCWA is raising funds to erect a monument honoring Michigan's contributions to victory and to Emancipation at the Battle of Antietam,

Sept. 17, 1862.

※ ※ ※

The Michigan Civil War Association is a Michigan 501(c)(3) non-profit corporation.

Its corporate purpose is to pursue cultural, historical, and economic development opportunities to preserve and promote the history of Michigan's role in the American Civil War.

Founded in 2013, the MCWA has acted as a careful steward of all donations received.

More information is available at michigancivilwarassociation.org.

Board of Directors

Bradley M. Egen
Kalamazoo
Brian James Egen
Monroe
Will Eichler
Washington
David D. Finney Jr.
Carmel, Indiana
Margaret O'Brien
Portage
Jacqueline Tinney
Livonia
Matt VanAcker
Lansing
Jack Dempsey
Plymouth

Publications Committee

Margaret O'Brien
Matt VanAcker
Jack Dempsey

Editorial Consultant

Dr. Martin J. Hershock
Professor of History
Former Dean of College of Arts,
Sciences, and Letters
University of Michigan-Dearborn

Contents

Illustrations vii
Special Photo Essay viii
Preface xv
Foreword xxi
Introduction & Editorial Note xxvii

❋ ❋ ❋

Part One: A Culture of Liberty in a New Northern State 1
Part Two: William Dollarson from Virginia to Michigan 25
Part Three: The Riot of 1863 77
Part Four: The 1st Michigan Colored Regiment 105

❋ ❋ ❋

Aftermath 167
Appendix 183
Bibliography 229
Index 251
Acknowledgments 259

Illustrations Follow Part Two

1. 1st Michigan C.T. marker
2. 1968 marker dedication program
3. Dollarson gravestone
4. Old Capitol
5. Second Baptist Church
6. 54th Mass. Inf. monument
7. Kinchen Artis
8. Henry L. Chipman
9. Map of main combat area of the 102nd
10. Battle of Honey Hill
11. I-375 sign
12. John Brown Seminar program
13. Governor Certificate of Tribute
14. Beaufort cemetery
15. Capitol plaque
16. Map of escape to freedom

Special Photo Essay

On October 31, 1861, an unidentified photographer visited the camp of Brigadier-General A.S. Williams, commanding officer of the 3rd Brigade, Banks's Division, near Muddy Branch or Darnestown on the Maryland side of the Potomac River. The photographer produced three images, each slightly different. Others have not been discovered or inventoried.

One is held by the Gilder Lehrman Institute of American History. Designated as GLCO5111.01.0338, it portrays a temporary log structure or hut in the midst of several tents bordering a grove of trees. Several soldiers are mounted or holding their mounts. Other than identifying the scene as Williams's headquarters, and perhaps suggesting the General among the soldiers in the image, no identities are stated.

Photograph, Headquarters of Brig. Gen. Williams [3rd Brigade, Banks's Division]. 1861 ca. (*The Gilder Lehrman Institute of American History, GLCo5111.01.0338*)

The second is in the collection of the Carlisle Barracks a/k/a U.S. Army Heritage and Education Center. The image is darker than Gilder Lehrman's, but this photograph includes several identities and signatures: Williams in the center, flanked by Quartermaster Edward V. Preston, A.A.C.S. Edgar C. Beman, A.A.G. Wm. D. Wilkins, and Aide-de-Camp S.E. Pittman.

U.S. Army Heritage and Education Center

The third is an albumen photograph owned by the Michigan Civil War Association. Acquired in August 2023, this image is both rare and unique among period photographs. Its rarity derives from how it similarly identifies Williams and members of his staff, but here by

Albumen photograph of headquarters camp of Brigadier-General Alpheus S. Williams, showing guards, orderly, staffers—and William Dollarson, Muddy Branch, Md., Oct. 1861. *Michigan Civil War Association*

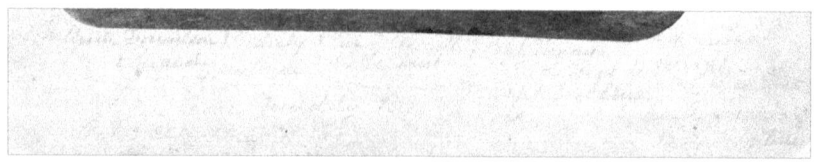

Detail of penciled identification on lower part of Muddy Branch photo; "Donnelson" is a misstatement for "Dollarson." *Michigan Civil War Association*

virtue of a numbering system keyed to the place and order of the persons in the print. Two close-ups from this image are also featured.

Its uniqueness is in this: it contains an image of William Dollarson, Detroit chef and civilian member of Williams's retinue, by name ("William Donnelson") and position within the photograph. To the MCWA's knowledge, no other Civil War photograph shows a person of African descent who was member of a General's inner circle. Moreover, this individual was self-emancipated and an escapee from the Deep South.

The MCWA's photograph is a national treasure. An artist's tribute is found below, before the Appendix.

Close-up of William Dollarson, self-freed ex-slave, Underground Railroad conductor, leader in Detroit's Black community, renowned chef, and volunteer on General Williams's staff, 1861-1862, within historic Muddy Branch photo. *Michigan Civil War Association*

In this green month when resurrected flowers,
Like laughing children ignorant of death,
Brighten the couch of those who wake no more,
Love and remembrance blossom in our hearts
For you who bore the extreme sharp pang for us,
And bought our freedom with your lives.

❈ ❈ ❈

American earth is richer for your bones;
Our hearts beat prouder for the blood we inherit.[1]

---

1. Dudley Randall, "Memorial Wreath" in Melba Joyce Boyd ed., *Roses and Revolutions: The Selected Writings of Dudley Randall* (Detroit: Wayne State University Press, 2009), 69.

This is essentially a people's contest — On the side of the Union, it is a struggle for maintaining in the world, that form, and substance of government, whose leading object is to elevate the condition of men — to lift artificial weights from all shoulders — to clear the paths of laudable pursuit for all — to afford all an unfettered start, and a fair chance, in the race of life — Yielding to partial, and temporary departures, from necessity, this is the leading object of the government for whose existence we contend —

As I would not be a slave, so I would not be a master. This expresses my idea of democracy—Whatever differs from this, to the extent of the difference, is no democracy —[2]

---

2. *Message to Congress*, July 4, 1861, Abraham Lincoln Papers, Manuscript Division, Library of Congress; handwritten note, Abraham Lincoln Presidential Library and Museum.

Preface

Virtually on the heels of Brigadier-General Chief Stand Watie (his Cherokee name was De-ga-ta-ga) surrendering the last Confederate force in the field, historians began to document, debate, and analyze the military aspects of America's bloodiest conflict. Even prior to when the muskets of the conflict quieted, soldiers erected monuments in the memory of their fallen comrades on the field.

Between June and October 1863, a detail of the 9th Indiana Infantry constructed what was to be known as the Hazen Monument—named after Colonel William B. Hazen whose brigade resisted four Confederate attacks on the first day of the battle at the Stones River battlefield in Tennessee.

The Patriots Monument on the Manassas Battlefield was dedicated on June 10, 1865, by a Union burial detail as one of their last actions prior to being discharged. Initially known as Decoration Day, Memorial Day's roots can be traced to 1868 when Major-General John A. Logan created a day for Union veterans wherein the graves of the fallen soldiers were decorated with laurel wreaths and flowers.

Several cities and towns claim to be the founder of "Memorial Day" but on May 1, 1865, nearly 10,000 formerly enslaved African Americans and some White missionaries paraded in recently Confederate evacuated Charleston, South Carolina, to honor the Union war dead. Accounts of African American children and ladies from the community decorating graves during this time illustrate the national effort to commemorate and memorialize the sacrifices made.

With millions of Civil War veterans returning to their communities—many bearing the physical and emotional scars of conflict—the preceding tsunami of grief lasted for generations. The collective memory of the nation was in large part allotted to these veterans and their military service. Although a warranted path to reconciliation and healing, the civilian experience and the lesser-known stories, especially of minorities, were relegated to the sidelines for decades.

The monumental outpouring of this veneration so critical in the process of reunification of the nation, so aptly said by Lincoln in his 2nd inaugural address "to bind up the nation's wounds," was eminent in a plethora of expressions in the postwar years. Veteran organizations such as the Grand Army of the Republic were created. Parades of nearly any occasion honored, with robust pomp and circumstance, survivors of the war. Battlefield sites were formally established and interpreted. Cities, towns, streets, military forts, and bases took on the names of Civil War participants. National reunions, that further helped to heal the schism, were hosted for Union and Confederate combatants. Battlefield relic souveniring, sometimes conducted during the battles, spurred a craze for magnificent exhibitions and even business ventures as a sector of the economy. Monuments, cemeteries, memorials, and other creations of commemorative remembrance became nomenclature of American society for generations.

Analysis and writings of the Civil War primarily focused on the campaigns and tactics, the military aspects of the conflict. Biographies, personal reminiscences, and general histories focused on higher ranking military personnel, politicians, notable personalities, and key events. This approach persisted well into the 20th Century up to the Civil War Centennial and in some cases like the National Park Service's Civil War sites, until the late 1990s.

The foundational and sustaining components of the collective memory were attributed to veterans, north and south, thus the acute focus on the military aspects of the conflict. The adherence to this collective memory remained poignantly prominent while the veterans remained as a part of the fabric of communities throughout the nation. As the veterans began to pass, attempts to keep their sacrifice foremost in the minds and hearts of subsequent generations emerged. The Sons of the Union Veterans, United Sons of Confederate Veterans, and various ladies' auxiliary groups took up the mantle providing advocacy and voice to those who could no longer speak.

The Civil War Centennial in the early 1960s brought about a deeper and more substantive look at a broader range of topics of this pivotal time. One example is the Michigan Civil War Centennial Observance Commission's series of books encompassing various topics, many of which were non-military. The themes, all focused on Michigan during the Civil War, included women, manufacturing, higher education, religion and faith-based organizations, agriculture, mining, and a myriad of other new source material of untold stories and impacts the conflict had on the state.

From their inception, interpretation at Civil War battlefield sites, understandably so, centered around who shot who, when, how, and where. Advocacy and preservation groups aided in this quest as they vehemently protected thousands of acres that ultimately added to the National Park Service's footprint at Civil War sites. As stewards and caretakers of these sacred places, their purpose was set and executed with alacrity, for over a century.

At the dedication of the 20th Massachusetts monument at Gettysburg in 1889, Joshua Chamberlain forecasted, with almost prophetic accuracy, what was to happen at these sites. In a poignant and powerful section of his remarks, he said:

> In great deeds something abides. On great fields something stays. Forms change and pass; bodies disappear, but spirits linger, to consecrate ground for the vision-place of souls. And reverent men and women from afar, and generations that know us not and that we know not of, heart-drawn to see where and by whom great things were suffered and done for them, shall come to this deathless field to ponder and dream; And lo! the shadow of a mighty presence shall wrap them in its bosom, and the power of the vision pass into their souls.

In the late 1990s the National Park Service began to receive criticism of their interpretation as being myopically focused on the military actions lacking the important aspect of cause and consequence and relevancy in visitors' lives. In 1998 a shift in interpretation commenced to include an expanded scope of relevance. The multi-year transformation was to provide broader perspectives that include civilian experience, States' rights, slavery, emancipation, constitutional amendments, and much more.

John Hennessey, retired Chief Historian for the Fredericksburg and Spotsylvania National Military Park, was instrumental in this transformation over his 40-year career in the National Park Service. In an article prior to the Sesquicentennial on this new interpretation he wrote, "The challenge faced by the National Park Service today is huge: to convey the significance and relevance of the Civil War while at the same time sustaining the Service's invaluable tradition of resource-based interpretation (a concept that is at the very foundation of the National Park Service mission) … To engage Americans in those sorts of conversations, the National Park Service needs to show the public that Civil War sites include more than just battlefields."

The Civil War Centennial saw the prolific emergence of public history and non-traditional professional historians. Civil War "buffs," "armchair historians," and living history enthusiasts began digging deep into other details and genres of Civil War history. The manifestation of this work has been shared through museums, living history demonstrations, Civil War Roundtables, publications, documentaries, movies, and other public history venues. Although many are based on military history, some of the best writings on the Civil War in recent years have been by attorneys, detectives, and law-enforcement individuals. History, at its core, is all detective work.

The wonderful result of this new research and deep dives into non-military histories is that previously untold voices and perspectives have emerged. Countless thousands of stories are yet to be explored— the core ingredients in sustaining a more wholistic collective memory of the distancing past.

The story of William Dollarson, a free African American from Detroit, is one of those otherwise incredible stories saved from the clutches of obscurity. Although much of Dollarson's story is attached to his service and association with General Alpheus S. Williams, it is one previously neglected, untold, and even passed over. Having self-emancipated and personally known the physical and emotional trauma of enslavement, he committed to supporting the Union as a member of General Williams's staff. Being so close to the front lines, and often in Confederate steeped regions, Dollarson assumed significant personal risk. Although he had not taken the oath for official military service, had he been captured by enemy hands he would have been killed or sent to the deep south. Even with constant threat of death or enslavement, Dollarson remained loyal in his support of the Union—and possibly more deeply motivated in defeating the Confederacy and crushing the evil system of slavery.

The Michigan Civil War Association strives to venerate the sacrifice and experience of Michiganders, especially of those that have yet to be shared. One of our previous works, *Heart in Tatters: Eunice Hunt Tripler and the Civil War*, allows us to hear the voice of a woman and her unparalleled experience. The value proposition of these efforts is that those of the past that would have previously been benched on the sidelines can now speak.

Through expertly researched publications, the Michigan Civil War Association has given an outlet for these incredible voices to be heard. Please allow the story of William Dollarson to inspire you and spark intrigue to learn more about the past. History is relevant and learning from it is crucial to navigate a better and more fulfilling tomorrow.

Tuebor!

—Brian James Egen
President, Michigan Civil War Association

Foreword

What is Freedom? According to the Oxford Dictionary, the word freedom evolves from an "Old English word frēodōm, which was a state of emancipation, liberty, or free will. This word is composed of free or frēo, indicating an exemption from something, and -dom, a suffix in Old English indicating judgement."

The Oxford Dictionary defines the word Freedom as "The state or fact of being free from servitude, constraint, inhibition, etc.; liberty."

The Merriam-Webster Dictionary defines the word freedom as 1) "the absence of necessity, coercion, or constraint in choice or action" and 2) "liberation from slavery or restraint or from the power of another: independence." Some of the many synonyms to the word Freedom, according to Merriam-Webster, include Autonomy, Sovereignty, Independence, Independency, Liberty, Liberation, Emancipation, Self-Determination, Self-Governance, Self-Government, Manumission, Enfranchisement, Release."

As an author, community historian, and civil rights activist the opportunity to speak during seminars and humanities gatherings as well as during educational sessions engaging students from K-12, University level adults, and the educators that open their minds to a broader world view is often. My question to all is, "What is Freedom?"

I am a 5th generation Underground Railroad Descendant of 2 formerly enslaved people, Allen Watkins and Caroline (Quarlls) Watkins who escaped to Canada in the early 1830s/1840sica respectively to find what they could not find in the United States. I am also the 13th

Great Granddaughter of Thomas Rogers and son Joseph Rogers, both Mayflower passengers who arrived in Plymouth, Massachusetts, in 1620 to find something they could not obtain in Great Britain. I am the descendant of the enslaved and the enslavers.

What is Freedom?

My ancestors sought the answer to that question in two different centuries, two different countries, and by different means. I seek the answer to that question from those that I am fortunate to encounter in educational settings, in books that I read, in lectures that I attend and public tours I may lead by engaging the audience in conversation and dialogue.

What is Freedom?

There are many stories that define the State of Michigan. We can relay stories and histories attached to many people. There are stories of courage, determination, perseverance, and there are also stories of danger, distrust, and inhumanity. The Historic Detroit River defines the Detroit River Region. The river has seen war, peace, and many heroes.

There is a man who is buried in our own Elmwood Cemetery under an obelisk that is his designated marker and unfinished. It is at his wish that the marker is not complete as that man, former U.S. Senator Jacob Howard, was asked by President Abraham Lincoln to sponsor what are called the "Freedom Amendments" of the U.S. Constitution. The amendments known as the 13th, 14th, and 15th grant significant rights to the citizenry in the U.S. including the end of chattel slavery in the U.S. by the 13th. The 14th Amendment granted citizenship most importantly to all the newly freed African Americans who had no country, and in the 15th amendment the "franchise" or the right to vote (for men) was granted. The 13th Amendment to the U.S. Constitution is engraved on Senator Howard's obelisk; it is the sign of his most important legacy and in turn, "unfinished business."

In this volume we will meet a man and hero named William Dollarson, born enslaved in Virginia who also now resides for eternity in Detroit's Elmwood Cemetery. A man buried with his wife next to him in a very unassuming grave that belies the remarkable story he is tied to of the international resistance story that surrounded the Detroit River Region known as the Underground Railroad. The trails to "Midnight" (Detroit) were seven in number and guided by many known and unknown heroes. Of the nearly 5 million people who were enslaved in the United States by the end of the Civil War, approximately 100,000 were Underground Railroad seekers of freedom and as best research will say nearly 25,000 used the great and mighty Detroit River to find the elusive answer to the question, "What is Freedom?"

What is Freedom?

As she began her escape across country from St. Louis, Missouri, on July 4, 1843, and eventually crossing an international border at Detroit in October 1843, Caroline Quarlls escaped from the only home she knew on the corner of Sixth and Pine, 2 blocks from the Mississippi River, and spent what was a 10-day journey by Ferry Boat and Stagecoach to Milwaukee, Wisconsin, where she was safe for nearly a month. After Bounty Hunters showed up with a warrant to take her back to St. Louis and slavery, Caroline Quarlls was spirited away by a local group of abolitionists and spent about a week in the surrounding farmland of Milwaukee hiding.

Engaging rescuers while plans were discussed to expedite her escape from those intending to return her to enslavement, Caroline asked about this thing "Freedom." Her questions to the rescuers were of someone willing and wanting to understand an explanation of her plight. Her questions? What is Freedom? ... Can I feel it? ... Can I taste it? ...

Caroline Quarlls married on November 21, 1844, a man named Allen Watkins who had escaped from enslavement to the Detroit River Region through Sandusky, Ohio, along Lake Erie in 1835. The escape was planned after the loss of his first wife to suicide due to her grief having been sold to another enslaver and facing a forever separation from her children and husband. The death left Allen with 3 children under the age of ten and the substantial threat of his own sale and the children to be left alone. A decision that was no less a lesson of courage of a father rescuing his children from a life he did not want them to face as he had.

What is Freedom?

The Oxford Dictionary and the Merriam-Webster Dictionary do not seem to agree succinctly on the definition of freedom.

I spend days with humanities scholars and historians. I talk to children and their parents. I speak with educators and librarians. I spend time with folks that go about life as letter carriers and nurses. I know many from diverse cultures and heritages and count among many—friends. I have been known to carry a rousing conversation surrounding the question, "What is Freedom?" I believe that we all must take the personal journey to the meaning of Freedom. Freedom is personal. It is carried in each of us. We should not allow someone to define our "freedom" for us. It is carried in our own hearts. The question is for all of us a lifelong search for its meaning. I believe one of the most defining statements on the question of freedom is this:

> Freedom is not about the size of your cage or the power of your wings or non-attachment to a person or a thing. Freedom is about being so truly, madly, and deeply attached to your own soul that you cannot bear if only for a moment a life that doesn't honor it. —Andrea Balt

I am still asking myself, "What is Freedom?" As I read the pages of this fascinating and powerful volume, I will take away more wisdom and additions to my own personal thoughts. I hope that you the reader will find more truths within its chapters.

I hope you discover your own answers.

Freedom Lives.

Kimberly Simmons
President/Executive Director
Detroit River Project

Kimberly L. Simmons is recipient of the 2022 Michigan Humanities Champion of the Year award. She received this honor for her "15+ years of commitment to telling the stories of Michigan and highlighting the participation of African Americans in the making of our state and in crafting complex meanings of freedom."[3]

---

3. https://www.michiganhumanities.org/kimberly-simmons-champions-efforts-to-make-detroit-river-a-unesco-world-heritage-site/

Introduction

In 1968, an election year full of civil strife across America, a State historical marker was unveiled in a joyous celebration on the grounds of the Duffield Elementary School near downtown Detroit.[4] In just over a hundred words, the monument commemorated a little-told story of a Civil War regiment unique among the 46 units that entered the service of the U.S. Army from Michigan. The location marked the site of the regiment's training grounds before heading off to combat. The marker stands today, its faded text announcing:

> The First Michigan Colored Regiment was organized at Camp Ward, which originally stood at this location. Formed from August through October 1863, a year of draft riots and protests against the war, this Negro regiment consisted entirely of volunteers. During training, a regimental band was formed and toured southern Michigan to recruit additional volunteers. Mustered here as the 102nd U.S. Colored Troops, February 17, 1864, the 900-man unit left Detroit March 28, 1864 for service in South Carolina, Georgia, and

---

4. The location achieved historical status by becoming a State Informational Site on March 1, 1968. Laura Ashlee, *Traveling Through Time: A Guide to Michigan's Historical Markers* (Ann Arbor: University of Michigan Press, 2005), 467. The address today is Bunche Preparatory Academy, 2715 Macomb St., behind the building, near Robert Bradby Drive on the city's east side. Bradby was an African American church leader, one of the presidents of the Idlewild Association, and a founding member of the Detroit NAACP. See https://www2.dnr.state.mi.us/publications/pdfs/ArcGISOnline/StoryMaps/mhc_historical_markers/pdfs/MHC821968002.pdf

Florida. More than 1,400 men served in the regiment during 19 months in the field; ten percent of this number died in service. The regiment was disbanded in October 1865, in Detroit.[5]

Much more could have been said. The regiment fought in 10 engagements against enemy forces. It supported the "March to the Sea" campaign that captured Savannah, Georgia, in December 1864 and the Carolinas Campaign of 1865. One of its officers received a Medal of Honor for valor in battle, made possible by actions of "his men who so faithfully followed their leader."[6] Its theater of war—the Deep South—meant capture would result in enslavement, or worse. Not many of its contingent were draftees; some volunteered as substitutes. They stood upon a record of inter-racial affairs during Michigan's antebellum history that was far from unsullied.[7] Altogether, the heroism and patriotism of such men cannot be denigrated or denied. By becoming an effective fighting unit, the Regiment "helped solve Union military manpower problems" and produced "significant military success."[8] In the largest sense, victory for the Union meant a

---

5. It bears the same text on each side. A sponsor strip notes that funds were supplied by the Detroit Branch of the Association for the Study of Negro Life and History. Another marker approved by the Michigan Historical Commission in 2012 for a site in Ypsilanti states: "In December 1863, the First Michigan Colored Infantry stopped here as part of its state-wide recruiting drive." https://www.hmdb.org/m.asp?m=101216 In June 2022, a memorial to Black Civil War soldiers buried in Ypsilanti's Highland Cemetery was dedicated, thanks to $60,000 in grants. Muster rolls for Ypsilanti volunteers can be viewed at https://southadamstreet1900.wordpress.com/102nd-united-states-colored-troops-regimental-and-company-records/

6. *The War of the Rebellion: A Compilation of the Official Records of the Union and Confederate Armies* (Washington: Government Printing Office, 1881), series I, XLIV, 435 [hereafter "*OR*", and with reference to series I unless otherwise stated].

7. See, e.g., Karolyn Smardz Frost & Veta Smith Tucker eds., *A Fluid Frontier: Slavery, Resistance, and the Underground Railroad in the Detroit River Borderland* (Detroit: Wayne State University Press, 2016).

8. Herman Hattaway & Archer Jones, *How the North Won: A Military History of the Civil War* (Urbana: University of Illinois Press, 1983), 686.

new day where "freedom and the right to it transcended racial lines." It meant the securing of liberty under the law for 4 million enslaved Americans immediately and many more millions to come. The contributions of American Blacks were instrumental through "their struggles through the centuries as well as by their services in the final battles" of the fratricidal war.[9]

One way to understand these contributions is to study each soldier's record of service. This monograph has insufficient space for such an endeavor. But take one case, that of Parker C. Bon. He enlisted in the regiment on September 16, 1863, at Detroit, for a 3-year term. He was 27 years old. According to one source, Bon was then working as a cook at Fort Wayne, the U.S. military installation on the Detroit River, providing meals for the White officers of the White regiments mustering there. He learned a great deal by observation and listening to those officers, and "[h]e also studied books written by top ranking military authors whenever his assigned duties were finished." Aware of his capabilities, Black community leaders recommended Bon for the position of drill master for the 1st Michigan Colored enlistees. The official records state that he entered the Volunteer service as Sergeant Major on September 21. He became 1st Sergeant on January 26, 1865, and served until his honorable discharge on September 30 of that year.[10]

Other Michiganders of color brought recognized leadership qualities to the great task. William H. Carter enlisted at Ypsilanti on November 15, 1863, age 18; he was promoted in 1865 to 1st Sergeant on March 2 and to Sergeant Major on August 19 before mustering out on September 30.[11] Marcus Dale became a Commissary Sergeant.

---

9. John Hope Franklin, *From Slavery to Freedom: A History of Negro Americans*, 4th Ed. (New York: Alfred A. Knopf, 1974), 234-235; Mabel M. Smythe, *The Black American Reference Book* (Englewood Cliffs: Prentice-Hall, 1976), 34-35.
10. *Record of Service of Michigan Volunteers in the Civil War 1861-1865* (Kalamazoo: Ihling Bros. & Everhard, 1900) [hereafter *Record of Service*], Vol. 46, 14; Reginald R. Larrie, *Black Experiences in Michigan History* (Lansing: Michigan History Division, 1976), 13; Norman McRae ed., *Negroes in Michigan in the Civil War* (Lansing: Michigan Civil War Centennial Observance Commission, 1966), 49.
11. *Record of Service*, Vol. 46, 22.

Waltham G. Wynn received promotion to Quartermaster Sergeant.[12] Altogether, at least 50 individuals attained the rank of a non-commissioned officer in the 1st Michigan Colored, some of whom had been enrolled at the rank of Corporal.[13] Convention did not permit men of color to become officers except in some limited circumstances, despite obvious qualifications.

Although the Michigan soldiers of African heritage were forced to wait until many months of the War had elapsed, it is especially notable how one such individual much earlier, in October 1861, went off to the front. History has not acknowledged his contributions for more than a century and a half. He served for a number of months in the District of Columbia, Maryland, and Virginia—all jurisdictions where human bondage remained legalized during the ongoing War. He took part in the defense of the Potomac River in Fall 1861, in the Shenandoah Valley Campaign the next Spring, and in the Union advance to Warrenton, Virginia, in July 1862 as part of support for the Peninsula Campaign. His service is especially notable because he did not—could not—wear a uniform and, consequently, had no protection as a service member who could be paroled or exchanged if taken prisoner of war.[14] He carried no weapon; nonetheless, his service was so important that he was personally invited aboard the small staff of Michigan's preeminent military leader when America's greatest crisis unfolded.

William Dollarson—not his birth name—was a most unlikely member of the military family of Alpheus Starkey Williams, Brigadier-General of Volunteers, Mexican-American veteran and student of military matters. Born in 1807-1808, Dollarson was a year or two older than "Old Pap," so nicknamed by soldiers for Williams's grandfatherly demeanor.[15] Not having been born into freedom, Dollarson

---

12. Id. 28, 114.
13. E.g., Paul W. Brooks, id. 16.
14. Mark M. Boatner III, *The Civil War Dictionary* (New York: David Mackay Co., 1988), 270, 620.
15. Pronounced "Pop." Jack Dempsey, *Michigan's Civil War Citizen-General:*

was self-emancipated. He well knew the risk of being retaken, having been brutalized while enslaved (more about that *infra*). He could not have known, however, how bloody this war would become—few other Americans did. When the Civil War wound down to its end, the best modern estimate is that over 750,000 service members had died while in uniform. Many succumbed from disease, despite the dauntless efforts of Union military medical staff.[16] Perhaps the absence of a military background aided Dollarson in accepting Williams's invitation. Perhaps a motivation to rid America of the pestilence of human bondage overrode all considerations of personal safety. As one historian put it:

> [T]he free black wanted to show that they were ready to fight for their rights and the freedom of all men. Blacks showed their willingness to serve by accepting non-military duties within the Army. Therefore, most of them worked as waiters, kitchen helpers, cooks, and medical or personal attendants to high-ranking officers.[17]

For those paying attention, the first six months of the Civil War gave more than a hint of the manifest dangers at the front. On May 24, 1861, accompanying a Michigan regiment in securing Alexandria, Virginia, from Rebel control, a member of President Lincoln's Illinois fraternity, Elmer E. Ellsworth, had become the first well-publicized Union officer casualty.[18] At the Battle of First Bull Run on July 21, the 1st Michigan Infantry "lost heavily" in terms both of killed and wounded and those who did not rejoin after the close of combat.[19] Colonel Orlando B. Willcox and Captain William D. Withington were both wounded, and they were taken prisoner. Official reporting

---

Alpheus S. Williams (Charleston: The History Press, 2019), 12.
16. See, e.g., Michigan Civil War Association, *His Sword a Scalpel: General Charles Stuart Tripler, MD, USA* (Traverse City: Mission Point Press, 2023).
17. Larrie, *Black Experiences*, 12.
18. Robert Garth Scott ed., *Forgotten Valor: The Memoirs, Journals, & Civil War Letters of Orlando B. Willcox* (Kent: Kent State University Press, 1999), 260-265.
19. John Robertson, *Michigan in the War* (Lansing: W.S. George & Co., 1882), 110.

gave the regiment's casualties as 6 killed (including an officer), 37 wounded, and 70 missing (most captured). That tally equaled "one-third of the officers" of the regiment.[20] Detroit newspapers published lurid details and lists of the killed and wounded. One subhead entitled "Fiendishness of the Rebels" reported that "no quarter" had been given to Federal troops.[21]

Despite these alarming reports, Dollarson departed home, left behind his wife of 26 years, and went to the front. He was renowned in Detroit culinary circles, and this kind of service was to be his role, being the staff cook for Williams and his aides. How critical was such service to Union victory? The "preparation of food" was a key component of soldier health in the view of leading medical authorities.[22] It must be said that Dollarson acted not from a mercenary cause; rather, he was "animated by the loftiest patriotism" to do what he could "for the triumph of constitutional liberty." He went to "battle for humanity, for the world, for posterity."[23]

In this year of the 160th anniversary of mustering in of Michigan's regiment of color, the rich annals of contributions made to victory in the Civil War by these soldiers and their civilian counterparts are deserving of special and continuing study.

Editorial Note

A significant portion of this work consists of previously published material no longer readily available in print, supplemented with appropriate annotations. In particular, the first-person accounts of the 1863 Detroit riot have been incorporated so that readers may share the experiences of those who suffered. Other portions consist of exposition of original sources. Combined, it is hoped that this volume

---

20. *OR*, II, 405, 411-413.
21. The basis was unstated.
22. Charles S. Tripler & George Curtis Blackman, *Hand-Book of the Military Surgeon* (Cincinnati: Robert Clarke & Co., 1861).
23. *Michigan in the War*, 110 (quoting a letter by Thomas W. Palmer, future U.S. Senator).

will educate and inspire modern-day readers on a little-explored subject area in Michigan Civil War studies, as well as lead to continuing scholarship. As recently lamented, "The pre-twentieth-century history of African Americans in Detroit has not received a great deal of scholarly attention."[24] It might also be said for the subject statewide.

Previous Civil War era Michigan-focused publications did not speak much to the participation by the State's regiment of color:

- Ida C. Brown, *Michigan Men in the Civil War* (Ann Arbor: University of Michigan, 1959 [later republished])—no reference
- Frederick D. Williams, *Michigan Soldiers in the Civil War* (Lansing: Michigan Historical Commission, 1960)—one paragraph (p. 2)[25]
- Philip P. Mason & Paul J. Pentecost, *From Bull Run to Appomattox: Michigan's Role in the Civil War* (Detroit: Wayne State University Press, 1961)—no reference

One book did include a chapter touching on the Underground Railroad and John Brown.[26]

The paucity of such studies is, perhaps, not surprising. As a 21st Century publication in the U.S. Army Historical Series noted, Americans classified as "White" by Federal Census takers "forgot" how persons of color had fought in the Revolutionary War[27] and

---

24. *A Fluid Frontier*, 252.
25. Printed in multiple editions and two versions.
26. Frank B. Woodford, *Father Abraham's Children: Michigan Episodes in the Civil War* (Detroit: Wayne State University Press, 1961), 7-16.
27. For example, the 1st Rhode Island Regiment of the Continental Army was almost completely composed of freed African Americans. The regiment fought through the entire war from the siege of Boston to the disbanding of the Army on November 3, 1783. See n.29. For a related perspective, see James G. Basker ed., *Black Writers of the Founding Era: A Library of America Anthology* (Library of America, 2023).

War of 1812, and "much the same thing happened after 1865."[28] Nineteenth-century works by Black authors were allowed to fade into obscurity.[29] The publication of new studies after World War II, attempting to educate on "what the Negro did to free himself," did not immediately prompt a Michigan counterpart.[30]

Perhaps it was a volume by a future Pulitzer Prize-winner[31]—and changing social and political conditions in America—that prompted the Michigan Civil War Centennial Observance Commission to issue a tidy monograph in 1966 entitled *Negroes in Michigan in the Civil War*. Under the editorship of Sidney Glazer, Professor of History at Wayne State University in Detroit, authorship was attributed within the publication to Norman McRae, who obtained his Ph.D. from the University of Michigan. Dr. McRae's papers were donated to the Reuther Library at Wayne State, including this biographical sketch: "Since the mid-sixties, Dr. McRae has been an avid researcher and writer on African American history, especially the history of Detroit's African American community; he played a major role in the development of multicultural and human rights curricula in the Detroit school system. In 1969 he taught the first black history course offered at Wayne State University." The 124-page publication represented that "it contains a detailed account of Negro life and a history of

---

28. William A. Dobak, *Freedom by the Sword: The U.S. Colored Troops, 1862-1867* (Washington: Government Printing Office, 2011), xiii.

29. William W. Brown, *The Negro in the American Rebellion: His Heroism and His Fidelity* (Boston: Lee & Shepard, 1867); George W. Williams, *A History of the Negro Troops in the War of the Rebellion 1861-1865* (New York: Harper & Bros., 1888); and Joseph T. Wilson, *The Black Phalanx: A History of the Negro Soldiers of the United States in the Wars of 1775-1812, 1861-'65* (Hartford: American Pub. Co., 1888). See an early 20th Century Master's thesis: Nellie C. Armstrong, *Negro Troops in the Civil War* (Champaign: University of Illinois, 1919).

30. Benjamin A. Quarles, *The Negro in the Civil War* (Boston: Little, Brown & Co., 1953); Dudley T. Cornish, *The Sable Arm; Negro Troops in the Union Army, 1861-1865* (New York: Longmans Green, 1956). Quote is from front cover jacket. Herbert Aptheker, *Negro Casualties in the Civil War* (Washington: Association for the Study of Negro Life & History, Inc., 1945).

31. McPherson, see *infra*.

the First Michigan Colored Infantry" (p. iii). A regimental roster was included.[32]

Michael O. Smith's "Raising a Black Regiment in Michigan: Adversity and Triumph" in Darlene Clark Hine & Earnestine Jenkins eds., *A Question of Manhood: A Reader in U.S. Black Men's History and Masculinity*, Vol. I (Bloomington: Indiana University Press, 1999), renewed the study of Michigan's Colored regiment.[33]

A 2005 Michigan Notable Book addressed the subject under the heading "We Are Coming, Father Abraham.[34]

Michigan and the Civil War: A Great and Bloody Sacrifice (Charleston: The History Press, 2011), another Michigan Notable Book, sought to respectfully tell the story of Michigan's African American soldiers in a chapter entitled "The Fighting 102nd."

A glossy and informative online publication associated with Michigan's current (and third) Capitol, first published in 2023, illuminates the story of the Regiment.[35]

The same year, a rare collection of letters by a soldier of the 1st Michigan Colored Volunteers was published in Sharon A. Roger Hepburn ed., *Private No More: The Civil War Letters of John Lovejoy Murray, 102nd United States Colored Infantry* (Athens: University of Georgia Press, 2023). The book indicated that Dr. Roger Hepburn was completing a history of the 102nd U.S.C.T.

The present volume has been brought to the reader as an effort to pay informed attention to this vital aspect of our heritage. It cannot be all-inclusive, but it is intended to be respectfully thorough in its coverage. It does not attempt coverage of the Reconstruction era or those that followed. As with every volume in this series, revenues from purchases will support the MCWA in its mission to erect a monument

---

32. See Appendix for further information on this Commission.
33. The article earlier appeared in another publication. Smith also wrote his Master's Thesis on the Regiment, *infra*.
34. Richard Bak, *A Distant Thunder: Michigan in the Civil War* (Ann Arbor: Huron River Press, 2004), 50-53.
35. http://capitol.michigan.gov/Content/Files/1st%20Michigan%20Colored%20Infantry.pdf

honoring Michigan's contributions to victory at the Battle of Antietam and to Civil War emancipation that bloody day made possible. As ever, any errors herein are the sole responsibility of the undersigned.

As for the title, the use of "liberty" is chosen as one of the inalienable human rights expressed in the Declaration of Independence upon which this nation was founded. It is also embedded in the U.S. Constitution. Kimberly Simmons's Foreword asks us to consider "What is Freedom?" "Warrior" is also appropriate as a term that connotes a person engaged in a struggle or conflict, who displays courage, and who is prepared to sacrifice self for the good of others.

—Jack Dempsey, Editor

WARRIORS *for* LIBERTY

Part One

A Culture of Liberty in a New Northern State

A Liberty-Loving Haven

Michigan achieved statehood on January 26, 1837. It had not been easy. Established as a U.S. Territory in 1805, more than four years had elapsed since voters endorsed a bid to become a State in October 1832. In January 1833, the territorial legislature had requested Congress to approve the drafting of a constitution. In December 1833, the Michigan delegate to Congress presented a formal petition for admission. In 1834, the Committee on Territories of the U.S. House of Representatives determined that admitting Michigan would be inexpedient. The Senate considered and tabled a similar bill. In September, the Territorial Council authorized a population count to demonstrate Michigan's entitlement to become a State. The returns showed 87,278 residents, enough to qualify. The Council early in 1835 authorized an election of delegates to a constitutional convention, which met in Detroit from May 11-June 24 inside the Territorial Capitol building on Griswold Street. That draft was adopted by referendum on October 5-6, but not until June 15, 1836, did Congress pass conditional legislation enabling Michigan to become a State. The First Convention of Assent rejected the condition—that Michigan exchange its claim to a strip of Ohio land encompassing Toledo for the entire Upper Peninsula. The Second Convention met in December and accepted the compromise. Both houses of Congress approved statehood legislation in January, and President Andrew Jackson attached his signature on the 26th.[36]

Underlying the delaying tactics in Congress was the practice "to

---

36. Don Faber, *The Boy Governor: Stevens T. Mason and the Birth of Michigan Politics* (Ann Arbor: University of Michigan Press, 2012), 48-74.

admit a free state and a slave state at the same time so as to preserve the balance in the Senate" between the two sections. Southerners undertook "to postpone the admission of Michigan until Arkansas also was ready for admission."[37] Arkansas's admission on June 15, 1836, coupled with Michigan as the 26th State in the Union, produced the desired 13-13 split in the upper body. Slaveholding States could be assured that no legislation could pass negatively affecting what they held as their "peculiar institution"—holding human beings in bondage, buying and selling them, and excluding them from protections afforded other persons under the law.

Michigan suffered this delay because it stood as a lighthouse of liberty on great lakes that shaped the outlines of its two pleasant peninsulas. Its founding documents outlawed slavery, and so political and legal institutions as well as the outlook of the majority of its citizens favored liberty, not bondage.[38]

This heritage derived from the Northwest Ordinance of 1787, adopted by the Congress of the Confederation of the United States to govern territory outside of the original 13 States in the region around the Great Lakes. Once a certain population level existed, a petition for statehood could be presented. Essential to the government and the society it served was this principle:

> There shall be neither slavery nor involuntary servitude in the said territory, otherwise than in the punishment of crimes whereof the party shall have been duly convicted…[39]

Michigan's Constitution of 1835 contained identical language. Proposed in the convention in Detroit on May 20, 1835, it received

---

37. Willis F. Dunbar, *Michigan: A History of the Wolverine State* (Grand Rapids: William B. Eerdmans Pub. Co., 1970), 312-313.
38. Roy E. Finkenbine, "A Beacon of Liberty on the Great Lakes: Race, Slavery, and the Law in Antebellum Michigan" in Paul Finkelman & Martin J. Hershock eds., *The History of Michigan Law* (Athens: University of Ohio Press, 2006), 83.
39. *Journals of the Continental Congress, 1774-1789*, Vol. XXXII (Washington: Government Printing Office, 1936), 334, 343.

not a single negative vote.⁴⁰ The provision, Article XI, entitled "Prohibition of Slavery," stated:

> Slavery prohibited.
> 1. Neither slavery nor involuntary servitude shall ever be introduced into this state, except for the punishment of crimes of which the party shall have been duly convicted.⁴¹

What did the term "slavery" mean in the 1787-1835 period? According to the classic source of word meanings, the two key terms were:

> Slavery, *n.* bondage, the state of a person wholly subject to the will of another.
> Slave-trade, *n.* the business of buying and selling men.⁴²

A less neutral yet accurate definition can be found in a period history:

> Slavery means to rob the poor of their wages, to rob men and women of their liberty (a God-given right), to rob the husband of his wife, wife of husband, father of son, mother of daughter, brother of sister, and has closed the door of knowledge against them, and deprived them of the religion of Christ. It includes licentiousness, concubinage, drunkenness, and in short every thing the human tongue is capable of uttering is found in the one word "SLAVERY"; it is, therefore, impossible to exaggerate it.⁴³

---

40. *Daily Journal of the Convention to Form a Constitution*, Wed., May 20, 1835 [p. 18], available at https://babel.hathitrust.org/cgi/pt?id=mdp.39015071175163&seq=1
41. *The Revised Statutes of the State of Michigan, Passed at the Adjourned Session of 1837, and the Regular Session of 1838* (Detroit: John S. Bagg, 1838), 42.
42. Noah Webster, *A Dictionary of the English Language* (New York: N. & J. White, 1833), 401.
43. W.M. Mitchell, *The Under-Ground Railroad* (London: William Tweedie, 1860), 99.

During the French and British control of the Michigan Territory prior to the extension of U.S. influence over the region, slavery did exist. The first Blacks arrived in 1731, "where they were held as slaves by French settlers in the Upper Peninsula.[44] In 1782 Detroit, a total of 179 individuals were held to servitude.[45] As of 1805, six free males and seven free females of African descent lived in Detroit.[46] The 1810 Census counted 24 slaves and 124 free Blacks.[47] An early history asserted that enslaved peoples were "well taken care of by our ancient inhabitants."[48] The Ordinance of 1787, however, extinguished any basis for the continuation of the practice.

By contrast, the U.S. Constitution of 1787 did not abolish slavery, which existed in 12 of the 13 original States. The Ordinance sought to remedy the "evils" of human bondage by dedicating the Northwest Territory to human freedom. In a powerful way, the measure kicked the traces out from legalized mistreatment of one human by another:

> Several decades were to pass before the soil of the Old Northwest endured its last pollution from the footprints of a slave, but the prohibition proved an effective ban against the widespread expansion of slavery over the territory, and eventually exterminated it here completely. In doing so, the ordinance prepared the way for its ultimate extermination in the nation; for when civil war came and North and South faced each other on the field of battle during four awful years, it was

---

44. Paul Finkelman ed., *Encyclopedia of African American History 1619-1895: From the Colonial Period to the Age of Frederick Douglass*, Vol. 2 (New York: Oxford University Press, 2006), 356.
45. Elaine Latzman Moon, *Untold Tales, Unsung Heroes: An Oral History of Detroit's African American Community, 1918-1967* (Detroit: Wayne State University Press, 1994), 23.
46. Id.
47. Finkelman, *Encyclopedia*, 356.
48. J.A. Girardin, "Slavery in Detroit" in *Michigan Pioneer and Historical Collections*, Vol. I, 2d Ed. (Lansing: Robert Smith Printing Co., 1900), 415-417.

the exuberant might of the free Northwest which decided the issue in favor of permanent Union and human freedom.[49]

The Ordinance and the first State Constitution had "set the tone for liberatory possibilities." As a leading historian of the period explained, "unadulterated moral hostility to slavery seems to have been more prevalent in Michigan than in many other northern states."[50] Early anti-slavery outposts sprang up in Adrian, Ann Arbor, Detroit, and Marshall.[51]

The leading apologist for American slavery, John C. Calhoun of South Carolina, vilified the Ordinance during his tenure in the U.S. Senate. He criticized it, among Federal enactments, as a measure "destroying the equilibrium" between North and South.[52] Michigan entered the Union in 1837 as a "Free State" in which all former measures that authorized human bondage were eliminated.[53] Regardless of pre-American practice, the Northwest Ordinance and the 1835 Constitution made it clear that within the State's limits "Americans, however, could not own slaves."[54]

Three months to the day that Michigan became a State in the Union, the Detroit Anti-Slavery Society was founded by prominent Black individuals Robert Banks, William Lambert, and Madison J.

---

49. Northwest Territory Celebration Commission, *History of the Ordinance of 1787 and the Old Northwest Territory* (Marietta: 1937), 83.
50. Martin J. Hershock, *The Paradox of Progress: Economic Change, Individual Enterprise, and Political Culture in Michigan, 1837-1878* (Athens: Ohio University Press, 2003), 112. Still, "abolitionism always remained a minority position within the state." Id.
51. Russel B. Nye, *Fettered Freedom; Civil Liberties and the Slavery Controversy 1830-1860* (East Lansing: Michigan State University Press, 1963), 214.
52. George W. Williams, *History of the Negro Race in America from 1619 to 1880: Negroes as Slaves, as Soldiers, and as Citizens* (New York: G.P. Putnam & Sons, 1885), 105.
53. A principal advocate for "popular sovereignty," the notion that only territorial legislatures held power to address slavery, was Michigan's preeminent political leader of the early 19th century. Willard C. Klunder, *Lewis Cass and the Politics of Moderation* (Kent: Kent State University Press, 1996), 241-244.
54. McRae, 3.

Lightfoot, along with well-known White leaders Edwin W. Cowles, Robert Steward, George F. and A.L. Porter, and Shubael Conant, the Society's first president (and for whom Conant Street and the Conant Gardens Historic District were named). The Society called for the abolition of slavery in America as well as advocating "the elevation of our colored brethren to their proper rank as men."[55] Such principles were not universally embraced, and issues of "Slavery and race proved to be especially divisive:"

> Michigan's small yet significant African American population stood resolutely against slavery and racial discrimination even as law and custom restricted African Americans' access to the public sphere. Abolitionists, both white and black, were always a minority in Michigan and elsewhere across the antebellum North. Their small numbers notwithstanding, abolitionists aroused Michiganians' deep misgivings regarding slavery.[56]

According to one contemporary source, the State in the year of its admission to the Union could claim a total of 27 societies organized for "anti-slavery" purposes. That number swamped those of New Jersey, Illinois, and Indiana.[57]

The story of abolitionism in Michigan remains to be fully told. Once upon a time, historians could describe "the Abolitionist movement ... as a white man's benevolent association." Doing so overlooked the contributions of Frederick Douglass, Harriet Tubman, and Sojourner Truth, to name a few.[58] In Michigan, both Blacks and

---

55. https://detroithistorical.org/learn/encyclopedia-of-detroit/detroit-anti-slavery-society
56. John W. Quist ed., "Preface" in *Michigan's War: The Civil War in Documents* (Athens: Ohio University Press, 2019), xvii.
57. Thomas Earle, *The Life, Travels, and Opinions of Benjamin Lundy* (Philadelphia: William D. Parrish, 1847), 296.
58. Herbert Aptheker, *The Negro in the Abolitionist Movement* (New York: International Publishers, 1941), 4. Tubman's life is now commemorated at two

Whites provided leadership to the effort, and an accounting of those individuals is a worthy effort. Ann Arbor was a community with "a strong antislavery tradition" as the site of Michigan's first statewide abolitionist gathering in 1836 and home to *Signal of Liberty*, "the state's most successful abolitionist newspaper."[59] In Oakland County, the Free Discussion and Anti-Slavery Society was organized and meeting in the summer of 1836.[60] Detroiter and ex-slave Henry Bibb published *The Voice of the Fugitive* in Ontario, and he worked with individuals regardless of race including Elijah Staunton Fish (1791-1861) of Birmingham, Nathan Power (1801-1874) of Farmington, and lawyer and writer George W. Wisner (1813-1849) of Pontiac. Dr. Isaac J. Bigelow (1809-1887) of Davisburg was associated with abolitionist William Lloyd Garrison in Boston; while at Western Reserve College in Ohio, Bigelow "was mobbed and burned in effigy many times for his anti-slavery lectures, often barely escaping with his life."[61] Churches became embroiled in the subject, sometimes dividing because of this issue.[62]

The Baptist church in Detroit incurred such a split. Founded in 1827, located at the corner of Fort and Griswold, the congregation employed a segregated seating arrangement. When a protest by Black members went unheeded, they left to form their own Baptist church, One of Detroit's noted historians included this entry:

---

national parks in Church Creek, Maryland, and Auburn, New York, and by a 2019 major motion picture. A leading 20th century historian wrote in 1961 that serious students of northern Black history must review the manuscript collections of White abolitionists since they include correspondence with prominent Black leaders and information on Black activities and conditions in the North. Leon F. Litwack, *North of Slavery: The Negro in the Free States, 1790-1860* (Chicago: University of Chicago Press, 1961), 287.
59. Quist, 32. The location was at 1001 Broadway Street. For an exemplar of its articles, see Appendix.
60. *Pontiac Courier*, July 1836.
61. *Michigan Pioneer and Historical Collections*, Vol. XIII, 2d Ed. (Lansing: Wynkoop Hallenbeck Crawford Co., 1908), 255.
62. See Appendix for one example out of Wayne County.

Second Baptist Church (Colored).

This church was organized in 1836, and held its first services in private houses. As early as March 30, 1836, the society contracted for a building to cost $480. The church, however, was not built, and in 1839 the society held meetings in a building also used for school purposes, on the south side of Fort Street, between Beaubien and St. Antoine Streets, subsequently known as Liberty Hall. On March 18, 1839, the society was incorporated.

> From August 16 to 20, 1850, the church was occupied by the annual meeting of the Amherstburg Baptist Association; to which the society belonged. In September, 1851, the society was received into the Michigan Baptist Association. On June 26, 1854, the church was burned. Services were then held for a time in an old school-house on the south side of Fort near Hastings Street. In February, 1857, the society bought their present property on the north side of Croghan near Beaubien Street for $3,800 of the First German Reformed Zion Church, which society had built it in 1851. …
>
> Number of members in 1840, 15; in 1850, 80; in 1860, 221 … Rev. W.C. Monroe, the first pastor, served from 1836 to 1847. Rev. S.H. Davis was pastor from 1847 to 1851, and was succeeded by Rev. D.G. Lett, who remained until 1856. In 1857 Rev. William Troy was pastor. He was followed by Rev. G.W. Anderson, who served from 1859 to 1861. Rev. S. Chase served from April 1, 1861, to April 1, 1874 ….[63]

The first meeting site was a small hall on Fort Street between Beaubien and St. Antoine. In February 1857 the site on Croghan—441 Monroe

---

63. Silas Farmer, *The History of Detroit and Michigan: or, The Metropolis Illustrated* (Detroit: Silas Farmer & Co., 1884), 607; Paul Taylor, *"Old Slow Town": Detroit During the Civil War* (Detroit: Wayne State University Press, 2013), 21-22. See Nathaniel Leach, *The Second Baptist Connection, Reaching Out to Freedom: History of Second Baptist Church of Detroit* (Detroit: 1988).

in modern times—was acquired, where the church has met ever since. It is the first Black congregation formed in Michigan. The congregation began its involvement in political and government matters when it led the formation of the Amherstburg Baptist Association and the Canadian Anti-Slavery Baptist Association as part of the effort to support abolitionism and the flight to freedom of escaping persons through the auspices of the Underground Railroad.

Network of Freedom in the Wolverine State

Before as well as after Statehood, Michiganders helped men and women escape from bondage via what became known as "the Underground Railroad." Up until the Civil War, "Michigan was home to a highly complex and adaptable network of operators assisting freedom seekers." These operators were of European and African heritage. Although its population grew more slowly than other Northern States, Michigan's "geographic situation and antislavery activity thrust it onto the national stage of resistance to the system of slavery." Located far north from the slave States, and positioned "as a gateway to Canada," provided an ideal setting for self-emancipators to maximize the chance to secure their liberty. The first Michiganders to interfere with slave-catching were free African Americans, both those born into freedom and who escaped into it. Anti-slavery groups populated primarily by White men and women emerged as important contributors to the network in the 1840s. From the time when it was a Territory, Michigan's people "thwarted every known attempt at recovering slaves."[64]

Those who participated in this pre-Civil War effort brought different motivations. Self-emancipators sought to aid others, including family members. Religious guidance provided the rationale for others. Some were humanitarians, pure and simple.[65] The inhumanity of the slave system motivated all.

During the decades leading up to the Civil War, after the slave

---

64. Carol E. Mull, *The Underground Railroad in Michigan* (Jefferson: McFarland & Co., 2010), 1, 163-165.
65. Id. 166-167.

trade with Africa was officially banned in 1808,[66] numerous planters in the Maryland-Virginia region raised capital by selling people they owned under their State's laws. One estimate is that "about one million people" were dispersed into the cotton States before the end of human bondage came with the Civil War. Instead of survival into eldership thanks to a more temperate mid-Atlantic climate, "the lives of the enslaved were often cut short by a labor regime of appalling brutality" in the Gulf States, where both the sun and owners were often merciless. Slave traders made large commissions by a system that broke up families, sending those both of pure and mixed race into a darker bondage than they had known when more proximate to the freedom available in the North and Midwest.[67]

The Fugitive Slave Law of 1850 was "a law to reactivate the recapture of fugitive slaves" imbued with "a number of gratuitously obnoxious provisions." Federal authorities could "summon" citizens to aid them in apprehending purported escapees. It deprived the target of the right to a jury trial. It sanctioned recovery of escaped individuals with no statute of limitations. Accordingly, it "left all free Negroes with inadequate safeguards against claims that they were fugitives," exposing them to forcible kidnapping and to enslavement regardless of their place of birth. The measure "inspired a great revulsion in the North." No Northern State had the power to veto the federal law, which posed new risks to those who had escaped and created the possibility that free Blacks could be arrested and taken South. The Federal

---

66. The U.S. Constitution, Art. I, Section 9, First Clause, prohibited Congress from enacting a ban before arrival of that year. On March 2, 1807, effectuating congressional response to a call for action in his State of the Union address, President Thomas Jefferson signed into effect Public Law 9-22, 2 Stat. 426, making it unlawful to "bring into the United States or the territories thereof from any foreign kingdom, place, or country, any negro, mulatto, or person of colour, with intent to hold, sell, or dispose of such negro, mulatto, or person of colour, as a slave, or to be held to service or labour."
67. Scott Shane, *Flee North: A Forgotten Hero and the Fight for Freedom in Slavery's Borderland* (New York: Celadon Books, 2023), 7, 69-70.

enactment "prioritized white enslavers 'property' ownership over the humanity of African Americans."[68]

One case underscored their alarm. Silas Rose had escaped from Kentucky to freedom and lived in Detroit for several years. The effect of the law was to drag him into Federal court, which declared that he must be remitted to his "master." Violent means to interfere with the verdict were averted when Lewis Cass and other subscribers purchased Rose's freedom.[69]

The decade of the 1850s made for a turbulent nation. It began with some hope in the Compromise of 1850. A package of bills passed Congress that sought to balance the sectional interests of free and slave societies. California was admitted as a free State, the slave trade in Washington, D.C. was banned, and the people of each territory would decide whether or not slavery would be permitted under the doctrine of popular sovereignty first outlined by Cass and taken up by Stephen A. Douglas. Abolitionists opposed the introduction of slavery into the territories, but they regarded as particularly odious the enactment of a more stringent Fugitive Slave Law.

If the hope had been that the American people had put the matter of human enslavement behind them, it was dashed when a popular novel appeared. *Uncle Tom's Cabin* was published in 1852, a tale of cruelty, family separation, and escape to freedom in Canada. It outraged slaveholders, but it was freedom-lovers' turn to rise in opposition when the Kansas-Nebraska Act became law in 1854. Their ire arose from its repeal of the Missouri Compromise of 1820, which had effectively prohibited slavery north of a lateral line in lands west of the Mississippi River. The 1854 enactment repealed that arrangement and became an immediate impetus to founding of the Republican Party that year to restrain the expansion of slavery.

Sectional feelings were further sharpened when the U.S. Supreme

---

68. Pinheiro, *infra*.
69. Clarence M. Burton & M. Agnes Burton eds., *History of Wayne County and the City of Detroit, Michigan*, Vol. II (Chicago: S.J. Clarke Pub. Co., 1930), 1124.

Court handed down the *Dred Scott* decision in 1857. The justices ruled 7-2 that a Black person with slave ancestry could not become entitled to the rights, privileges, and immunities guaranteed to citizens by the U.S. Constitution. "Citizens," the majority opinion by Chief Justice Roger Taney of Maryland opined, was a term synonymous with "people of the United States." It did not include persons of color born free, or later freed, on account of their very nature:

> a subordinate and inferior class of beings who had been subjugated by the dominant race, and, whether emancipated or not, yet remained subject to their authority, and had no rights or privileges but such as those who held the power and the Government might choose to grant them.[70]

One of the dissenting opinions challenged this interpretation. Were persons of African ancestry deemed to be citizens of the States at the time of the adoption of the Constitution?

> Of this there can be no doubt. At the time of the ratification of the Articles of Confederation, all free native-born inhabitants of the States of New Hampshire, Massachusetts, New York, New Jersey, and North Carolina, though descended from African slaves, were not only citizens of those States, but such of them as had the other necessary qualifications possessed the franchise of electors, on equal terms with other citizens.[71]

A Lansing newspaper castigated the decision as "a direct denial of the Declaration of Independence."[72] In less than a decade, *Dred Scott*

---

70. 60 U.S. 393, 403-405 (1857). For a modern view on this decision, see Samuel E. McCargo, "Taney's Negroes: Can the Court Un-Ring the Bell" in *Michigan Bar Journal*, Vol. 94, No. 5, May 2015, 42ff.
71. 60 U.S. 572-573.
72. Nye, 280.

would be consigned to the ash heap of history. Much blood would be spilled during the interim.

On March 12, 1859, Frederick Douglass was in town to speak at the congregation of Second Baptist Church. His remarks came on the heels of a meeting he attended with prominent African American leaders in Detroit and John Brown.[73] The Douglass/Brown meeting took place at the home of William Webb, located at 185 East Congress Street.[74] Present also were George de Baptiste, Joseph Ferguson, John Jackson, William Lambert, Rev. Monroe, and Willis Wilson, leaders in the fight for freedom. Brown had brazenly brought 12 Missouri fugitives by rail from Iowa to Detroit for the crossing to Windsor aboard the ferry.[75] The leaders "heard Brown's latest plans" to foment a slave insurrection. The two men had first met in 1848, and "the two abolitionists spent many hours and days in each other's company." They rendezvoused in Syracuse, N.Y., on June 26-28, 1855, at the self-described Convention of Radical Political Abolitionists. Douglass had signed the call for the meeting, and at least one Michigander attended—Charles C. Foote of Detroit. As Brown's vision for abolition via violence turned to assaulting a U.S. arsenal, Douglass began to part ways. Inside Webb's house that Saturday evening, Douglass (and the Detroiters as well) went "cold on Brown's scheme." It did not mean they had gone soft on abolition, but they did not find the plan a sensible one.[76]

---

73. National Register of Historic Places Nomination Form, Mar. 19, 1975. In 1863, the first celebration of the issuance of the Emancipation Proclamation in Detroit was held there.
74. *Detroit Free Press*, Mar. 21, 1920, D5. A parking garage occupies the site today. A Michigan Historical Marker on East Congress Street at San Antoine commemorates the meeting.
75. Finkenbine, "A Beacon of Liberty," 91.
76. David W. Blight, *Frederick Douglass: Prophet of Freedom* (New York: Simon & Schuster, 2018), 280-281, 293, 298, 300. Foote moved to Detroit in 1854 after nomination in 1848 as vice-presidential nominee of the Liberty Party, and he served as agent for the Refugee Home Society, whose object was to provide homes for escaped slaves in Canada, Henry Bibb being its founder. Abram W. Foote, *Foote Family, Comprising the Genealogy and History of Nathaniel Foote, of*

When Brown attacked the U.S. Arsenal that Fall and was executed for treason, Detroit African Americans met at the Church to address the crisis. They approved a statement of sentiment and resolutions, the preamble of which spoke to their own experience:

> We, the oppressed portion of this community, many of whom have worn the galling chains and felt the smarting lash of slavery, and know by sad experience its brutalizing effects upon both the body and the mind, and its damaging influence upon the soul of its victim ....

The declaration courageously identified Brown as "our much beloved and highly esteemed friend," and it vowed to "hold the name of Old Capt. John Brown in the most sacred remembrance."[77] Given the church's position as the congregation for Blacks in Detroit, membership and attendance by the Dollarsons was likely. It is also likely they were present when Douglass spoke in March 1859, and that they attended the December 2nd session at which the sentiments as to his insurrectionary effort were expressed. William Dollarson had worn the chains and felt the lash; the declaration represented his experience before gaining liberation.[78] Perhaps both of them contributed "when African American women in Detroit held a concert to raise funds for a monument to John Brown's black associates."[79]

The courageous and public response to the Harpers Ferry raid should be measured with the situation facing at least some of those who were identified with Brown. Douglass was warned that his

---

Wethersfield, Conn., and His Descendants, Vol. I (Rutland: Marble City Press, 1907), 339.

77. Benjamin Quarles ed., *Blacks on John Brown* (Urbana: University of Illinois Press, 1972), 20-23. See Appendix.

78. A description of the punishment devices used on the enslaved is in Trudeau, *infra* at 313, quoting a soldier in Sherman's army.

79. Julie Roy Jeffrey, *The Great Silent Army of Abolitionism: Ordinary Women in the Antislavery Movement* (Chapel Hill: University of North Carolina Press, 1998), 209.

apprehension was sought, and he quickly repaired to his hometown of Rochester, New York, thence traveled across to Canada for safety.[80] His autobiography reprinted a message from the Governor of Virginia to Michigan's Governor, in which Douglass's arrest was sought:

[Confidential.]
Richmond, Va., Nov. 13, 1859.
To His Excellency, James Buchanan, President of the United States, and to the Honorable Postmaster-General of the United States:
Gentlemen—I have information such as has caused me, upon proper affidavits, to make requisition upon the Executive of Michigan for the delivery up of the person of Frederick Douglass, a negro man, supposed now to be in Michigan, charged with murder, robbery, and inciting servile insurrection in the State of Virginia. My agents for the arrest and reclamation of the person so charged are Benjamin M. Morris and William N. Kelly. The latter has the requisition, and will wait on you to the end of obtaining nominal authority as post-office agents. They need be very secretive in this matter, and some pretext for traveling through the dangerous section for the execution of the laws in this behalf, and some protection against obtrusive, unruly, or lawless violence. If it be proper so to do, will the postmaster-general be pleased to give to Mr. Kelly, for each of these men, a permit and authority to act as detectives for the post-office department, without pay, but to pass and repass without question, delay or hindrance?
Respectfully submitted by your obedient servant,
Henry A. Wise.[81]

Douglass was nowhere close to Michigan; even had he been, the response by Michigan Governor Moses Wisner would have

---

80. Blight, *Frederick Douglass*, 305-307.
81. *Life and Times of Frederick Douglass, Written by Himself* (Hartford: Park Pub. Co., 1881), 314.

disappointed Wise. A Republican elected in 1858 and in his first year in office when the raid occurred, Wisner was a staunch defender of his State's personal liberty law. He would not have countenanced any attempt to apprehend a free Black for purposes of putting him on trial south of the Mason-Dixon line.[82]

Insistence on the right of Blacks to remain within Michigan's boundaries dated well back. The Territorial Legislature adopted a measure in 1827 that partly sought "to Punish the Kidnapping" of free Blacks.[83] That year, a Maryland slave hunter sought the return of "Hamlet" by publishing notice of a $200 reward in a Detroit newspaper for a number of months—without success.[84] A case in 1833, before Statehood, helped its reputation for liberty. In the so-called "Blackburn Riots" of 1833, slavecatchers from Kentucky sought to reclaim a well-known Black couple who had resided in Detroit since 1831. Their efforts were thwarted when subterfuge and martial conduct resulted in Thornton and Ruth Blackburn escaping across the Detroit River to eventual freedom in Ontario.[85] Detroit—and Windsor—became vital ports of exit and entry since Britain had no treaty obligations to the United States by way of a duty to deport persons who had escaped from bondage.[86] By one count, some 30,000 fugitives escaped to Canada through Michigan.[87]

In 1860, the State's population totaled 749,113 and Detroit's 45,619. The U.S. Census counted 6,799 "free colored" persons

---

82. For Wisner's attitude on fugitive slave and personal liberty laws, see his final address to the Michigan Legislature. George N. Fuller ed., *Messages of the Governors of Michigan*, Vol. II (Lansing: Michigan Historical Commission, 1926), 376, 410-412 [hereafter "*Messages*"].
83. Finkelman, *Encyclopedia*, 356. It also discriminatorily denied residence without compliance with certain conditions. *History of Michigan Law*, 84.
84. Finkenbine, "A Beacon of Liberty," 87.
85. David M. Katzman, *Before the Ghetto; Black Detroit in the Nineteenth Century* (Urbana: University of Illinois Press, 1973), 8-11. See Veta Smith Tucker, "Forging Transnational Networks for Freedom: From the War of 1812 to the Blackburn Riots of 1833" in *A Fluid Frontier*, 53-54.
86. Taylor, "*Old Slow Town,*" 17.
87. Finkenbine, "A Beacon of Liberty," 88.

residing in the State, with 1,673 within Wayne County.[88] That more Blacks had settled outside of the Detroit area derived from several factors. The first settlements were in rural areas, including Washtenaw County, where the majority of pioneers of color had "shunned the towns and mechanic trades" of Michigan. In second place, however, came Cass County, located along the border with Indiana near the southwest corner of the State, named for Michigan's most prominent pre-1861 politician—who, ironically, held "no moral abhorrence to slavery."[89] Its total of 1,368 African Americans represented nearly eight percent of the population.[90] After anti-slavery Quakers homesteaded in Calvin and Porter townships, they began to aid formerly enslaved persons to settle in the County. It became an Underground Railroad haven.[91] Ex-slaves from different States settled and made their farmsteads here.[92] In 1847, the County became the scene for one of the most famous confrontations between slave-catchers and the formerly enslaved. In mid-August, "a large group of Kentuckians" arrived in southern Michigan with the purpose "to capture African Americans." Having taken nine individuals hostage, they were persuaded by "a crowd of black and white farmers" to let the matter be adjudicated. The outcome: the captured individuals were released by the Cass County court and escaped.[93] A related and less sanguinary

---

88. The number may represent an undercount, since fugitives "did not voluntarily communicate with the census taker." Finkelman, *Encyclopedia*, 356.
89. Klunder, 4.
90. https://www2.census.gov/library/publications/decennial/1860/population/1860a-20.pdf
91. To some extent, adjacent St. Joseph County could make a similar claim. White Pigeon has been described as "an abolitionist stronghold." Fergus M. Bordewich, *Bound for Canaan: The Underground Railroad and the War for the Soul of America* (New York: HarperCollins Publishers, 2005), 205.
92. Booker T. Washington, "Two Generations Under Freedom" in *The Outlook*, Vol. 73, No. 6, Feb. 7 (New York: Outlook Company, 1903), 292-305. The article contains photographs of Black officials, farmers, and others who were prominent in the community. See also Harold B. Fields, "Free Negroes in Cass County Before the Civil War" in *Michigan History*, Vol. 44, No. 4, Dec. 1960, 375ff.
93. Veta Smith Tucker, *A Twenty First Century History of the 1847 Kentucky*

outcome: the affair contributed to demands for more rigorous Federal legislation regarding "fugitive slaves."[94]

State Historical Markers help tell the story of the freedom-embracing culture of the county at the site of the Chain Lake Baptist Church and Cemetery along Chain Lake Street in Calvin Township, in Vandalia at State and Water streets, and in Sumnerville Cemetery at Wood Road and Pokagon Highway in Pokagon Township.[95] According to a recent article, "the tradition of Black farming in the area" lives on.[96]

Life in antebellum Michigan did not mean complete equality. Although those of African heritage could legally settle soon after Statehood, and they could testify in court and vote (after 1855) in school elections, they still faced discrimination in the full exercise of civil rights. Michiganders of color lived in a State in which some other citizens "demonstrated hostility (sometimes violently) towards African Americans."[97] By comparison with its sister States of the lower Midwest, Michigan was more advanced and earning a reputation as a beacon of freedom.[98] Notwithstanding a less than color-blind legal structure, "mixed couples lived unmolested in Detroit," and some

---

Raid (Kalamazoo: Fortitude Graphic Design & Printing, 2010), 14-15, 17-18. See also "Perry Sanford: In and Out of Slavery" in *Michigan History*, Vol. 95, No. 1, Jan./Feb. 2011, 50.

94. Benjamin C. Wilson, "Kentucky Kidnappers, Fugitives, and Abolitionists in Antebellum Cass County Michigan" in *Michigan History*, Vol. 60, No. 4 (1976), 339–358. See also David G. Chardavoyne, "Michigan and the Fugitive Slave Acts" in *The Court Legacy*, Vol. XII, No. 3 (Detroit: Historical Society for the United States District Court for the Eastern District of Michigan, Nov. 2004), which details resistance to fugitive recaptures in Michigan dating to 1807.

95. Ashlee, 78, 81, 82.

96. Dustin Dwyer, "After more than 150 years, the legacy of a thriving Black community in Cass County continues on," Michigan Radio, Feb. 17, 2022, available at: https://www.michiganradio.org/community/2022-02-17/after-more-than-150-years-the-legacy-of-a-thriving-black-community-in-cass-county-continues-on

97. Holly A. Pinheiro Jr., "USCT Kin's Generational Battle for Equality" in *Journal of the Civil War Era*, Sept. 19, 2023.

98. Finkenbine, "A Beacon of Liberty," 86-87.

Blacks did vote "in some places in some elections." In 1860, nearly half of all African American children attended school. Those more than 1,100 students "exceeded all the free black children in school in the eleven states that would form the Confederacy."[99]

Some Blacks gained antebellum access to higher educational opportunity in Michigan. Rufus Lewis Perry, born into enslavement on a Tennessee plantation in 1834, attended the Kalamazoo Theological Seminary from 1860 to 1861 after self-emancipation. One source indicates he graduated, and that he received a Ph.D. from the institution. On October 9, 1861, he received ordination as a minister for the Second Baptist Church of Ann Arbor. He later served congregations in Buffalo and Brooklyn, New York.[100]

One of Michigan's staunchest anti-slavery females, Laura Smith Haviland, "referred with pride" to its regional identity as a place and culture where human rights were being advanced.[101] She "interacted closely with the black community that lived near Adrian" as part of an "interracial network" that helped escapees. Together, Haviland and "her African American neighbors and friends" housed and hid fugitives on their treks to liberty.[102]

Michigan had become home to many who fit the description of the so-called benighted "class" of persons under *Dred Scott*: a "negro" person born into servitude who had gained liberation but, the Court

---

99. Finkelman, *Encyclopedia*, 357.
100. William Cathcart ed., *The Baptist Encyclopedia* (Philadelphia: Louis H. Everts, 1881), 907; William J. Simmons, *Men of Mark: Eminent, Progressive and Rising* (Cleveland: Geo. M. Rewell & Co., 1887), 620ff; Clarence Taylor, *The Black Churches of Brooklyn* (New York: Columbia University Press, 1994), 16, 26. In 1853, the Union Church, described as a "colored church," was located on the south side of Fuller Street, between Detroit and Elizabeth; in late 1857 it met at 504 High Street. *Ann Arbor News*, Feb. 27, 1996. The Bethel A.M.E. Church of Ann Arbor has roots in this same period.
101. Tiya Miles, "'Shall Woman's Voice Be Hushed?': Laura Smith Haviland in Abolitionist Women's History" in *Michigan Historical Review*, Vol. 39, No. 2, Fall 2013, 18.
102. Stacey M. Robertson, *Hearts Beating for Liberty: Women Abolitionists in the Old Northwest* (Chapel Hill: University of North Carolina Press, 2010), 167.

adjudged, had no legal claim to equal status with "the dominant race." The life of one such Michigander refuted any legitimacy for this "pernicious"[103] and jaundiced view that the U.S. Constitution had—despite its flaws—described not as property, or chattel, or sub-human, but as "persons."[104]

---

103. Opinion of Justice John Marshall Harlan, *Plessy v. Ferguson*, 163 U.S. 537, 559 (1896).
104. Art. I, Sec. 2, Clause 3, Sec. 9, Clause 1; Art. IV, Sec. 2, Clause 3.

Part Two

William Dollarson
From Virginia to Michigan

A Saga of Self-Liberation

In Spring, magnolias are in soft bloom and apple trees are in full flower, as if to preserve the memory of the George Hunt Farm from which this burying ground originated in the 1840s. The 1856 chapel of quarried limestone and the 1870 office building remain. Frederick Law Olmsted, world-renowned American landscape architect and conservationist, enhanced its original beauty with a picturesque design in the 1890s. Majestic groves of trees and lush vegetation denote that the site seeks to evoke peace, tranquility, harmony, quietude. Veneration and remembrance are to be vital here, lest any forget.

This is Elmwood Cemetery in the venerable city of Detroit. It is among the oldest, non-denominational, continuously operating cemeteries in Michigan.

The land is steeped in history. Native Americans well knew the creek that continues to flow through its grounds. Governors, mayors, judges, lawyers, doctors, ministers, business leaders, abolitionists, and other notables have been interred here, along with family members who shared in their lives. Many who served their country in peace and in war have their final resting places here. A special section, S, holds the graves of loyal soldiers who fought in the Civil War for Union and liberty, including those of the 1st Michigan Colored Regiment, the State's contribution to a national military that became officially open to all males. The headstones offer proof that the veterans were not separated by race. The U.S. flag flies continuously here as a tribute to the patriots who committed to offering up the ultimate sacrifice. Each Veterans Day, a ceremony is held to honor those who took up arms on behalf of the nation's rebirth of freedom. It demonstrates an altogether fitting and proper level of care.

In 2016, Elmwood received designation by the National Park Service as a significant site connected to the National Underground Railroad Network to Freedom. In 2020, Elmwood expanded its educational offerings to include a self-guided map, completed in collaboration with the NPS, "identifying the locations of those who participated in or supported the underground railroad network to freedom." Twenty-one individuals are listed on the map with biographical information and, in some cases, a portrait. One soldier of the 102nd, Kinchen Artis of Battle Creek, is included, a rarity, for few such images exist.[105]

In an open space at Historic Elmwood, not far from the honored gravesites of veterans of the army of liberation, with no mighty oaks or flowering cherries to shade and shelter their markers, the remains of two 19th century Michiganders lay in the long-lived grass, unnoticed, unremarkable. Unlike the graves in the Civil War soldier section, no veterans' signage marks these two weather-worn stones. Nothing inscribed on their humble stones indicates what service they might have performed for their generation of Americans and for all those to come.

The man was of an age in life not conducive to the vagaries of encampments or battles. His spouse witnessed him go off to war, perhaps never to return, leaving her to sustain the life they had led together. No one compelled them to undertake this risk. No conscription law applied; no government policy yet allowed his bearing of arms. The couple chose purely of their own volition to volunteer. The man would return from the war and die of a good old age, while

---

105. https://www.elmwoodhistoriccemetery.org/images/9364_Elmwood_small_UGRR_Map_13x19.pdf Artis is not identified; see Jack Dempsey, *Michigan and the Civil War: A Great and Bloody Sacrifice* (Charleston: The History Press, 2012), 90, and *Record of Service*, Vol. 46, 8. See Illustrations for the image.

she, a decade younger, would follow him to the grave only two years afterward. Love and loss are bound up inextricably in their legacy.

Because he wore no uniform, he would draw no post-war pension, be entitled to no badge of honor, be hailed for his heroism. Only for those who knew him and of him was his service known and appreciated, especially among the small circle of a General's staff in which he became integral and who cared about him as he cared for them. His task was to sustain them through the food he cooked—a pillar of any successful military endeavor, if not all human enterprises. In this open part of Section G, their headstone identifies those buried here with a simple inscription:

> William Dollarson
> Died May 9, 1889
> Aged 81 Years
> Maria
> wife of
> Wm. Dollarson
> Died Dec. 22, 1891
> Aged 72 Years

Below these inscriptions, what appears to be a verse is illegible. The graves are never specially marked, never honored with a U.S. flag, never designated as the remains of a Civil War veteran. Equally absent is any hint of the couple's participation in the Underground Railroad. The observer cannot help, standing graveside, possessing knowledge about the role of liberator played by William, and supported by his wife, to be drawn to a knee, or both knees if physically able, in awe and appreciation for the courage, sacrifice, and love represented in these names.

The 1860 Federal (Eighth) census disclosed a population of over 31 million including nearly 4 million enslaved persons. Information recorded on free persons included the name of each person in an abode, their age, gender, race, and occupation, and place of birth, among other data. As to race, the Census provided three choices for the category: W for White, B for Black, and M for mulatto, i.e., someone of mixed race. This fuller inquiry resulted in an entry for one head of household as follows:[106]

Name: William Dolarson
Age: 49
Birth Year: abt 1811
Gender: Male
Race: Black
Birth Place: Virginia
Home in 1860: Detroit Ward 7, Wayne, Michigan
Dwelling Number: 478
Family Number: 551
Occupation: Cook
Household Members:

Name	Age
William Dolarson	49
Maria Dolarson	39
Catharine Gifford	25

Much is revealed by the report made to the census taker. His birthplace: Virginia, a slave State. His characterization as "Black" and not "Mulatto"—ostensibly identifying one of largely, or fully, African American heritage. His birth year: not fixed, but stated as "about" 1811. Combining these three indicia, it can be deduced that William had been born into slavery. As for Maria, she was 10 years younger, consistent with the disparity found on their grave marker. She, too, is listed as "B" and born in New York (in 1820 or 1821). That State did not completely abolish slavery until 1827, so, apparently, she became emancipated after the change in New York law. Their last name is spelled with a singular "l," reflecting perhaps pronunciation alone,

---

106. Page 65 of Census, Detroit Ward 7, Wayne County.

perhaps a spelling approach that is not attentive. His occupation as "Cook" dovetails with the kind of service he performed for Alpheus Williams and the rest of the staff. The third person in the household also was recorded as "B" with a birthplace of Kentucky, a slave State. The relationship, however, is unclear. A final note: the three who formed "Family No. 551" lived adjacent to non-blacks on either side, with families of "M" individuals recorded nearby.

Ward 7 on the east side of downtown Detroit was bounded by the Detroit River to the south, Gratiot Avenue on the north, Rivard on the west, and Dequindre to the east. The 165 Russell address in the two city directories was on that north/south street one block east of Rivard and north of Jefferson Avenue, where the street began. Today, Russell is truncated south of Gratiot, and Antietam Avenue takes up its line before it, too, no longer runs south. The Lafayette Park development replaced the street, which in later years had become part of the Black Bottom neighborhood.

In King George County, Virginia, in 1860, three of every five persons were enslaved, evidencing that a plantation economy had long found fertile soil on the Northern Neck.[107] William remembered that he had been born here—his tombstone suggests 1807 or 1808—and taken to Fredericksburg at age 6. In 2022, Congress designated it a National Heritage Area, official recognition of unique history that includes the birthplaces of three U.S. Presidents.[108] Robert E. Lee was born in next-door Westmoreland County in 1807 to one of the "first families" of Virginia.[109] Although the two Americans were nearly the same age, much separated them. Lee received his name from parents. William Dollarson was a name later assumed; retelling his life story many years later, he remembered the name he was assigned in Virginia: Samuel Lacey.

William could identify the family he had belonged to, but

---

107. *Map of Virginia: Showing the Distribution of its Slave Population from the Census of 1860* (Washington: Henry S. Graham, 1861), Library of Congress.
108. S. 1942, Pub. L. No. 117-339, 7-8.
109. See http://www.stratfordhall.org

apparently not the one that belonged to him. "His mistress, who when a baby nursed at his grandmother's breast, was Mrs. Lucy Alexander."[110] She was, he reported, a niece of George Mercer Brooke, who built a distinguished career in the U.S. Army. Commissioned 1st Lieutenant in the 5th U.S. Infantry on May 3, 1808, he fought in the War of 1812 and was promoted to Brevet Major-General for service in the Mexican-American War.[111] In 1844 he was put in command of the military department that encompassed Michigan. Brooke was born in nearby King William County, Virginia; the family had a long history in Virginia and Maryland, including U.S. Supreme Court Justice Roger Brooke Taney of the infamous 1857 *Dred Scott* decision.[112] As for the niece, the 1820 Federal Census recorded an individual of that name in Stafford County, the location of Fredericksburg. Her household comprised 6 White persons and 35 persons of color, all enslaved. Nine male slaves under age 14 were included—which would encompass someone of Samuel Lacey's—William's age.[113]

At age 18, William "was sold for debt" to a trader, who paid $350 and took him to Richmond.[114] He spent six weeks in a "slave pen." In an auction of 175 "human cattle," he was acquired by another trader for the New Orleans market. William fetched $460. The trip from Richmond was made in the brig *Robert Burns*; at New Orleans, the young man again stood on the auctioneer's block. A planter living

---

110. Detroit *Evening News*, Nov. 16, 1883, 2, reflecting a personal interview, under the headers "Slavery And Freedom / An Aged Detroiter Who Has Tasted Both. The Romantic Life History of Wm. L. Dolarson, and His Connection with the Famous Underground Railroad." Much of the detail that follows is drawn from this source.
111. Francis B. Heitman, *Historical Register and Dictionary of the United States Army*, Vol. 1 (Washington: Government Printing Office, 1903), 248.
112. R.A. Brock, *Virginia and Virginians* (Richmond: H.H. Hardesty, 1888), 88-90.
113. *Fourth Census of the United States*, Virginia, Stafford, 1.
114. For a life account of Charles W. Thompson, an escapee from Richmond who settled in Detroit, see William Still, *The Underground Rail Road: A Record of Facts, Authentic Narratives, Letters, &c.* (Philadelphia: Porter & Coates, 1872), 146-150.

six miles from Natchez, Mississippi, Alexander T. Dunbar, acquired Dollarson for $660. Dunbar owned a cotton plantation of 1,200 acres on which 115 slaves labored. The 1830 Census taker entered two persons with that last name for Adams County, one with 84 slaves and another with 93.[115]

Despite being sold off, William held some positive memories of his time in Virginia. Recalling his time with the Alexanders as not burdensome, "in turn he had become very much attached to the family." After being sold, "one of his mistress' sons met him in the road, and, with tears at the separation, took off his coat and urged him to take it to remember him by." His journey to New Orleans "on the whole was a measurably pleasant one for the young man, who seemed to find favor with his new owner." Dunbar, however, proved to be "one of the most cruel of men." Whippings of the enslaved workers were not uncommon, and William had not been exempted:

> Once Dunbar told Dolarson to take a woman who had been slow in her day's work down to the old shop and give her 500 lashes! He attempted to obey, but the blows were not severe enough to suit Dunbar, who made Dolarson strip off and then whipped him until the "blood squeaked in his boots."
>
> After eight years of such experience he was one evening ordered to whip another woman. This he could not do. He prayed God to help him to run. "And God said, Go!" and he went.

Flight took him into the nearby woods the first night, finding safety in darkness,[116] then into Natchez where he hid himself among people of color. Near sunset, he "ventured to go aboard an up-river boat.

---

115. Both appear on the same page 19.
116. For an evocative insight into this experience, see Jeanine Michna-Bales, *Through Darkness to Light: Photographs Along the Underground Railroad* (New York: Princeton Architectural Press, 2017). The journey portrayed begins in Louisiana, traverses Michigan through Coldwater, Jonesville, Jackson County, Lodi Township, Ann Arbor, Farmington, Oakland County, Macomb County, Romeo, St. Clair County, and Port Huron to Sarnia, Ontario.

Strangely enough no one disturbed him." Unable to find a place to hide, he exited the vessel near 11 p.m. at a woodyard known as Smith's Landing, Arkansas, having exchanged aboard ship "the colored fireman's free papers for a pair of boots and some trinkets." His newly acquired name: "Jomer Dolarson." How he ended up as "William" was not explained.

The escapee worked in the yard for almost three weeks. The manager treated him kindly, paying him $7 for his work, and then recommended him to a steamboat captain for carriage to Cincinnati at half price. The emotional state of the fugitive can only be imagined as the vessel plied the Ohio River eastward from the Mississippi and docked—not in slaveholding Kentucky—at the wharf in free Ohio. He worked in a restaurant there for a month before traveling to Chillicothe and Cleveland, and then to Buffalo. He resided in that New York city across from sure freedom in Canada for two years, finding employment aboard a Great Lakes vessel. Around 1835, he was in Canandaigua, N.Y., where he married Maria Fletcher.

In 1836, they made their home in Detroit. William continued to sail the lakes for another dozen years. During the ice-bound winters, "he cooked and did the work of a caterer. As such he provided the wedding and other feasts of many who are now among Detroit's most prominent citizens." In the winter of 1837-8 he became one of the founding members of the Second Baptist Church on Croghan street.

The U.S. Census of 1840 did not seek or contain much family information, its main purpose being an enumeration for purposes of congressional reapportionment. Later iterations would expand upon the queries and reveal more categories of interest to historians and genealogists. Found in Detroit is this entry: "Wm Dolanson" or (more correctly) "Wm Dolarson" (someone misreading the "r" for an "n"), with a home specified within the categories of "City, County, State" as Pontiac, Oakland, Michigan. In his household are:

Free Colored Persons—Males—Under 10: 2
Free Colored Persons—Males—24 thru 35: 1
Free Colored Persons—Females—10 thru 23: 1

Total Free Colored Persons: 4
Total All Persons—Free White, Free Colored, Slaves: 4

Important information is revealed here. First, this household is "colored"—and "free." Second, there are three males, two under ten years of age, one between the ages of 24 and 35. It can be surmised that "Wm"—a common abbreviation for William—was born between 1805 and 1816 or so. William appears to be accompanied by a spouse born between 1817 and 1830. Maria Dollarson's life span is specified on the common gravestone: she died in 1891 at age 72, making her birth date either in 1819 or 1820. Both possibilities fit these census data. The couple had two sons, both listed as under the age of 10 in the 1840 census.

William's interest in working for the liberation of the enslaved, and on behalf of equal treatment of free Blacks, is demonstrated by his participation in the October 1843 Convention of the Colored Citizens of Michigan, which met in Detroit. He was a delegate, one of 12 from Detroit, with others traveling from Jackson, Marshall, and Washtenaw County to participate. When the convention met on Thursday evening, an item of business was to determine how to defray the expenses of the meeting. The delegates approved a motion to establish a finance committee, with its members appointed by President William C. Monroe. Of the three so appointed, the name of "Wm. Dolerson" appears in the record. It would appear that his financial acumen held the respect of the others. Another indication might be from the order of the names as listed among the delegation: Reverend Monroe; Richard Gordon; Henry Jackson; William Dolerson; William Lambert; Willis R. Wilson; Alford Derrick; Madison J. Lightfoot; Robert Allen; George R. Sims; Henry Bibb; and Othello P. Hoyt. On Friday evening, after singing "a Liberty song, the convention was opened with prayer by Wm. Dolerson."[117] His contributions to the proceedings were varied and vital.

---

117. *Minutes of the State Convention, of the Colored Citizens of the State of Michigan, Held in the City of Detroit on the 26th and 27th of October, 1843 for the Purpose of Considering Their Moral & Political Condition, as Citizens of the State*, available at https://omeka.coloredconventions.org/items/show/245 . "Dolerson" appears in this document at 183, 187, 190.

In 1847, the Dollarsons bought and moved onto a farm near Royal Oak. Their vision through this land ownership was to set an example "in order to encourage the colored people of Detroit to become landholders." When the Fugitive Slave Act was passed in 1850, they "sacrificed" the farm, losing $800, and moved to Canada to escape capture and re-enslavement.[118] They moved back to Detroit after a few months when "his white friends assured him that they would never permit such a wrong" as allowing a "slave catcher"—someone hired to retrieve an owner's human property—to take him.

> The enactment of the second Fugitive Slave Law, that of 1850, had a depressing effect upon the colored people of Detroit. Many of them sacrificed their property to get away, not knowing how soon they might be carried back into slavery, and it was found necessary by the leading men of the community to assure them that the danger was more imaginary than real. But a sense of security could hardly be established among them. The aiding of fugitives to escape, however, continued to prosper, the number of fugitives crossing at this point became larger than ever, as many as forty-three having been run over in one night, and if the negroes were afraid to live in Detroit, the slave-hunters also gave the place a wide berth. Isolated minor cases of slave arrests happened from time to time, but little excitement attended them, and no more Slaves were returned from this point.[119]

In 1851, Dollarson was appointed custodian of the Old State Capitol school, located on Griswold at State, and the couple moved into the building. The location was an apt one: here, in 1835, delegates to

---

118. They are not enumerated in the Federal Census (Seventh) of that year. The 1850 law, Pub. L. 31–60, 9 Stat. 462, was the first since the original, 1 Stat. 302, "An Act respecting fugitives from justice, and persons escaping from the service of their masters," enacted in 1793.
119. Burton & Burton, 1125.

a constitutional convention had crafted a document enabling the Territory of Michigan to obtain statehood from the U.S. Congress. Within its walls, words had been set as if into stone, forever outlawing the notion that one human could hold property in another.

The Dollarsons' participation in the Underground Railroad began energetically at this juncture:

> They began through his acquaintance with Asher Ray, a wealthy colored resident of Pittsfield, Washtenaw county. One night Mr. Ray ran to him and said he had a lot of escaped slaves out in his wagon, and wanted to know what he should do with them. "I'll take them" said Mr. Dollarson. He took them, hustled them down cellar, and early the next morning went out to see the lay of the land. Rash and dangerous as the action seemed to be and really was, he told them to follow him and boldly led the way to the ferry, paid their fare and told the captain to take them across. The captain did as he was bid, and the underground railroad was in successful operation.

At times when such openness proved too risky, escapees were ferried across the Detroit River in small vessels under cover of darkness. Similar occasions presented themselves with as many as 11 escaping. Sometimes they were hidden in the Finney Hotel barn across from the Capitol; Dollarson held a key to lock the barn.[120] Sometimes he got them over the river without delay. He joined with the hotel proprietor, Seymour Finney, in ushering formerly enslaved to their freedom in Canada.[121] More specifically:

---

120. A State Historical Marker has marked the site since 1980. Ashlee, 465. The proprietor is cited in Mary Ellen Snodgrass, *The Underground Railroad: An Encyclopedia of People, Places, And Operations*, Vol. One (Armonk: Sharpe Reference, 2008), 192.

121. See Philip P. Mason & Paul J. Pentecost, *From Bull Run to Appomattox: Michigan's Role in the Civil War* (Detroit: Wayne State University Press, 1961), 14.

Whenever a "train" in the shape of a covered or straw filled wagon arrived, the driver seemed to know that he was to rein up his team at the back door of the Capitol school, where the utterance of a peculiar call was sure to bring out the janitor in less than no time. Mr. Dolarson in turn lost no time in getting over to the hotel, where he awakened Mr. Finney with the news that a team wanted stabling. If by chance the hostler was awakened, he was always sent back to bed with the assurance that his services were not needed. Going over to the barn, the landlord put up the team, while Mr. Dolarson took the fugitives in tow, and, by a direct route or by circuitous ways which led through the woods of Hamtramck or Springwells, brought them to the river, across which he or some other person would row them to that which was really "the land of the free," as well as "the home of the brave."

At times, the slave catchers stayed in Finney's hotel while seeking out the lost "property." On at least three occasions while their teams were put up in the hotel's barn, the escapees were in the hayloft above.

Another source of support came from Alanson Sheley and his wife, who pledged $5 for every refugee who received assistance on their road to freedom. The Sheleys also "contributed generously of their wardrobes for the destitute."[122]

In 1854, Dollarson traveled to California to engage in gold prospecting, but his efforts proved unrewarding. After a couple of years, he returned to Detroit poorer. His liberation activities suffered as a result. An 1857 municipal directory contained a listing for "William

---

122. Sheley came to Detroit in 1831 and became a major figure in the lumber industry. "Originally a Whig, he was one of those who organized the Republican Party ..." His wife was Ann Elizabeth Drury. Their son George A. Sheley served in the 1st Michigan Light Artillery. *Cyclopedia of Michigan: Historical and Biographical Synopsis of General History of the State* (New York: Western Pub. & Engraving Co., 1900), 288-289 (with image). The Sheley Family House on Mackinac Island is a bed and breakfast. http://www.smallpointmackinac.com/home

Dolarson (col'd) b. 165 Russell."[123] The Census taker in 1860 reported his occupation as cook. It was a year marked by extreme grief. An item in the listing of "City Mortality for the Month of March" included this: "Infant child of William Dolarson deceased."[124] The Census taker came by on June 19, three months after their loss. A 23-year-old son was a waiter and musician on the steamer *Lady Elgin* and went down with her on September 8.[125] The Dollarsons had 20 children together; by the time William recounted his story to a reporter in 1883 "all are now dead."[126] Johnston's Detroit City Directory, published under date of 1861, contained this entry (on page 149):

Dolarson Mrs, embroider, 165 Russell

It also listed "Dolarson Geo W, colored, baker, 167 Russell," evidently referring to one of their sons who also had employment in the culinary trades and lived next door.[127]

Alpheus Williams was also recorded in the 1860 Census in Detroit. He lived in Ward 3, with Gratiot again marking the northern boundary, Randolph and St. Aubin the west and east limits. He was listed as 48 years of age, making William Dollarson narrowly his senior.[128] He, too, knew loss. Married in 1839, his wife Jane Larned had passed in December 1848, age 30. They had lost an infant child. He had served his country in the Mexican-American War, not in a major battle but against guerilla fighters. He knew the dangers inherent in warfare, both from study and direct experience. If another war came, and he became involved, he well knew the importance of gathering people around him he could trust. No doubt, they would be people whom he did not want to lose.

---

123. *Polk's Detroit City Directory for 1857*, 172.
124. *Detroit Free Press*, Apr. 4, 1860, 1.
125. A State historical marker in Milwaukee commemorates the disaster.
126. *Detroit Evening News*, Nov. 16, 1883, 2, and Nov. 28, 1883, 3.
127. Milo M. Quaife ed., *From the Cannon's Mouth: The Civil War Letters of General Alpheus S. Williams* (Detroit: Wayne State University Press, 1959), 46 n.8 [hereafter "*FTCM*"], states that the two were "of the same address" and surmises that William was son, not father.
128. Page 148 of the Census, Detroit Ward 3, Wayne County.

A list of Underground Railroad sites in Michigan as designated by the State and as of the date of publication can be found in the most modern study of the topic. A welcome resource, it has the misfortune of telling only half the story when it comes to the Finney Hotel Barn.[1]

Across Griswold from the stable, the Capitol—the only such structure during Territorial days, and the first upon Statehood—stood tall as a symbol of self-government. Not at first—on September 22, 1823, the cornerstone was placed within the triangle of streets where the Woodward Plan had laid out a public space. The building faced south, designed to impress visitors approaching it from the Detroit River where debarkation occurred. Completing the project was no rush job; five years passed before it could be dedicated. When completed, observers who climbed interior stairs to its cupola tower had a breathtaking view of Detroit. The tower reached 140 feet, making it the building that exceeded all others in height. The building served as home to the Territorial government and location for the Governor and Legislature until 1848. It was home to the Michigan Territorial Library from 1828 to 1837, when it became the State Library.

The plan of the building included: a basement level for the executive branch; a first floor devoted to the hall, library, and offices for the Legislative Council, plus the Governor's office; and an expansive second floor to accommodate more offices and meeting rooms. Its design followed Greek Revival principles, with an elegant portico supported by six Ionic columns. Those who contributed to its architecture evidently had vision, for it far surpassed immediate needs and revealed intentions to enter the Union with a capitol commensurate with Michigan's elevated status. It served as "a superb ornament to Detroit, the rising metropolis of Michigan."

On this ground, delegates met in 1835 to devise a constitution to qualify Michigan for Statehood. Among its provisions was the prohibition on slavery, modeled after the similar language of the Northwest Ordinance. The provision slammed the door on the practice that had existed for over a century under French and British governance. The Convention also debated Black suffrage; Dar-

---

1. Mull, 179-180 (Appendix 3).

ius Comstock of Lenawee County moved, unsuccessfully, to omit "White" in the voting provisions of the new charter. In 1846, the Legislature declined to extend the franchise or to repeal an 1838 prohibiting interracial marriages. When the first revised code of Michigan was adopted in 1838, the act requiring free Blacks to register in order to remain was not incorporated.

Across the street, abolitionist Seymour Finney purchased a plot of land in 1850 and erected a tavern with a large barn. He continued to own the site into the 1860s. As proprietor of the Temperance Hotel on Woodward Avenue, he pressed the barn into use as a hiding place for runaways. The Finney stop on the Underground Railroad could not have been located at a more appropriate place, across from where Michigan's constitutional prohibition on slavery had been penned.

On March 25, 1865, as the final week of the War in Virginia was about to unfold, a collection of 5,000 books became accessible to the public when the Detroit Public Library opened for service. The site was a room in the old Capitol High School, repurposed from its days as the center of government for Michigan. Now it was a center of learning.

Soon after the Civil War concluded, the media began to publish stories about the mysterious, covert, and dramatic aspects of the Michigan routes on the Underground Railroad. Sites were hailed as waystations—not all accurately so. On one that had indisputably served as a haven was posted, by George DeBaptiste in 1870, a sign "identifying its importance as a place to hide runaway slaves before the war." On the famous Finney Barn appeared:

> Notice To All Stockholders In The Underground Railroad
> This Office Is Closed
> Hereafter All Stockholders Will Receive Dividends According To Their Merits[2]

From the east side of the Park, and at its southern boundary at the corner of State, one can look south and see the Detroit River.

---

2. Finkenbine, "A Beacon of Liberty," 83-101.

It takes little imagination to envision the reaction of an escapee from slavery to have in his or her eyesight the destination so earnestly hoped for, where liberty awaited. Such a setting makes this Park unique among Underground Railroad sites in Michigan—and perhaps as the only place where the gateway to freedom in Canada can be glimpsed from the seat of government of, initially, a U.S. Territory and, thereafter, a sovereign State of the Union.

And the War Came

In an event that in modern times had a similar domestic impact to the attack on Pearl Harbor, December 7th, 1941, or the September 11th, 2001, terrorist attacks that included the Pentagon building across from the nation's capital, the Federal military installation of Fort Sumter in the harbor of Charleston, South Carolina, took fire beginning early in the morning of April 12, 1865. Outnumbered and outgunned by hostile forces of the so-called Confederate States of America and of South Carolina, the garrison of U.S. soldiers were forced to surrender after holding on for more than a day. The justification for the attack: a national presidential election that jeopardized the security of the slave system of the South.

The formation in Jackson, Michigan, of a new political party in 1854 sought to establish as the majority view that slavery ought to be put on a path to extinction. It united under the "Free Soil" banner a diverse collection of Whigs, Liberty Party members, and others who sought a nation that promoted growth through non-slave policies. Free Soilers maintained that the Founders had intended in the Constitution "to separate the national government from the institution of slavery and to prevent the institution's spread."[129] The party's roots lay partially in the Liberty Party, whose national candidate for President in 1840 and 1844, James G. Birney, was a prominent Saginaw-area abolitionist.[130] The national Free Soil Party had a presence in Michigan at its formation in 1848,[131] and Free Soil

---

129. Hershock, 112.
130. Finkenbine, "A Beacon of Liberty," 89.
131. Id.

Township and the village of Free Soil were named for the party in Mason County.[132] Most Republicans identified themselves either as Free-Soilers, former Whigs, or anti-slavery Democrats.

That year's November elections produced "a political revolution" in Michigan. The "fledgling Republican Party handily defeated its Democratic opponents," with Republican Kinsley Bingham winning 53 percent of the vote for Governor. Republicans gained control of the Legislature and won in three of the four U.S. House races. When Bingham delivered his inaugural address, the "bulk of his message was devoted to the issue of slavery."[133] He laid out the Republican vision for a national policy, calling for "the divorce of the General Government from slavery:"

> Neither Congress or the President should take any part in upholding or extending such an evil. Without any interference whatever, with the internal concerns of States, not committed by the Constitution to the supervision of Congress or the Executive, the power and influence of both departments, should be exerted for the benefit of freedom, rather than for the benefit of slavery. There should be no slavery in the District of Columbia—none in national Territories—no slave catching under national law—no slave trade in American vessels, allowed or regulated by acts of Congress—no slave auction under process, out of the Federal Courts. These things done, the example and influence of the National Government would be on the side of freedom, and the power of reason and the force of sympathy, might be safely relied upon, to bring about universal emancipation.[134]

Two years later, Bingham won reelection as Republicans continued in

---

132. Walter Romig, *Michigan Place Names* (Detroit: Wayne State University Press, 1986), 212.
133. Id. 135-136.
134. *Messages*, 298-299.

control of the Legislature and captured all four seats in the U.S. House of Representatives. Their presidential candidate, John C. Fremont, also won Michigan by a vote of 71,762 - 52,136, though losing the national contest to Democrat James Buchanan. At the State level, the outcome was an "overwhelming" Republican triumph. Lewis Cass joined the Buchanan cabinet, opening up one of Michigan's seats in the U.S. Senate. Zachariah Chandler, one of the leaders at Jackson in the formation of the Republican Party and a staunch anti-slavery advocate, succeeded to the post. The 1858 State canvass resulted in the same, if not as robust, outcome as two years prior, with Republican Moses Wisner elected as Governor. Continued control in Lansing meant that the expiration of the term of U.S. Senator Charles E. Stuart on March 3, 1859, a Democrat, enabled election of a Republican to the other of Michigan's seats in the upper house. Former Governor Bingham "was handily elected."[135]

Elections at Federal and State levels in late 1860 came when America "was in a state of highly unstable equilibrium." After the votes were tallied and announced, "something was bound to break." Secession—withdrawal from the United States—had become a Southern threat if the outcome produced a Republican as President.[136] On Tuesday, November 6, in a contest against three other tickets, Republican Abraham Lincoln of Illinois won a national Electoral College majority. In his home town of Springfield as well as in Michigan, "joy that the Northwest had at last sent one of its sons to the White House" reigned.[137] In the Wolverine State, "the Republican victory was complete." Another founder of the party, Jacksonian Austin Blair, was handily elected as Governor.[138]

The national Republican platform, and Lincoln's personal creed, relied on the language of the Declaration of Independence that "all

---

135. Hershock, 143-144, 154-156.
136. Bruce Catton, *The Coming Fury, The Centennial History of the Civil War, Volume One* (Garden City: Doubleday & Co., 1961), 87-88, 100-101.
137. Id. 110.
138. Hershock, 161-162.

men are created free." To anti-slavery advocates, "all" meant "everybody." Lincoln's Democratic opponent, Stephen A. Douglas, asserted that the Declaration was of limited scope: "all men" meant "the white race alone."[139] Even if not in agreement on full equality under these founding documents, "northern farmers and artisans gave their allegiance to a Constitution that was unrecognizable to the Slave Power."[140] Because of this egalitarian view, the October 1843 Convention of the Colored Citizens of Michigan approved a message to the people of Michigan for redress of grievances predicated on this statement: "the Declaration of Independence is the textbook of this nation and without its doctrines be maintained, our government is insecure."[141] The 1860 national canvass validated the Free Soil interpretation. The Republican national ticket won Michigan with nearly 89,000 votes against some 66,000 for the three other candidates.

Lincoln's election served as the linchpin to more than rhetorical division. Secessionists feared that the new Administration would consign the South to a future where the formerly enslaved population would gain equal political rights and, since they might be the majority population, political power.[142] South Carolina held a convention in Charleston and on December 20 approved an Ordinance of Secession; on the 24th, a "Declaration" gave the causes, initially

---

139. Robert W. Johannsen, *Stephen A. Douglas* (New York: Oxford University Press, 1973), 570, 735.
140. James Oakes, *The Crooked Path to Abolition: Abraham Lincoln and the Antislavery Constitution* (New York: W.W. Norton & Co., 2021), xiv-xv.
141. McRae, 9-10.
142. See Charles B. Dew, *Apostles of Disunion: Southern Secession Commissioners and the Causes of the Civil War* (Charlottesville: University Press of Virginia, 2001), 46, 77-80. It is a main theme of Edward A. Pollard, *The Lost Cause; A New Southern History of the War of the Confederates* (New York: E.B. Treat & Co., 1867), from which that mythology derived its title. A contrary, and illusory argument, is in Edward Spencer, "Confederate Negro Enlistments" in *The Annals of the War* (Philadelphia: Times Pub. Co., 1879), 536ff, arguing that the enslaved "behaved in the most exemplary manner everywhere," provided no aid to Union forces, and "had no fight in them" since they were treated kindly by and were attached to their masters. Maryland native Spencer of Randallstown wrote for Baltimore newspapers.

centered on non-compliance with the Fugitive Slave Clause of the U.S. Constitution by Michigan and other non-slaveholding States. This policy was decried at length:

> Those States have assumed the right of deciding upon the propriety of our domestic institutions; and have denied the rights of property established in fifteen of the States and recognized by the Constitution; they have denounced as sinful the institution of slavery; they have permitted open establishment among them of societies, whose avowed object is to disturb the peace and to eloign the property of the citizens of other States. They have encouraged and assisted thousands of our slaves to leave their homes; and those who remain, have been incited by emissaries, books and pictures to servile insurrection.

The defining event, however, was election of a Republican President:

> A geographical line has been drawn across the Union, and all the States north of that line have united in the election of a man to the high office of President of the United States, whose opinions and purposes are hostile to slavery. He is to be entrusted with the administration of the common Government, because he has declared that "Government cannot endure permanently half slave, half free," and that the public mind must rest in the belief that slavery is in the course of ultimate extinction.[143]

Others unwilling to accept the outcome in the Electoral College took the same step: in January, the States of Mississippi, Florida, Alabama, Georgia, and Louisiana; in February, Texas and Tennessee. These

---

143. Frank Moore ed., *The Rebellion Record*, First Volume (New York: G.P. Putnam, 1861), Diary of Events, 3-4, Documents, 3-4.

seceding States joined together in the so-called Southern Confederacy under a constitution containing explicit protections for slavery. It sought to enshrine "the right of property in negro slaves," and it proudly spoke of "slaves and other property" and of "negro slavery," evidencing a racially biased foundation for the new government and its society. The organizing document sought to make permanent the chattel status "of the African race" within Confederate jurisdiction. The specific provisions—four pillars of a government founded on racial differences—included:

> Article I, Sec. 9(1). The importation of Negroes of the African race from any foreign country, other than the slave-holding States or Territories of the United States of America, is hereby forbidden; and Congress is required to pass such laws as shall effectually prevent the same.
>
> Article I, Sec. 9(2). Congress shall also have power to prohibit the introduction of slaves from any State not a member of, or Territory not belonging to, this Confederacy.
>
> Article I, Sec. 9(4). No bill of attainder, ex post facto law, or law denying or impairing the right of property in negro slaves shall be passed.
>
> Article IV, Sec. 2(1). The citizens of each State shall be entitled to all the privileges and immunities of citizens in the several States; and shall have the right of transit and sojourn in any State of this Confederacy, with their slaves and other property; and the right of property in said slaves shall not be thereby impaired.
>
> Article IV, Sec. 3(3). The Confederate States may acquire new territory; and Congress shall have power to legislate and provide governments for the inhabitants of all territory belonging to the Confederate States, lying without the limits of the several states; and may permit them, at such times, and in such manner as it may by law provide, to form states to be admitted into the Confederacy. In all such territory, the

institution of negro slavery as it now exists in the Confederate States, shall be recognized and protected by Congress, and by the territorial government: and the inhabitants of the several Confederate States and Territories, shall have the right to take to such territory any slaves lawfully held by them in any of the states or territories of the Confederate states.[144]

Human beings of a particular race as "property"—such a notion formed the cornerstone of the Southern nation. Indeed, the Vice-President of this break-away government, Alexander H. Stephens, openly declared this the aim in a speech given that same month:

> The new constitution has put at rest, *forever*, all the agitating questions relating to our peculiar institution—African slavery as it exists amongst us—the proper *status* of the negro in our form of civilization. This was the immediate cause of the late rupture and present revolution.

Stephens reviewed how the Founders had approached the issue during the American Revolution and in the Federal structure that arose to govern the United States of America. He mentioned by name the "author" of the Declaration of Independence, and declared how Thomas Jefferson and his colleagues—Benjamin Franklin, James Madison, George Washington, among them—knew not a great truth:

> The prevailing ideas entertained by him and most of the leading statesmen at the time of the formation of the old constitution, were that the enslavement of the African was in violation of the laws of nature; that it was wrong in principle, socially, morally, and politically. It was an evil they knew not well how to deal with, but the general opinion of the men

---

144. *Constitution of the Confederate States of America* (Montgomery: Shorter & Reid, 1861).

of that day was that, somehow or other in the order of Providence, the institution would be evanescent and pass away. This idea, though not incorporated in the constitution, was the prevailing idea at that time. The constitution, it is true, secured every essential guarantee to the institution while it should last, and hence no argument can be justly urged against the constitutional guarantees thus secured, because of the common sentiment of the day. Those ideas, however, were fundamentally wrong. They rested upon the assumption of the equality of races. This was an error.

This new nation, then, was conceived to protect the liberty of only some and dedicated to the proposition that not all humans are created equal. To his listeners in the Athenaeum theatre on Chippewa Square in Savannah, Georgia, the second-highest Confederate statesman then declared:

> Our new government is founded upon exactly the opposite idea; its foundations are laid, its corner-stone rests upon the great truth, that the negro is not equal to the white man; that slavery—subordination to the superior race—is his natural and normal condition.

At this utterance, so the record reflects, the audience responded with "Applause." Stephens continued:

> This, our new government, is the first, in the history of the world, based upon this great physical, philosophical, and moral truth.[145]

When the Confederate President sought to attempt "the vindication"

---

145. Henry Cleveland, *Alexander H. Stephens in Public and Private with Letters and Speeches, Before, During, and Since the War* (Philadelphia: National Publishing Co., 1866), 717, 721-722.

of the conduct of the Southern States leading up to secession and war, he asserted that "[n]o moral nor sentimental considerations were really involved" in the issues that "finally ruptured the Union." Although the idea of slavery was "repellent to the moral sense of mankind," Davis argued that the "rupture" arrived because the Republican party capture of the Presidency in November 1860 threatened a slaveholder's ability to take "his slaves" into territory "into which the non-slaveholder could go with <u>his</u> property of any sort."[146] Human beings as property: it was a fundamental premise of the Confederate cause.

Davis anticipated that an attempt at disunion would in no wise "be peaceably exercised." His background and experience justified his appointment to command Mississippi's troops as Major-General. He undertook to prepare the State's war footing, an intent superseded when he was elected President of the Confederate States of America on February 9, 1861. He allowed himself to be inaugurated, believing he would soon return to command of the Army of Mississippi and to position it for the "long and bloody" war coming. His inaugural address avoided the "repellent" term as the underlying cause for secession and formation of a new government that was making preparations for war; instead, Davis spoke of a failure "to obtain respect for the rights to which we were entitled," now enshrined in "a Constitution differing only from that of our fathers in so far as it is explanatory of their well-known intent"—i.e., an "intent" to preserve the right of property in human beings.[147]

Representatives of this government were sent to Washington, D.C., to negotiate matters of difference—presumably including how to handle Federal installations, mails, and other nationally funded operations and resources. Years later, Davis excoriated the hostility of Michigan's two U.S. Senators to negotiating with the so-called "Confederacy." Kinsley S. Bingham opposed any "concession which the imperious slave power so insolently demands." Similarly,

---

146. Jefferson Davis, *The Rise and Fall of the Confederate Government*, Vol. I (New York: D. Appleton & Co., 1881), 1, 6-7.
147. Id. 227-236.

Zachariah Chandler urged the sending of "stiff-backed men" to any peace conference, or none, and was pleased when Governor Austin Blair declined the participation of Michigan.[148]

In Blair's inaugural remarks of January 2, 1861, he had spoken to the issue of secession—with dramatic bluntness:

> The existence of the government is threatened, not by enemies from without, but by traitors from within. The State of South Carolina, possessing a free white population of less than three hundred thousand, of all ages and sexes, has assumed to dissolve the national government. By a convention called under State authority, and without consulting any other State or people, and without the least discussion which seems to have been interdicted, she passed an ordinance annulling the laws and Constitution of the United States. In her own cherished phrase, she has seceded from the Union. If it could be properly done, I presume the country, generally, would be willing to let that restless, heady little nation, retire from the confederacy forever. But that cannot be, without admitting the right of secession to exist in all the States. This done, and no government remains to us; but only a voluntary association of States, dissolvable at the pleasure of any of them.[149]

The new Governor had become the seminal representative of Wolverine Free Soilers. Michigan's 1835 Constitution had been crafted, like other Midwestern polities, "during an age of growing democratic and egalitarian commitments." It was "a land of democratic vigor, cultural strength, racial and gender progress, and civic energy" that had reached an apogee in world history as "the most advanced democratic society." It was not a utopian society. But it was one rooted in liberty for all:

---

148. Id. 248-249.
149. *Joint Documents of the State of Michigan, for the Year 1860*, No. 2, 1-24 (Lansing: Hosmer & Kerr, 1861); *Messages*, 425-442.

> [T]here was a communally agreed to ideal, a model for behavior, a goal to be striven for, a moral code, a way of inspiring the young, a motivation for civic duty, a virtuous patriotism, a recognition of civic obligations, and, perhaps most telling, a willingness to bleed and die for one's home, especially as against sinful rebels who put the young republic at risk.[150]

Blair had no military background, but he became Commander-in-Chief of his State's military apparatus on the eve of its greatest challenge since becoming a U.S. Territory in 1805.

In his own inaugural, Abraham Lincoln had spoken of his hope for peace and disavowed any intention to initiate armed domestic conflict. He also promised to "hold, occupy, and possess the property and places belonging to the Government" of the United States. His words were unmistakably clear. So, too, was the language of a proposal by some to smooth the roiling waters of the American polity.

In that winter and spring of 1860-1861, members in Congress sought to resolve and restore fractured relations between South and North. Not since 1804 had the U.S. Constitution been amended. A 13th Amendment was proposed to be added in a desperate bid to bring back the seven States that had declared their secession from the Union and the formation of the Confederate States of America. President Lincoln took office the day this amendment received approval by Congress, and he tendered it to the States for ratification as by law he ought to have done. The text provided:

> No amendment shall be made to the Constitution which will authorize or give to Congress the power to abolish or interfere, within any State, with the domestic institutions thereof, including that of persons held to labor or service by the laws of said State.

---

150. Jon K. Lauck, *The Good Country: A History of the American Midwest, 1800-1900* (Norman: University of Oklahoma Press, 2022), 3-4, 29.

The phrase "persons held to labor or service" tracked the language of the Constitution itself. Nowhere did that 1787 document use "slavery" or "enslaved" to refer to an institution through which people largely from the continent of Africa were captured, bound, shipped, and put to a lifetime of work, all under force and against their will, on plantations and farms in the temperate sections of the United States. Instead, temporal language was employed, suggesting slavery would not become a permanent fixture in a land launched for purposes of expanding and protecting human liberty. Indeed, the Constitution's call for the ending of the international slave trade in 1808 had held open the vision of a nation inhabited wholly by free people.[151]

On April 12, 1861, military forces under the direction of the Confederate government attacked the Federal installation of Fort Sumter in Charleston harbor. Uniformed members of the U.S. Army defended the fort, which flew "Old Glory" from its flagpole. The American Civil War had begun. In his second inaugural speech, Lincoln recalled the moment:

> While the inaugural address was being delivered from this place, devoted altogether to *saving* the Union without war, insurgent agents were in the city seeking to *destroy* it without war—seeking to dissolve the Union, and divide effects, by negotiation. Both parties deprecated war, but one of them would *make* war rather than let the nation survive; and the other would *accept* war rather than let it perish. And the war came.[152]

---

151. See James Oakes, *The Crooked Path to Abolition*, and *Freedom National: The Destruction of Slavery in the United States, 1861-1865* (New York: W.W. Norton & Co., 2013). *The New York Times Magazine* sponsored the "1619 Project," a reinterpretation of American history. "Our democracy's founding ideals," its lead essay proclaimed, "were false when they were written," resting on slavery and White supremacy, whose existence made a mockery of the Declaration of Independence's "self-evident" truth that all men are created equal. Accordingly, the nation's birth came not in 1776 but in 1619, the year, the Project stated, when slavery arrived in Britain's North American colonies.
152. *Collected Works*, Vol. VIII, 332-333 (spelling revised; emphasis in original).

Michigan and Dollarson Go to War

On Tuesday, April 16, 1861, Michigan Governor Austin Blair arrived in Detroit to develop the State's initial response to the attack on Fort Sumter. President Abraham Lincoln had issued a call to the States for volunteers to put down the Southern rebellion. Blair met with civic leaders and the State Military Board, on which sat Michigan's premier military figure in the antebellum era, Alpheus Williams. As a militia leader, an officer in the Mexican-American War, and student of warfare, Williams, at 50 years of age, composed both a sturdy and expert martial figure. Within days, the First Michigan Infantry Brigade was authorized with Williams in command as Brigadier-General, and the 1st Michigan Infantry Regiment was organized. During the next several months, Williams served as the commander of the camp of instruction at Fort Wayne in Detroit, seeing capably to the organization and training of volunteers in additional Michigan regiments.[153]

Preparing raw recruits for fighting at the front proved less than fully satisfying for Michigan's top General. Williams felt drawn to lead troops in battle. In August 1861, his efforts at a battlefield post paid off when Congress approved his presidential nomination to become a Brigadier-General of Volunteers. He began to assemble his staff in preparation for orders from the War Department. At first, he was assigned right where he was, "to duty with the Michigan regiments in course of organization." On September 17, 1861, he received orders to "repair to Washington and report for duty to the

---

153. *Michigan in the War*, 3, 22, 166, 221-222.

commanding general Department of the Potomac."[154] Having a staff became urgent. For his Adjutant-General, he tapped William D. Wilkins, son of a prominent Detroit judge and a veteran of the war in Mexico. Lawyer Henry M. Whittelsey would serve in the capacity of quartermaster. Both were officers in the Detroit Light Guard militia unit.[155] For his principal aide-de-camp, he chose Samuel E. Pittman, an official in a Detroit bank and brother of James Pittman, another figure known to Michiganders for his military acumen. Son Charles ("Larned") Williams came along as a civilian adjutant for the first several months.[156] And Williams asked aboard a man who had known slavery first hand, who had liberated himself, who had been a conductor on the Underground Railroad, and who agreed to go. On September 27, the staff—William Dollarson included—departed Detroit by train for Washington, D.C., with horses and baggage. The General followed the next day. Their route was to Cleveland, on to Philadelphia and Baltimore, and finally to the nation's capital.

Once reunited, the small contingent awaited a command, staying in Washington. On Monday, October 7, they mounted and with three wagons drawn by mule teams moved out toward their post, billeting overnight together in a small village inn in Rockville, Maryland, due to a storm. General Williams had been ordered to take charge of a brigade of 5,000 soldiers in the Army of the Potomac, commanded by Major-General George B. McClellan, in the division commanded by Nathaniel P. Banks, former Governor of Massachusetts.[157]

A letter home from Williams on October 12, 1861, located the command group "near Darnestown, Md.," northwest of the national capital and fifty miles below the Mason-Dixon line that formed a cultural barrier between North and South. Above the boundary were the free States of Pennsylvania and New Jersey; below were Delaware,

---

154. *Michigan's Civil War Citizen-General*, 39-41.
155. Friend Palmer, *Early Days in Detroit* (Detroit: Hunt & June, 1906), 188; *Michigan in the War*, 965.
156. *Michigan in the War*, 166, 966; *Michigan's Civil War Citizen-General*, 41.
157. *FTCM*, 16-19.

Maryland, the District of Columbia, and Virginia, all of which continued to legalize the holding of humans as slaves. Williams described the bucolic setting: a collection of tents pitched on a hillside, a stream flowing in the valley below, higher hills rising on the opposite side. Woods and shrubs helped cloak the location from any enemy. The horses were sheltered, and the tents of the servants were also set up within the trees. They had "all set to work" to arrange the camp. Williams began another paragraph with a simple statement, heavy with meaning:

Nearby is William Dollarson's cooking apparatus.[158]

Though not under a military oath, Dollarson's presence underscored his commitment to support the Union war effort, to suppress the Rebellion, and to ensure American democracy would last. To the enemy, his status was nothing more than of a "fugitive slave"—but the danger did not deter him from aiding the U.S. military in its work of defeating the Rebellion.

The area around Darnestown, between Edwards Ferry and Muddy Branch, remained the scene of deployment for the Williams command group into December. Within days after arriving, the Battle of Ball's Bluff had required General Williams to lead his brigade to the banks of the Potomac in preparation for crossing over into combat. He was then sent to Edwards Ferry with the anticipation of going into battle. A short letter to daughter Irene revealed concern about what might happen: "if I fall or am taken prisoner you must help Larned to support yourself and Minnie … God bless you my daughter and have you always in his holy keeping." He placed this burden on her because his son, at the front as well, "is pretty well used up and nervous."[159] Charles Larned Williams was then 20 years of age and had never been so close to armed conflict. Neither had William Dollarson,

---

158. Id. 18.
159. Id. 23.

and emotions arising from the uncertainty of the military situation likely occupied his thoughts.

Williams and his troops were not thrown into the maelstrom of this Union defeat in which a thousand casualties, including the fatality of former U.S. Senator Edward Baker, had been incurred. Instead, they would continue guard duty along the Potomac into the Spring of 1862, always prepared should the enemy appear. Violence against Union troops had erupted in Baltimore during the first days after Fort Sumter. The Maryland Legislature had met in Frederick to consider secession, and the presence of loyal armed volunteers had helped dissuade that body from taking the State out of the Union. Across the Potomac at Harpers Ferry, and reaching as far southeast as Leesburg, Rebel troops brandished arms to protect the northern boundary of the Confederacy. Rebel units had occupied Maryland Heights at the juncture of the Potomac and Shenandoah rivers, had taken control of portions of the Chesapeake and Ohio Canal on the left bank of the Potomac, had interrupted service on the Baltimore and Ohio Railroad (requiring months for it to resume). In the western triangle of Maryland, skirmishes had occurred between Confederate forces and local home guard companies. As the first calendar year of the war became the second, Confederate forces conducted several raids against the Canal near Williamsport.[160] Hostile action seemed ever present; secessionists were all around.

Juxtaposed with a constant state of readiness for war was the everyday routine of army camp. The General's cook contributed to the state of well-being critical for the success of arms. Williams would record how Dollarson provisioned the contingent:

> … we were all pretty snugly located before dark and William had opened our mess chest and prepared a very comfortable meal of broiled ham and soda biscuits, and upon this diet we were obliged to feed for a couple of days before we could find fresh meat or bread.

---

160. *OR*, V, 1-4.

Williams also wrote about the morning routine of waking and reveille, followed by:

> William gives us a cup of strong coffee soon after and breakfast in an hour.

A letter in December 1861 contained this news item:

> Larned [Williams's son] promised, and I thought did write you all about our Thanksgiving under canvas. It was no grand affair, but we had turkeys and chickens, and William made a big effort.[161]

That "early cup of coffee" and Dollarson's efforts to keep his leader in fine fettle became an essential part of the General's routine on duty at the front.[162]

The Detroit cook, chosen no doubt for his skill, reputation, and, perhaps, personal acquaintance with General Williams, needed to become resourceful. Camp fires and camp kettles replaced the heat source and utensils he had used in Detroit. Rations arrived from the army subsistence department; he did not visit a city market to acquire ingredients. Fresh food might be in short supply. Five thousand soldiers depended on Dollarson to equip their commanding officer with sustenance such that he could lead well and make good decisions, not inhibited by hunger or a lack of nutrition.

Did the chef rely only on his own experience, or might he have consulted some kind of published resource to aid in the performance of his duties? If so, it might have been a slim publication that appeared under date of January 1862. A hardback entitled *Camp Fires and Camp Cooking; or Culinary Hints for the Soldier* was an official government publication authored by an officer serving as "Commissary of

---

161. *FTCM*, 19, 43.
162. Id. 20.

Subsistence for Volunteers" in the Army of the Potomac. In a dozen pages, it offered some ideas, schematics, and recipes for "the most savory and gratifying results." It also contained "The Cook's Creed," which provided a high-principled standard for someone performing Dollarson's role:

> Cleanliness is next to godliness, both in persons and kettles: be ever industrious, then, in scouring your pots. Much elbow grease, a few ashes, and a little water, are capital aids to the careful cook. Better wear out your pans with scouring than your stomachs with purging; and it is less dangerous to work your elbows than your comrade's bowels. Dirt and grease betray the poor cook, and destroy the poor soldier; whilst health, content, and good cheer should ever reward him who does his duty and keeps his kettles clean. In military life, punctuality is not only a duty, but a necessity, and the cook should always endeavor to be exact in time. Be sparing with sugar and salt, as a deficiency can be better remedied than a surplus.[163]

Sage advice, and a wisdom that likely already had found itself in the Detroiter's tool kit.

The weather also dramatically affected the quality of life at this post. "Furious" gales and winds and northeasters unleashed torrential rains, with ice forming when the night-time temperatures dropped to the freezing mark. These conditions contributed to a growing sick list. Healthy culinary practices became ever more vital. On November 9, Williams wrote from camp near Muddy Branch, Maryland, and Canal Lock No. 22. He mentioned a visit by Michigan Governor Blair and that the State's chief executive "and suite" had "dined with us."[164] Had Dollarson prepared their meal? Not long after, Williams

---

163. James M. Sanderson (Washington: Government Printing Office, 1862), 3-4.
164. *FTCM*, 29.

reported on the "booming of cannon above and below us."¹⁶⁵ It was a reminder of the reason they had left home, to be amid thousands armed for battle.¹⁶⁶

On November 28, the date appointed for Michiganders to observe Thanksgiving,¹⁶⁷ orders issued from McClellan's headquarters directing Banks's division to take up position with a base near Frederick in order to guard the Potomac between the Monocacy River and the town of Cumberland one hundred miles away in western Maryland.¹⁶⁸ An aqueduct constructed in the 1830s carried the Canal over that tributary, forming the eastern line of Banks's responsibility.¹⁶⁹ Williams and his command moved out on December 4, leading the brigade and supply train of over one hundred four-horse wagons for a first day's journey of fifteen miles. They had followed the "Mudpike" from Rockville to Frederick, encamping the first night at the road's junction with Little Seneca Creek.¹⁷⁰ The march began on the 5th just after sunrise. Unlike the ease of the previous day's trek, stragglers from preceding units impeded the route before reaching Clarksburg only two miles ahead. Men of one Maryland regiment "fairly lined the road, drunken and furious with liquor and committing all sorts of depredations and outrages." Among the latter were attempts to share "rum canteens" with Williams's command and recklessness with their weapons:

> ... occasionally manifested their high regard by a grand discharge of loaded muskets, fired without especial regard to

---

165. Id. 31.
166. Id. 33.
167. *Detroit Free Press*, Nov, 17, 1861, 2.
168. OR, V, 668-669.
169. https://home.nps.gov/choh/learn/historyculture/themonocacyaqueduct.htm
170. *FTCM*, 38. The location appears to be where the creek intersects the Frederick Road (Md-355) in Montgomery County near GPS coordinates 39.214784, -77.250786.

range or aim. On one occasion a wagon-load fired a volley at some of their comrades lying drunk by the roadside.[171]

William Dollarson had not bargained for such misbehavior; danger presented itself from Rebel arms, Southern sympathizers, and inebriated soldiers of a State divided over which side to join.

Overcoming this obstacle, Williams's brigade covered fifteen miles again and reached the Monocacy junction where the main line of the Baltimore & Ohio spun off a spur into Frederick, three miles northwest. The supply train lagged, so, without their tents, the General and his staffers "found quarters in a nice house."[172] They were all up and again moving soon after sunrise. The brigade halted outside Frederick, formed up their ranks, "and marched through the city in grand style, colors flying and music playing." Williams rode "at the head of the brigade with my staff of six." They continued onward until reaching Catoctin Mountain some four miles west of Frederick, "perched up in the hills," on a "southern slope on a gravelly soil, with several small mountain streams running close to us, with plenty of wood." Headquarters was in a farmhouse, with "one large room for office and eating-room, one bedroom (small) for myself and Larned, and one large one for my staff."[173] The change presented the cook with a much better situation than the day before.

Williams's staff consisted of Detroiters. A post-war speech by Pittman identified the membership:

> [W]e will make mention of his [Williams's] headquarters organization as it left Detroit, which probably in these latter

---
171. *FTCM*, 38.
172. Id. 39.
173. Id. 37-39. The location, 3.5 miles west of Frederick, places it on the National Road just beyond Old Camp Road. The route can be glimpsed from U.S. War Department, *Atlas to Accompany the Official Records of the Union and Confederate Armies, 1861-1865* (Washington: Government Printing Office, 1891-1895), Plate XXVII-1 [hereafter "*OR Atlas*"].

days might be called a "Michigan Outfit." We name them in order of rank:

General, A. S. Williams,
Captain, W. D. Wilkins,
Captain, H. M. Whittlesey,
Lieutenant, S. E. Pittman,
Mr. C. L. Williams, Quartermaster's Department,
Mr. Charles Dannals, in charge of horses,
Mr. Victor Ulrich, mess attendant,
Mr. Wm. Dollarson, colored cook.[174]

Wilkins's birth was in 1826, Whittlesey in 1822, Pittman in 1831. Charles Dannales [Daniels] was an unmarried 23-year-old employed as a servant. Ulrich was a 24-year-old waiter according to the 1860 Census, with a 20-year-old wife named Isabella and two young children.[175] He had worked at the preeminent Russell House, a Detroit hotel, according to Pittman.[176] Though Wilkins and Whittlesey had militia officer experience, and the latter had been Wayne County Register of Deeds, the General and Dollarson were senior members of this little fraternity.

Pittman also provided two important causes for the "cook of color" to be included:

Dollarson having a wide reputation as a Detroit chef of the first order, who had also been a prominent personage in working the Underground Railroad.[177]

---

174. Samuel E. Pittman, *A Sketch of the Operations of General Alpheus S. Williams' Command Known as the Red Star Division of the 12th and 20th Corps of the Army of the Potomac and Army of the Cumberland, respectively, October 1861 to June 1862* (Michigan Commandery of the Loyal Legion, 1899), 3.
175. Ages are based on grave markers and 1860 Census; page 11 of Census, Detroit Ward 7, Wayne County; page 91 of Census, Detroit Ward 4, Wayne County. H.M. "Whittlesea" is found on page 129, Detroit Ward 2, Wayne County.
176. Pittman, 3.
177. Id.

Not just a cook—a "chef." Not just any chef—one "of the first order." And not just any typical Detroiter—a "prominent" person who had worked in the network to freedom of escaped persons from slavery. Dollarson's credentials to join the Williams team were every bit as significant as the others.

Stability proved fleeting. Orders could arrive suddenly demanding the brigade be ready for a rapid march. All would be packed up and ready for the movement. Then, an order would arrive to countermand the march. The result: "domestic arrangements" would be "left in great disorder."[178] Dollarson would need to be as ready for and cope with such developments as any soldier.

Here, amid picturesque scenery, with Sugar Loaf mountain to the southeast, South Mountain to the west, the valley of cultivated farms and "the white farmhouses" to the east, an event occurred that must have conflicted someone who had once been enslaved. In the center of a field used for drilling, a scaffold was erected during the morning of December 23. The brigade was obliged to witness the execution of a soldier in a Pennsylvania regiment. Major Arnold C. Lewis had served as a sergeant in the Mexican-American War. On the second day of the regiment's first march towards Darnestown on September 22, the major placed under arrest a soldier who was insubordinate and under intoxication. Private John Lannagan picked up a loaded musket and shot the Major dead. A court martial found him guilty and sentenced him to be hanged. The violence and the mode of discipline could well have reminded of the brutality of slavery and its not infrequent reliance on the noose.[179]

The turn of the year brought the brigade to a new post at Hancock, halfway to Cumberland and on the north bank of the Potomac again. The town had been shelled on January 5 by the hero of the Battle of

---

178.   *FTCM*, 41, 43.
179.   Id. 42-43; *OR Atlas*, Plate XXV-6; Headquarters, Army of the Potomac, General Orders No. 54, Dec. 13, 1861, in U.S. War Department, *Index of General Orders, Army of the Potomac, 1861* (Head-quarters Printing Office, 1862).

First Bull Run, Thomas J. "Stonewall" Jackson, and orders came of an emergency nature. The brigade faced cold and ice over a mountainous route, finding a panicked populace upon its arrival. Across the river in Virginia lurked 8,500 troops of Jackson's command, as near as several hours' march from the force of 6,000 that Williams employed to protect miles of Canal, rail, and river. He was also ordered to be in readiness to aid other commands, so Williams kept his force under marching orders "with cooked rations for days." March 1st brought those new directions.[180]

On that date, the brigade marched east more than twenty miles to Williamsport, where the Potomac turns south. Crossing into Virginia, the advance reached Martinsburg and then Bunker Hill, encountering no opposition. Williams established his headquarters in a small house, occupying a bedroom while "the others, servants and all, occupy our office-room rolled in blankets at night." Dollarson bedded down in the Old Dominion, in the Shenandoah Valley region, within the Confederacy. His thoughts can be imagined. Hostile forces were encountered when scouts approached Winchester a dozen miles away; Wilkins's horse was hit in the shoulder. The command began its advance on March 11, skirmishing all day and reaching a point a few miles from the town before encamping. On the 12th, the brigade formed at 4:00 a.m. and moved forward, expecting a great battle to take Rebel earthworks guarding Winchester. Instead of initiating hostilities, Jackson retreated, leaving the town to the Federals. It had been "an easy and bloodless victory."[181]

A remarkable change began to occur, one that must have made Dollarson proud to play his role in this campaign. In 1860, Frederick County had a population in which one in seven persons—a total of 2,259—were enslaved.[182] The presence of the Union military now made it possible for such individuals to gain their freedom, and they

---

180. *FTCM*, 52-56; *OR*, V, 390, 392.
181. *FTCM*, 61-64; *Atlas*, Plate XXVII-1; *Michigan's Civil War Citizen-General*, 47 n.80.
182. *Map of Virginia*, *supra*.

exercised that power. Slaveholders came to Williams and demanded return of their "property." Consistent with "An Act to confiscate Property used for Insurrectionary Purposes," approved on August 6, 1861, which placed the burden on the person claiming to be due "labor or service under the law of any State"—euphemism for slavery—to enforce the claim the "owner" must show the individual had not been used "in hostile service" against the United States.[183] Consequently, Williams declined.[184]

Dollarson's chief was rewarded with a promotion on March 20, though without advance in rank, to command of the 1st Division, 5th Corps, in the Army of the Potomac. Unlike many of his peers, he had not missed a day on the sick call since arriving in Washington to seek assignment.[185] Despite discouragement, weather, and logistics issues, Williams would not report personal disease until April 29 when he "had my first ill day." He quickly recovered thanks to "my universal remedy—diet."[186] This record was all the more remarkable considering the poor state of health of many Union soldiers on duty in western Maryland. Over a thousand were ill in the division posted near Cumberland.[187] The Medical Director of the Army of the Potomac had issued a prescription for health: "The indispensable conditions for securing the health of men in the field are good shelter, good clothing, <u>good food</u>, and good water, dry camp grounds, and an abundant supply of pure air."[188] Dollarson contributed in a major way to the well-being of the division's leader.

The bulk of the Army of the Potomac, located in the vicinity of Washington, began embarking for transit to the James Peninsula.

---

183. 37th Congress, 1st Session, 12 Stat. 319, § 4.
184. *Michigan's Civil War Citizen-General*, 48.
185. Commanding General McClellan became ill from the effects of typhoid just before Christmas 1861. Stephen W. Sears ed., *The Civil War Papers of George B. McClellan: Selected Correspondence, 1860-1865* (New York: Ticknor & Fields, 1989), 148 n.4, 152-153.
186. *FTCM*, 72.
187. *OR*, V, 86.
188. Id. 108 (emphasis added). See generally *His Sword a Scalpel*.

McClellan ordered Banks's V Corps to leave the Shenandoah Valley and take up position near Manassas, protecting the capital. Williams packed up his division and marched east, reaching the crossing of the Shenandoah River on March 22, only to be ordered to reverse direction back to Winchester. Williams rushed back and reached the town in advance of his troops, fed himself "and horse," and rode up the Valley pike toward the scene of the Battle of Kernstown, a Union victory over Stonewall Jackson on the 23rd. Two of Williams's three brigades caught up to him with their wagons after the General had "found comfortable lodgement in a farmhouse and sufficient to eat." The Union advance continued over the next days deep into Virginia, to Harrisonburg, nearly one hundred miles distant from the Potomac. No major battle developed, but casualties were incurred and Rebel artillery rounds "fell in unpleasant vicinity to our quarters." Nearly as unpleasant were the "rank Secessionists" populating the homes nearby. Coupled with sleet, snow, rain, and storms, the excursion into the Valley had proved harsh. Orders to march would come late at night, requiring a hurried packing "[a]s we carry all our cooking utensils and mess furniture, to say nothing of the office desks, table, etc. etc." Far from its supply base, acquisition of food proved "no small task." Escapees in small numbers came into the Union lines, the number hindered by fear and the distance to safety.[189]

Having driven Jackson so successfully, Banks's force was reduced as of May 1 and withdrawn to New Market and Strasburg.[190] With McClellan approaching Richmond, Jackson was ordered to attack Banks. His force approached 17,000 strong;[191] Williams had but 4,500 infantry, a part of which garrisoned Front Royal. On May 23, most of that detachment were captured. Jackson and Williams were almost equidistant from Winchester to the north. On the 24th, Banks's small

---

189. *OR*, XII, pt. I, 163; *FTCM*, 65-69, 71, 73.
190. *OR*, XII, pt. III, 122, 135; *FTCM*, 73.
191. Robert G. Tanner, *Stonewall in the Valley: Thomas J. "Stonewall" Jackson's Shenandoah Valley Campaign, Spring 1862* (Garden City: Doubleday & Co., 1976), 201-202, 204.

command "under direction of Williams" raced toward Winchester to avoid being cut off. Though one in six wagons were lost to the enemy, few men were captured. Williams took "a hurried cup of coffee" (by Dollarson brewed?) as he attempted to thwart superior Rebel numbers from driving his defenders away from Winchester, but the Battle of Winchester on May 25 commenced another race for safety, this time on the Maryland shore. Aside from casualties and equipment necessarily left behind, all—including William Dollarson—were safely across by 9:00 a.m. the next morning. Again, Williams had succeeded in extricating his command with comparatively few losses.[192]

Williams's letter home on May 27 detailed how dangerous the situation had been for the General, his staff, and the Division. Anxiety produced by "laborious days and sleepless nights" would have made "old age come prematurely." Reports had made it seem likely that Winchester had already been taken by a Confederate force; however, great labor by the men of the 1st Division beat the Rebels to the town. Greatly outmanned in the coming attack meant for Williams "[t]hat we should all be prisoners of war." Several of his staff were ordered to the wagon train; defense held until forced to withdraw; the front of the train reached the Potomac but could not cross, the rear extending back some three or four miles. As each wagon descended into the 300-foot wide river, it "stalled on the start and then the poor animals would struggle and flounder in the rapid stream, which reached nearly to their backs, till many a horse and scores of mules were drowned." Looking back from security on the north bank, it all seemed "a great and horrible nightmare dream." What had cheered him during the ordeal was "hearing that my personal baggage had arrived early and was across the river," the danger to Dollarson and crew having been surmounted.[193] Williams's military family remained intact. Contrasted with the successful retreat was Jackson's failure to reap all that had been possible.[194] Williams was safe—but sobered.

---

192. *Michigan's Civil War Citizen-General*, 49-51.
193. *FTCM*, 76-84.
194. Id. 87; Tanner, 258.

Within a few days, the Federals were back across the boundary waterway as the Rebel Army of the Valley retreated south. Williams was feeling his oats again, "quite well and over my fatigue. Indeed, I see nobody quite as tough as I am."[195] His personal chef helped make that statement possible. Headquarters moved to Martinsburg before settling in Winchester once more, the location of bed and office in the Baker-Hardy House on Loudoun Street, site of the French and Indian War fort built by George Washington.[196] The group soon moved to near Front Royal[197] and became involved in a reorganization. Long a part of the Army of the Potomac, the Division now was numbered in the II Corps, still under Banks, within the newly formed Army of Virginia commanded by Major-General John Pope. By then, Jackson had gained fame for defeating several Union contingents during his "'celebrated' Valley Campaign."[198] He had next helped Robert E. Lee defeat McClellan in the Seven Days Battles, June 25-July 1, before returning to the Virginia piedmont near Gordonsville. Pope's mission was to occupy Jackson east of the Blue Ridge.[199]

On August 9, units of Pope's command met Jackson in the Battle of Cedar Mountain. It was a costly affair, with Wilkins taken prisoner. Williams's military family had lost one of its members—actually, the second loss. Another of the coterie who had departed Detroit the previous summer was gone. Pittman remembered it well more than a third of a century later:

> The first break came here in our military family by the departure to Detroit of our colored cook Dollarson, and it was a genuine trial to part with him. Although, as manager of our mess, I had much to do with him from time to time, it did not come from himself, but the boys about head quarters had

---

195. *FTCM*, 96.
196. Id. 97.
197. Id. 98.
198. Tanner, xv.
199. *OR*, XII, pt. II, 3, 20-21.

it, that Dollarson could not but believe that his connection with Seymour Finney's branch at Detroit of the Underground Railway was well known at the South, and if caught his body would ornament a limb of the first tree that could be found. Dollarson had kept his ear to the ground and the result was his conviction that Union and Confeds were getting too close together. Their proximity at Winchester had already satisfied his military ambition, and no matter if our digestion was to suffer from inferior skill in cooking he could not be induced to remain.

Where was "here," and when? It was after Williams's retinue and command "got settled in camp on the 17th of July at and around Warrenton." On July 6, the II Corps had marched through Manassas and Chester Gaps in the direction of that town, with "sundry halts for a few days at a time, side marchings, etc." The weather was "simply insufferable" until arriving at Warrenton.[200] Dollarson had endured all, but he would not suffer to be treated less than as a prisoner of war. He went home, back to Detroit, back to his community where he had felt safe. The prospect of being captured had become all too real.[201]

---

200. Samuel E. Pittman, *Sketch of the Operations of the Red Star Division of the 12th Corps Army of the Potomac and 20th Corps Army of the Cumberland Commanded by Gen'l Alpheus S. Williams in the Pope Campaign June 1862 to Sept. 2nd 1862* (Michigan Commandery of the Loyal Legion, 1900), 15-16.
201. During incursions by Confederate forces into Maryland and Pennsylvania, free Blacks were captured and taken South into captivity. See, e.g., https://emergingcivilwar.com/2020/05/06/the-confederate-slave-hunt-and-the-gettysburg-campaign/

"Then We Will Sacrifice"

Michigan immediately responded in support and compliance with the President's call for the enlistment of the 1st Michigan Volunteer Regiment to meet head-on the Rebellion's forced surrender of Fort Sumter. The State treasury had not the resources to support the financial burden of the $100,000 necessary, and a loan was arranged in substantial part because of a civilian pledge of over $81,000. Among the subscribers those early days was "John Lewis (colored) Adrian."[202] Among the ranks of Michigan soldiers, one by the name of John Lewis Jr. can be found to have enlisted, in a regiment denominated as the 1st Michigan. It had a modifier, though, in "Colored," and Mr. Lewis had to await permission to join until after the Battle of Gettysburg in July 1863.

It was not for lack of desire that Michigan African Americans in the first days and weeks of the War lacked uniforms. On April 25, 1861, reacting to Fort Sumter and mobilization of troops to answer Lincoln's call, Black Detroiters met at the Second Baptist Church to declare:

1. That we love this land of our nativity, above all lands.
2. That when the government of the State of Michigan manifests a deposition to recognize us as men and citizens, … then we will sacrifice our lives, if necessary, in defense of the flag of our country.
3. That … as men whose hearts are with the union and the flag, we beg the government of Michigan to place us in such a

---

202. *Michigan in the War*, 17, 20.

position that we may be able to prove the courage, devotion and patriotism of our people.
4. Nevertheless, that if the State of Michigan is ever invaded we hold ourselves ready and willing, in common with other men to repel such invasion at all hazards and to the last extremity.[203]

African Americans elsewhere in Michigan made similar offers.[204]

Readers of the *Detroit Free Press* found an item in early May 1861 entitled "A Negro View of the Crisis" in which Frederick Douglass responded on the issue of Black support for Union arms:

> "What are you colored men going to do?"
> He answered, let a few colored regiments go down South and assist in getting their brothers free, and they could and would do this work effectively for our government.

The newspaper scoffed at Douglass saying he "was ready to go," but it added that "this did not imply much courage, for he knew he would not be accepted."[205]

Michiganders of color agreed with Douglass. Although nothing officially encouraged their volunteering to take up arms, some sought to do so. A group in Ypsilanti "resolved to organize a military company and offer themselves to the President on the same terms as white troops."[206] In Detroit, a military unit organized in May 1860, the "Detroit Liberty Guards" captained by Obadiah C. Wood, "a local

---

203. Michael O. Smith, *The First Michigan Colored Infantry: A Black Regiment in the Civil War* (Wayne State University, M.A. Thesis, 1987), 6.
204. Id. 7.
205. May 5, 1861, 4. This newspaper took a racially discriminatory slant toward African Americans, while the *Detroit Advertiser and Tribune* championed their cause.
206. Jean Joy L. Fennimore, "Austin Blair: Civil War Governor, 1861-1862" in *Michigan History*, Vol. 49, No. 3, Sept. 1965, 212.

black abolitionist," sought to enlist.[207] A letter from a Black physician exemplified this desire:

> Battle Creek Oct 30th 1861
> Hon Simon Cameron
> Secy of War.
> Dear Sir:
> Having learned that in your instructions to Gen. Sherman you authorized the enrollment of colored persons I wish to solicit the privilege of raising from five to ten thousand free men to report in sixty days to take any position that may be assigned us (sharp shooters preferred). We would like white persons for superior officers. If this proposition is not acceptable we will if armed & equipped by the government fight as guerillas.
>
> Any information or instructions that may be forwarded to me immediately will be thankfully received and implicitly obeyed.
>
> A part of us are half breed Indians and legal voters in the state of Michigan We are all anxious to fight for the maintenance of the Union and the preservation of the principles promulgated by Pres Lincoln and we are sure of success of [sic] allowed an opportunity.
>
> In the name of God answer immediately.
> Yours fraternally
> G.P. Miller M.D.
> Box 725 Battle Creek Michigan.
> To the Hon Simon Cameron
> Secretary of War
> Washington DC[208]

---

207. William Dunn, *A History of the First Michigan Colored Regiment*, M.A. Thesis, Central Michigan University, Jan. 1967, 3; Finkenbine, "A Beacon of Liberty," 98.

208. *OR*, Series III, I, 609-610; National Archives Identifier 3854722 (original available online).

The offer was answered in the negative.[209] The Militia Acts of 1792 and 1795 limited service to "free able-bodied white male" citizens.[210] When the President called for 75,000 volunteers to suppress the armed rebellion represented by the attack on Fort Sumter, he invoked this authority. The U.S. War Department acted in accordance with its Commander-in-Chief. Michigan law dovetailed with the Federal legislation, providing that "the militia shall be composed of all able-bodied white male citizens" between 18 and 45.[211]

Dr. Miller's reference to "Gen. Sherman" being authorized to enroll persons in color arose from the War Department's instructions dated October 14, 1861, to Brigadier-General Thomas W. Sherman in the conduct of a joint expeditionary force to take control of Port Royal Sound in South Carolina. In relevant part, they authorized him to "in general avail yourself of the services of any persons, whether fugitives from labor or not, who may offer them to the National Government." Although not "a general arming" for military service, the persons accepted could be organized "in squads, companies, or otherwise."[212]

In May, the issue of "fugitives from labor" had been joined when a slaveowner demanded the return of three escapees who had taken refuge inside the lines of Union forces near Fort Monroe, Virginia. Major-General Benjamin F. Butler refused, and out of this action came the notion that humans escaping bondage were "contraband of war." On July 30, Butler requested guidance from the War Department, having some 900 self-emancipated individuals under his protection.[213] Secretary of War Cameron answered, having the "First Confiscation Act" as the guide. On August 6, Congress had passed, and the President signed, "An Act to confiscate Property used

---

209. *OR*, Series III, I, 626.
210. *Statutes at Large*, I, 264, 271.
211. Constitution of 1850, Art. XVII, Sec. 1.
212. *OR*, VI, 176-177.
213. Frank Moore ed., *The Rebellion Record*, Second Volume (New York: G.P. Putnam, 1862), 437-438.

for Insurrectionary Purposes."[214] Cameron declared, accordingly, that "no claim can be recognized by the military authorities of the Union" for return of persons held to service and employed "in hostility to the United States."[215]

As Michigan regiments took the field, they encountered this question themselves. During the summer of 1861, for example, a group of slaves in Fairfax County, Virginia, offered their services to their benefactors from the 2nd Michigan Infantry—and were accepted.[216] An enslaved person found near Alexandria, Virginia, by the 1st Michigan Infantry returned to Michigan with one of its companies and began working on a farm near Coldwater.[217]

Not until Summer 1862 did the wide possibility of uniformed service become more real. Congress enacted "An Act to suppress Insurrection, to punish Treason and Rebellion, to seize and confiscate the Property of Rebels, and for other Purposes" in which "the President of the United States is authorized to employ as many persons of African descent as he may deem necessary and proper for the suppression of this rebellion, and for this purpose he may organize and use them in such manner as he may judge best for the public welfare."[218] Acting on authority conferred in this "Second Confiscation Act," Lincoln issued the preliminary Emancipation Proclamation on September 22, 1862, after the Union victory in the Battle of Antietam five days prior.[219] Congress also acted to amend the Militia Act on July 17 and authorized the President to:

---

214. Pub. L. 37–60, 12 Stat. 319.
215. *OR*, series II, I, 761-762.
216. *Detroit Free Press*, June 26, 1861, 1.
217. McRae, 26.
218. Pub. L. 37–195, § 11, 12 Stat. 589. Note: Blacks served in the U.S. Navy from its founding through the Civil War to a number that some calculate at 18,000. Black men in the U.S. military during the War totaled some 200,000. Raymond Gavins, *The Cambridge Guide to African American History* (New York: Cambridge University Press, 2016), 63-64.
219. See Jack Dempsey & Brian James Egen, *Michigan at Antietam: The Wolverine State's Sacrifice on America's Bloodiest Day* (Charleston: The History Press, 2015).

receive into the service of the United States, for the purpose of constructing intrenchments, or performing camp service, or any other labor, or any military or naval service for which they may be found competent, persons of African descent, and such persons shall be enrolled and organized under such regulations, not inconsistent with the Constitution and laws, as the President may prescribe.[220]

When the vote for the bill came up in the summer of 1862, both U.S. Senators from Michigan were steadfast in seeking the maximum opportunity for Blacks to serve in the military.[221]

Not everyone believed that African Americans would fight, if put in uniform. In August 1862, just weeks before Lincoln issued the preliminary edict, an article appeared in the *Detroit Free Press* quoting an unnamed Captain in the 8th Michigan Infantry under a headline about "the Negro Soldier Movement." It categorized the policy as an "Utter Failure." Although the subject was the arming of former slaves in an area of South Carolina under Union control, the letter expressed a broad opinion about the fighting nature of Blacks: "If there is anything a negro fears it is a gun of any kind." As for "negroes and abolitionists," the writer intoned, "neither are fit for the battle-field."[222]

This opinion, held by not an insubstantial number of Americans about the fighting spirit of their neighbors of African heritage, in and of itself produced surprising consequences far from the front.

---

220. George P. Sander ed., *The Statutes at Large, Treaties, and Proclamations of the United States of America*, Vol. XII (Boston: Little, Brown & Co., 1863), 597, 599.

221. *Journal of the Senate of the United States of America*, 37th Congress, 2nd Session, July 15, 1862, 843–845.

222. *Detroit Free Press*, Aug. 9, 1862, 4.

Illustrations

State Historical Marker commemorating Michigan's Black Civil War unit, Macomb Street, Detroit. *Michigan History Center*

SOUVENIR PROGRAM
Marker Unveiling Ceremonies

Memorial To First Michigan Colored Regiment
102nd UNITED STATES COLORED TROOPS
ARMY INFANTRY VOLUNTEERS

DUFFIELD SCHOOL GROUND
JOS CAMPAU AT CLINTON STREET
3:00 P.M.

Marker Dedication Program
Buffet Supper

ROMA HALL
3009 Gratiot at McDougall Street

Sunday, May 19, 1968 – 4:30 P.M.

— Sponsored By —
Association For The Study Of Negro Life And History
DETROIT BRANCH

1968 Program, 1st Colored Regiment Marker Unveiling Ceremonies. *Michigan History Center*

The Dollarsons' uncelebrated gravestone, Historic Elmwood Cemetery, Detroit. *Editor Collection*

First Michigan Capitol, Detroit, ca. 1840. *Bentley Historical Library*

Second Baptist Church, Detroit, ca. 1839. *Burton Historical Collection*

Massachusetts 54th Regiment Memorial, Boston. A number of Blacks from Michigan volunteered and served in this renowned unit. *National Park Service*

Image of Corporal Kinchen Artis, ca. 1861-1865; born 1831 in Ohio, enlisted at Battle Creek Dec. 1863, discharged Sept. 30, 1865; died Sept. 18, 1905. *Archives of Michigan*

Colonel Henry Laurens Chipman of Detroit, commander of 102nd U.S. Colored Troops, Apr. 15, 1864—Sept. 30, 1865.
U.S. Army Heritage and Education Center

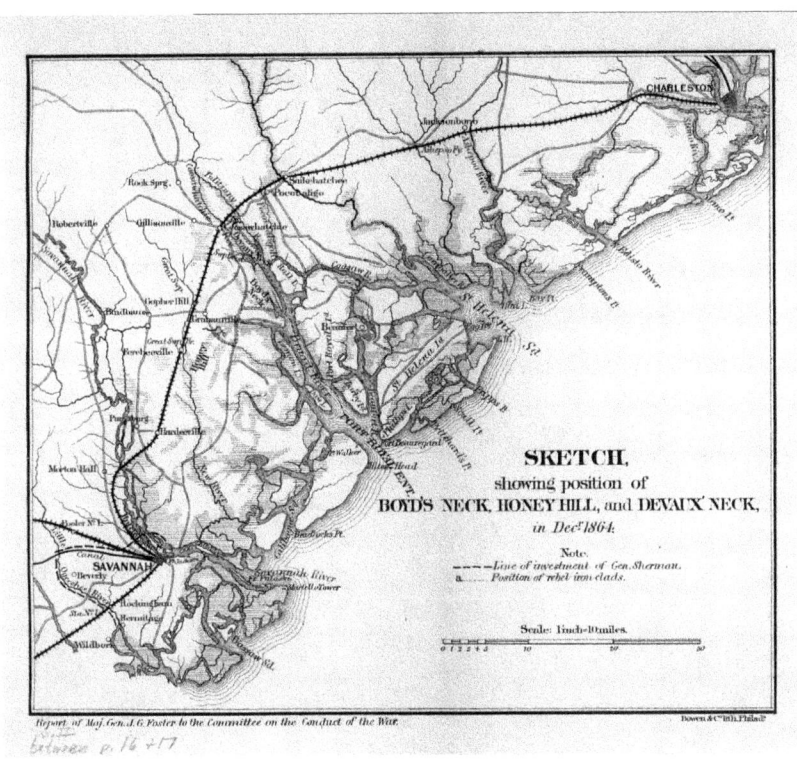

"Sketch" of coastal and inland waters with adjacent areas between Savannah and Charleston, the main area of the 1st Colored Regiment's service. *Library of Congress 99448801*

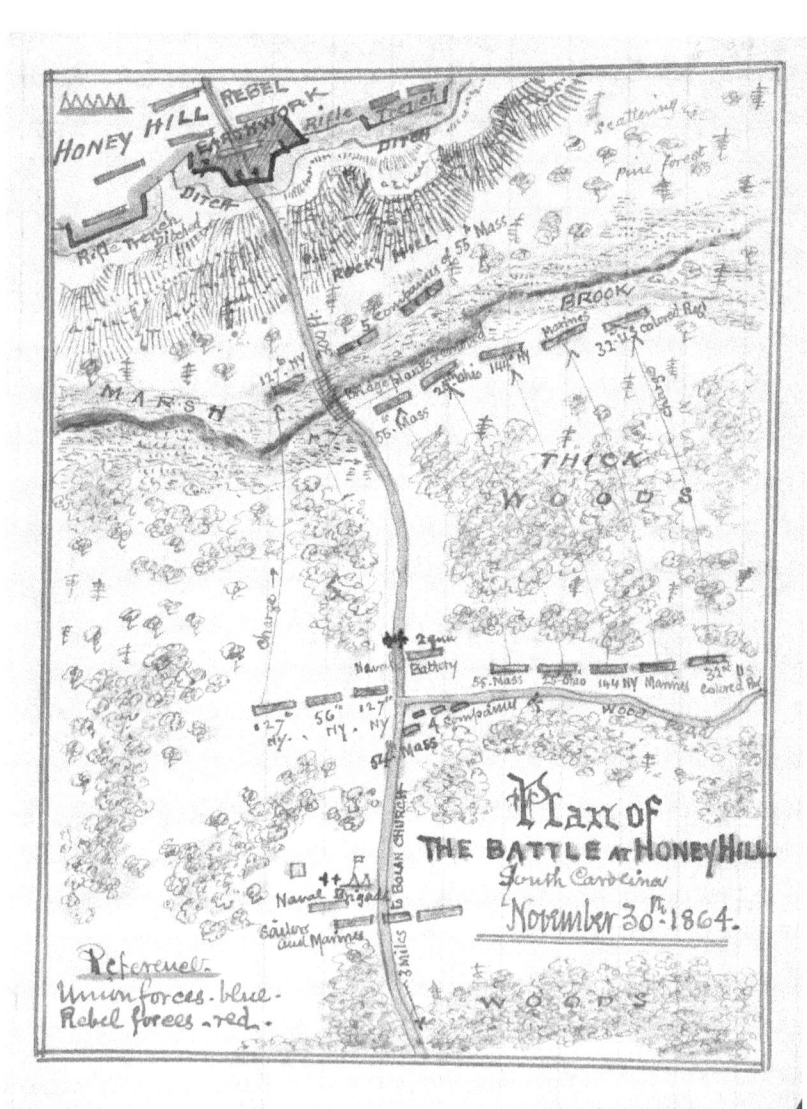

Map of Battle of Honey Hill, Nov. 29-30, 1864, by soldier-artist Robert Knox Sneden. *Library of Congress/Virginia Historical Society*

102nd United States Colored Troop I-375 Memorial Highway sign, Detroit. *Maurice Imhoff*

A Commemoration of the 150th Anniversary of
the Detroit Meeting of John Brown and Frederick Douglass

March 12, 2009

On March 12, 1859, John Brown met with the noted abolitionist and former slave, Frederick Douglass. They met at the Detroit home of William Webb, now the location of a Michigan Historical Marker. Along with members of Detroit's African-American community, they discussed tactics for ending slavery in the United States. Though well acquainted with each other, the two men intensely disagreed on the proper course of action. Brown insisted on armed intervention and Douglass promoted a more peaceful, political end to slavery. Unable to convince Douglass of the necessity of his approach, the two men parted company and Brown began preparation for his assault on the federal arsenal at Harper's Ferry, Virginia, while the nation prepared for war.

His Soul Goes Marching On
John Brown, Frederick Douglass, Detroit, and the Path to Freedom

Presented by

African/African-American Studies Program, The University of Michigan-Dearborn,
Charles H. Wright Museum of African-American History,
The University of Michigan-Dearborn, and
the Michigan Historical Commission

This event is funded by the Office of the Chancellor, the Office of the Provost and the State of Michigan King/Chavez/Parks Visiting Professor Program at The University of Michigan-Dearborn.

Program for John Brown/Frederick Douglass seminar, Charles H. Wright Museum, Detroit, March 2009. *Editor Collection*

Certificate of Tribute from Governor of Michigan for Brown/Douglass seminar. *Editor Collection*

Ceremony honoring interred heroes of the 1st Michigan Colored Regiment, Beaufort National Cemetery, April 2013. *Courtesy of participating Michigander*

Plaque honoring the 1st Michigan Colored Regiment, Rotunda, Capitol of Michigan, Lansing. The numbers portrayed differ from other sources. *Michigan State Capitol Commission/Save The Flags*

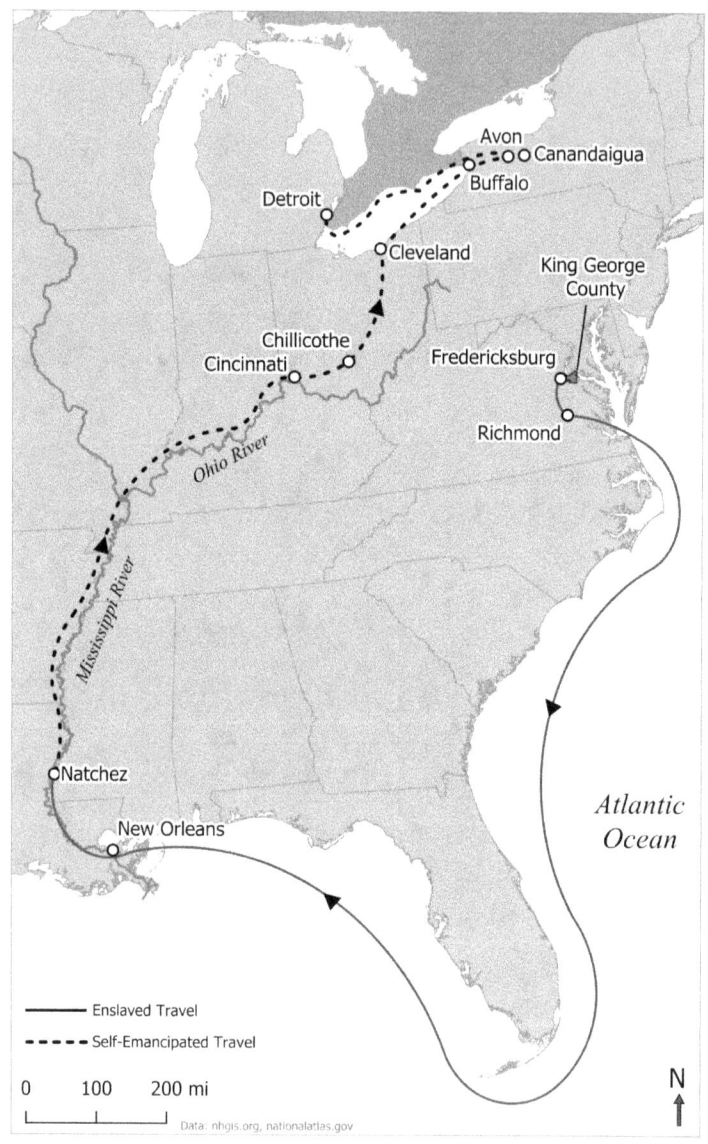

William Dollarson's odyssey from Virginia birthplace to Detroit home, first under compulsion, then by self-emancipation. *Map created by Jason Glatz. Credit also: Steven Manson, Jonathan Schroeder, David Van Riper, Katherine Knowles, Tracy Kugler, Finn Roberts, and Steven Ruggles. IPUMS National Historical Geographic Information System: Version 18.0 [dataset]. Minneapolis, MN: IPUMS. 2023. http://doi.org/10.18128/D050.V18.0*

Part Three

The Riot of 1863

So That Our Blood May Be Spilled

At the Battle of Antietam near Sharpsburg, Maryland, on September 17, 1862, Alpheus Williams and Samuel Pittman proved essential to Union victory.[223] Five days later, President Lincoln issued the preliminary form of an Emancipation Proclamation, giving the Rebels until January 1, 1863, to lay down their arms and return to the Union. Their failure to do so would result in the liberation of any person held in bondage within the control of the Confederacy. An additional aspect of the measure announced that freed "persons of suitable condition, will be received into the armed service of the United States to garrison forts, positions, stations, and other places, and to man vessels of all sorts in said service."

While Dollarson and all others who sought the end of American slavery rejoiced in these events, others did not. They were either indifferent or believed the Rebellion could and should be ended with slavery untouched where it had existed when the first gun fired on the flag over Fort Sumter. At commencement of the War and deep into its duration, most Union soldiers joined up to save the Union, not to save the slaves. Only as the conflict lasted longer than anticipated, and as awareness of manpower needs came to be understood both to fill Union ranks and to deny the resource to the Confederacy, did emancipation and African American military service gain in acceptance.[224]

On the same date as the Emancipation Proclamation issued under the signature of the President, the Governor of Michigan delivered

---

223. See *Michigan at Antietam, supra*. Dollarson had been their colleague.
224. Gary W. Gallagher, *The Union War* (Cambridge: Harvard University Press, 2011), 2.

his Second Inaugural Address. Austin Blair had been reelected but by a narrower margin than in 1860, a result attributed to the lack of success by Union arms and the costliness of the War. His remarks gave the status of the State's military manpower profile. Michigan had in the field 26 infantry regiments, one regiment of Mechanics and Engineers, six cavalry regiments, and eight Batteries of artillery. Active recruiting sought to add two regiments of infantry, one regiment of sharpshooters, three regiments of cavalry, and two batteries. It had been assigned a quota to fill in July 1862 by the War Department, and it remained nearly 3,000 short of compliance.[225]

Jefferson Davis signed a measure on April 16, 1862, authorizing the first military draft in the history of the people who had declared their independence from Great Britain in 1776. The law conscripted all White males between 18 and 35 for three-years' service. Five days later, the Congress approved a list of exemptions.[226] It was a surprising development for a government founded on the principle of State's Rights, made necessary by a failure to enlist the requisite military force to meet that of the Union.

On the Federal side, abortive efforts to raise troops via a form of the draft culminated in March 1863. The "Act for enrolling and calling out the National Forces" was signed by Lincoln on the 3rd, imposing "the first effective" draft in U.S. history. This "Enrollment Act of 1863" made every male citizen and certain male immigrants between 20 and 45 years of age subject to being conscripted into military service.[227]

The *Detroit Free Press*, no friend of African Americans, had supported a rally in July 1862 designed to spur enlistment. The newspaper editorialized in favor of a call for more volunteers on a non-abolitionist basis: "everyone who goes there will be inspired by the spirit of patriotic devotion to *the Union as it was, the Constitution as it is.*"

---

225. *Messages*, 457-477.
226. E.B. Long & Barbara Long, *The Civil War Day by Day: An Almanac 1861-1865* (Garden City: Doubleday & Co., 1971), 200, 202 , 708.
227. 12 Stat. 731; Long & Long, 325.

Tensions in the crowd over economic differences between the working class and others resulted in mob behavior by some. It was the first clear indication that a significant pro-peace, anti-war, anti-abolition element existed in the city.[228]

These sentiments were revived on January 1 in their proponents with issuance of the Proclamation. With the President's signature, "a righteous war for Union and Constitution had now, overnight, become a highly controversial war for black emancipation." Some men in Southeast Michigan responded to emancipation and the draft by fleeing to Canada,[229] an ironic step that replicated the flight of Black fugitives during peacetime. Those who met an exemption did not need to cross the international border; those who with ability to pay a fee of $300 were relieved of their obligation. It was a sum "well beyond the financial means of workingmen and seemed to fly in the face of what democracy in America was supposed to represent." Affluent Michiganders anted up nearly $600,000 in commutation fees. Another way out came through the hiring of a substitute, the payment being negotiable by those involved.[230]

The action of the national government seemed overweening to those who found these policy changes offensive. Federal power reached "into communities as never before."[231] That far-removed control could not be reached, seemed inaccessible. White workingmen of little means faced the prospect of Blacks attaining their freedom and being allowed into the job market. Would they undercut wage levels? For someone who did not regard a person of African descent as equal in civil, legal, or human dimensions, the War had come dramatically too close for comfort despite the distance from Washington or the battlefield. Then there was the racist fear involving issues of sexuality.[232]

---

228. Taylor, *"Old Slow Town,"* 79-81,
229. Id. 88-89.
230. Id. 89-90.
231. Id. 91.
232. Id. 93.

A major contributor to the disquiet in Detroit was the *Free Press*. It employed "blatant racism and stories that tied African Americans to incendiary issues to form a racial rhetoric designed to portray blacks as not only inferior, but also as a threat" to Whites. It sought "to incite fear and anger in its readers" in part by "showing how blacks were a threat to whites." Simply put, it was "a racist paper, and it printed racist stories." Between February 13th and 27th, the paper printed eight front-page stories "about either interracial relationships or black crime."[233]

For someone who had placed himself in jeopardy at war's jagged edge, the actions by the Lincoln Administration and the Congress must have been met with mixed emotions. Enslaved people behind Confederate lines were ostensibly freed, yet William Dollarson knew that only the U.S. Army could effectuate actual liberation. Whites who might be reluctant, or hostile, to enlistment in Union blue now were compelled to become eligible, while Blacks who were eager to fight found no change in the policy of excluding them as a general matter. His relief at having returned to a domestic scene of personal security would be sorely tested just a few days after approval of the Enrollment Act.

On Friday, March 6th, mob violence broke out again in Detroit with far greater range. Unlike in July 1862, when the violence occurred at Campus Martius, the danger would be confined to one of the city wards. According to one historian, "[i]nformation about the riot is sparse, but there are a few secondary sources that examine it closely."[234]

A contemporaneous account of the day appeared within several months, penned by an author from the viewpoint of persons of color. Following is the relevant portion of that scarce publication.[235]

---

233. Matthew Kundinger, "Racial Rhetoric: The Detroit Free Press and Its Part in the Detroit Race Riot of 1863" in *Michigan Journal of History*, Winter 2006 (Ann Arbor: University of Michigan Press).
234. Id.
235. *A Thrilling Narrative from the Lips of the Sufferers of the Late Detroit Riot, March 6, 1863, With the Hair Breadth Escapes of Men, Women and Children, and Destruction of Colored Men's Property, Not Less Than $15,000* (Detroit: n.p., 1863), 2-13, republished with font changes and with an offensive epithet

The Cause of the Riot

Thomas Faulkner[236], charged of committing the outrages upon Ellen Hover, a colored girl and also a white girl[237], was to all intents a white man. This is beyond doubt, for he was a regular voter, and the journals of the city that understood his politics state that he voted the Democratic ticket. And an old veteran of over one hundred years of age declares, that in conversing with F. he said: "If he thought he had one drop of colored blood in his veins, if he could, he would let it out." And this was the man that caused the mob on colored men!

On the 6th of March an organized mob made their way from the jail down Beaubien street. They were yelling like demons, and crying "kill all the d–d n---." In the cooper shop, just below Lafayette street, were five men working, namely: Robert Bennette, Joshua Boyd, Solomon Houston, Lewis Houston, Marcus Dale.[238] These men were busy at work in the shop until the mob made an attack upon the shop. The windows were soon broken and the doors forced open. The men in the cooper shop were determined to resist any that might attempt to come in. The mob discovered this, and did not attempt to come in, but stood off and threw stones and bricks into the windows, a perfect shower. There happened to be one old shot gun in the shop, a couple of discharges from

---

replaced by "n--."
236. In the 1870 (Ninth) Census, Faulkner was listed as 51, Black, keeping an "eating house." Born in North Carolina, he likely had been enslaved. Detroit City, 3rd Ward, 18.
237. In the 1860 Census, 7 years old, Mulatto, born in Canada. Her father, Dennis, age 40, was a barber; her mother (unnamed) was 30; her brother, Robert, was 16. Detroit City, 6th Ward, 158.
238. In the 1860 Census, Bennette, 25 years old, Black, born in Maryland, listed tailor as his occupation. Neither he nor wife Anna could then read or write. Their children: Louise, 3, and August, 2. Detroit City, 7th Ward, 57. The other four were not listed. The 1870 Census records "Salamon Huston," age 57, born in Ohio, "M" for mulatto, "Cooper," having $300 in personal property. Detroit City, 7th Ward, 182.

which drove the mob back from the shop. The dwelling house was attached to the shop, in which were three women and four children, namely: Mrs. Reynolds,[239] Mrs. Bonn and one child, Mrs. Dale and three children.

Some ten minutes after the mob had fallen back from the shop, they made a rush upon the house in which were the women and children. The men in the shop seeing this, rushed out of the shop into the house to protect the women and children. The windows of the houses were soon all broken in; stones and bricks came into the house like hail. The women and children were dodging from one room to another to escape the stones. The men frequently stood before the women and children to shield them from the stones. Very soon after the men went from the shop into the house, the shop was set on fire by the mob. There were plenty of shavings in the shop, which facilitated the burning. The flames soon reached the house in which were the women and children. The mob by this time had completely surrounded the building. Mrs. Reynold attempted to go out at the back door but could not get out, for hundreds of stones were flying at that part of the building. Mr. Dale, in shielding his wife, got a blow in the face with a stone, which his wife might have gotten had he not stood before her. Some person outside was heard to say "the women will be protected—no protection for the men." Hearing this, Mr. Dale told the women to go out at the front door. Mrs. Dale seeing the blood running from her husband's face, said my dear you are bleeding—you will be killed. Said he to her, go out with your children; they say there is protection for the women, but none for the men. I will look out for myself. Mrs. Bond started for the door, with her child in her arms, followed by Mrs Dale, with one child

---

239. In the 1860 Census, 34 years old, Black, born in Maine. Husband Alex, age 30, born in Ohio, was a tailor. Detroit City, 4th Ward, 90.

in her arms and two children hanging to her. Mrs. Reynolds next followed. When the women approached the door, some fiend in human shape drew back a large club to strike them, but some spectators, having within them a spark of humanity, rushed to the women and rescued them—drawn probably by the screams of Mrs. Bond. After the women had got out, the men, one by one, made their way out—were knocked down with stones when they came out, and beaten[.][240] Father Clark happened to be in the house, was beat on after he came out.[241] The last one who came out was Mr. Dale. When he came out into the back yard the heat was so intense that he came near being overcome by it—he had his face badly burned. When he came out of the door some twenty dirty-looking Irishmen rushed at him with clubs, crying "kill the nager." But being thoughtful enough to come out with something in his hands, and having a good deal of physical strength he made them get back, and he got out without receiving further injuries. Three families living in the building near the cooper shop, lost all they had; namely, Mr. Reynolds, Mr. Dale and Mr. Bonn.

The mob, not satisfied with burning the cooper shop, and building adjacent, proceeded up Fort and Lafayette streets, robbing and burning some fifteen houses belonging to colored people. Of the men who were in the cooper shop one has died from wounds received; namely, Joshua Boyd.

– M. Dale.

The mob, in its first appearance to me, was a parcel of fellows runing [sic] up Lafayette street after two or three colored men. They then returned back, and in a short time I saw a tremendous crowd coming up Croghan street on drays, wagons, and foot, with kegs of beer on their wagons, and rushed

---

240. Ed. note: additional periods are supplied here without brackets.
241. Ephraim Clark (1816-1871), sexton of the A.M.E. Church.

for the prison. Here they crowded thick and heavy. After this, while I was standing on the corner, with half a dozen other gentlemen, a rifle ball came whistling over our heads. After which we heard several shots, but only one ball passing us. In a short time after this there came one fellow down, saying, "I am shot in the thigh." And another came with his finger partly shot off. A few minutes after that another ruffian came down, saying: "If we are got to be killed up for n--s then we will kill every n-- in this town." A very little while after this we could hear them speaking up near the jail, and appeared to be drinking, but I was unable to hear what they said. This done, they gave a most fiendish yell and started down Beaubien street. On reaching Croghan street, a couple of houses west on Beaubien street, they commenced throwing, and before they reached my residence clubs, brick, and missiles of every description flew like hail. Myself and several others were standing on the side-walk, but were compelled to hasten in and close our doors, while the mob passed my house with their clubs and bricks flying into my windows and door, sweeping out light and sash!

They then approached my door in large numbers, where I stood with my gun, and another friend with an axe, but on seeing us, they fell back. They approached four times determined to enter my door, but I raised my gun at each time and they fell back. In the mean time part of the mob passed on down Beaubien street. After the principal part had passed, I rushed up my stairs looking to see what they were doing, and heard the shattering of windows and slashing of boards. In a few moments I saw them at Whitney Reynolds, a few doors below Lafayette street. Mr. R. is a cooper; had his shop and residence on the same lot, and was the largest colored coopering establishment in the city—employing a number of hands regular.

I could see from the windows men striking with axe, spade, clubs, &c, just as you could see men thrashing wheat. A sight the most revolting, to see innocent men, women and children, all without respect to age or sex, being pounded in the most brutal manner.

Sickened with the sight, I sat down in deep solicitude in relation to what the night would bring forth; for to human appearance it seemed as if Satan was loose, and his children were free to do whatever he might direct without fear of the city authority."

– Thomas Buckner.

Louisa Bonn—I had gotten home from a funeral of a young woman, and, after changing my apparel, commenced to get supper. I heard a yelling up Beaubien street, and looking out saw a crowd of men and boys throwing at Mr. Buckner's house. My husband told me I had better go into my mother's, and he would shut up the house so that they would not think any one was home. I went in, and in a few moments they were down to my father's house. They then commenced breaking in the front room windows, and the doors and windows of the cooper shop. Myself and child, mother, and Mrs. Dale, and her three children and brother, kept in the back part of the house while they were throwing stones, and then someone broke the front door open with an axe. Then the dining room caught fire. I started to go out the front door with my babe in my arms, thinking that, as I had not done anything at all to those fiends in human form, they would let me pass. On going to the door, a man met me with a large boulder in his hand, and would have knocked me in the head, had his hand not been caught by another man! I then returned in the house, the sheets of flames approaching me and my babe. I then went to the front door and found it locked, but the top pannel [sic] of the door was all knocked out. Finding I could not get out I commenced screaming! At this a crowd rushed across the street to me. And I feared it was some of the mob, and ran back into the house again. Two gentlemen ran to me and kicked the lower part of the door open—one taking hold of me and the other caught my child, and told me I should not be hurt. I could not then tell whether mother was burned up or not. So I commenced screaming for my mother. Dr. Calhoun told the gentlemen to take me on up street, and he would go in and get my mother out. A Dutchman went in with the Doctor and got Mrs. Dale out, and took her to Mr. McCutchens, and I went on up the street.

Before the house was fired, heard them say: "Let us surround the house and burn the n--s up." So I thought my mother was burned up! No tongue can describe the feelings of my mind on that occasion; everything that we had were in burning sheets of flame! My husband, mother and other friends were all exposed to murderous assaults from those fiends; and to all human appearance there was not a friend in all the thousands that thronged and gazed upon our ruins. Who can form an idea of a female's distress, under such circumstances?

After I escaped the mob, I went up to Mrs. R. Clark's, Lafayette street. I thought, of course, my mother was dead, and was gazing intensely to see if I could discover any one coming up from there, and while thus watching, I saw my dear mother coming up the street all wet, with a trunk in her hands. I ran out to meet her. I then took the trunk from her and went into Mr. C's, and told her to come after me. When we got in, I told her she had better break the trunk open and get out father's money. Mrs. Clark handed her a hammer, and just at that moment a rush of the mob approached, and hailed in a shower of bricks and other missiles, smashing in the doors and window. Mrs. Clark and all of us were frightened to desperation. She attempted to run up stairs, but Ma told her not to do that, but go out of the house. At this Ma opened the back door, and went down the yard, and jumped the fence, leaving the trunk and all its contents sitting behind the stove. My mother knew that the trunk had all my father's money in it; that he was then just preparing to lay in a large stock of copper stuff. She had dragged it several squares from our dwelling, that the mob had destroyed, to be compelled to leave it in the house of Mrs. Clark to be seized by those vile fiends. The amount of money in the trunk was twelve hundred dollars, besides a large lot of valuable clothes. We then proceeded from there up the alley to St Antoine street, and from thence on to Clinton street—as poor wanderers, not knowing where to go to seek an asylum from the coldness of the approaching night. My babe was entirely naked, with the exception of a little dress and skirt, having lost all his clothes, even to his bonnet, in the fire and trying to escape the mob.

Wandering up and down about eight o'clock at night, we got on Mullett street and found Mr. E. Harberd was not burned out.[242] We went there and found a shelter from the mob and cold.

During all this time, myself and mother was out of doors without bonnet or shawl. My distress was indescribable, on account of the absence of my husband and father. The former I saw last when the dining room fell in. He advised me to stand aside as much as possible out of the flames, as he heard the bell ringing, and thought the guards would soon come, and I could get out. From this time I never saw him any more till three o'clock on Saturday morning, when he and Mr. Dale came to father Harberd's. Mr. Dale was much wounded in the flames.

---

242. In the 1860 Census, William, 66 years old, born in Maryland, "M" for mulatto, laborer, married to Emily, 61, born in Kentucky. Detroit City, 4th Ward, 6.

My father had gone to the country to see about lumber, and told us that if he was not back by five o'clock, we need not feel uneasy about him, as he would not be back till morning. But still I had the grief and burden of mind for him; for we did not know but what he had come in and fallen into the hands of the mob; and this suspense of mind we had till about 9 o'clock the next morning, when he came home.

Mrs. Reynolds—I found, on my daughter going to the front door, she had to hasten back to save her life from the mob; so I returned into the room and gave up to be burned up; for I saw from all appearances that if I went out in such a shower of stones, I should be certainly killed, and I just gave myself up to the mercy of God.

I remained in this position and heard my daughter scream again, and then soon it was over. I could not tell whether herself and babe had fallen speechless at the foot of the bloody assassin, or fell in the flames!

Not long after this, a couple of gentlemen came in and helped me and Mrs. Dale and children out of the flames. I had taken care of the trunk.

Whitney Reynolds—I was out at Oakland that day, and on coming heard that my wife, daughter and her husband and child were all burned up, with all my property. This struck me with such force, that when I came home and found my family all safe it filled me with such satisfaction that I did not feel the loss of the property scarcely at all. I have lost in cash $1,200, and in property over four thousand, and all swept away in an hour for no cause, only the wickedness of a class of men who hate the colored man.

Louis Houston and Solomon Houston—We were working in Mr. Reynold's cooper shop, between Fort and Lafayette streets. An immense crowd came to the shop, and the first thing we know they smashed in the front window and door, and said: "Come out ye sons of b–h." They came around in the alley and smashed in the back windows. We did not go out, but they seemed too cowardly to come in, and they continued to smash and break up Mr. R.'s house. Finding the mob directing their fury on the dwelling house where there were none but the wife of Mr. Reynolds, Mrs. Bonn and child, and Mrs. Dale and four children, all exposed to all kinds of missiles that could be thrown through the doors and windows, we all went to the house to try to defend the women. Then the mob set the shop on fire. During our stay in the shop, none of them dared to come in; but after we left it they then put the torch to it, and soon it was in flames! The mob then surrounded the house in every direction, as if determined to burn up the property and all the men, women and children that were therein; during which time they were throwing brickbats and missiles from every direction. I came to the front door of the house, and it was then partly consumed. A gentleman that I know called me to come to him, and I made my way to him, and he forbade the mob interfering with me. He knew me well, and I was a peaceable man. Several laid hold of me and said they were intent on taking my life; that they saw me shoot. A German man rushed on me with a spade, and struck me twice with it over the head, inflicting a severe wound at each blow. A person who stood by him, as he raised the spade the third time, asked him what he intended to do! Said he, "I intend to kill him!"

The man said to him: "You ought to be ashamed to strike a man with such a weapon, whom you have never seen, nor has done you any harm!" At this, the assassin threw the spade down.

A gentleman, who I did not know at that time, being much excited, but I very well know him afterwards, came to me and took me down Lafayette street to Mr. Thairs', and the mob surrounded me again, and prevented the friend from taking me on. Here they knocked me down again. Mr. T. then came out and bade them not to interfere with me any more, and came and took me in. He sent for a doctor to examine my wounds, and washed me and took care of me kindly, till the next day.

I suffered for a couple of weeks severely; but, thank the Lord, I am now recovering, but have not been able to do a stroke of work since the 8th of March, five weeks, with a helpless family depending on me for protection!

– Solomon Houston.

Louis Houston—Finding the house about being entirely consumed, as before stated, as I was one of the last that came out, I went to the back part of the lot to go through a hole in the fence. The stones and bats were flying so that life was in danger at every stop that I took; but on reaching the spot, I found one of our hands who, a few moments before that, worked right at my side, sitting on the railing of the fence, knocked in the head with an axe. He appeared entirely lifeless, but was being held up by the fence.

I then went back to the house, but saw my only chance was to get through that place. I returned and found my friend had fallen from his position, entirely lifeless. I made my way out to get through the fence, and was knocked down with a stone or brick, I don't know which. Here we both lay side by side; I suppose it was ten or fifteen minutes before I made an attempt to get up.

By this time a barn, or some building, took fire, and the flames became very intense. Mr. Boyd lay perfectly unconscious, nearest the fire; and two white men came up to us and dragged us up from the flames on a cabbage hole, and there we lay.

After some time I came to myself, enough to get up, and I then went up the alley to St. Antoine street; here the mob overtook me again. They commenced on me again, and with all kinds of weapons they beat me in the most cruel manner over the head till I heard some one say, "he is dead!" then they left me alone. I can't say how long I lay in the position they left me, but after some time, near night, I came to enough to rise from the place and try to get home. As I was coming on, a young white man overtook and asked me if would not rather go to jail? He advised me to go to jail, and I concluded it would be best, as I feared the mob might follow me home. The young man hurried on, and by the time I got there he had the door open; but I don't think the keeper was there. When the jailor came I found myself sadly disappointed, as he ordered me out, and told me to go over to Mr. Steward's, and asked me "what I came in there for." Humanity sickens at such cruelty! Here I had lived and paid my taxes for the last ten or twelve years, and it was the first time I had ever been in prison; and then when a most brutal mob was raging through the city, the civil authorities doing not one thing to defend me; and when I went to the prison for protection of my life, was turned out to the exposure of the mob! "Publish it not in Gath, tell it not in the streets of Askelon."

I than [sic] started away from there, not knowing but I would be again set upon by the most barbarous of the age. My wife went out to seek after me—not knowing what had become of me, whether I was consumed in the flames or slain by the mob. Between seven and eight o'clock she came to Dr. Steward's and found me, having become almost frantic with grief from the rumors she had of my condition.

No one could tell the state of their friends, that were out from each other. The mob went like a volcano, sweeping along the dwellings of colored people, and if escaping at one point, perhaps the next turn would bring you right in the hands of your persecutors.

I can not describe my horrors in being forced by the expulsion of the jailor to go to Dr. Steward's, for I thought his house would soon be attacked, and the same sad scenes renewed as I had already twice passed through! My head was beaten almost to a pummel from the blows I received. I received three bad burns, which, with the wounds on my head, have caused me indescribable sufferings. And, although five weeks are passed, I have not been able to do anything for myself nor family, and am yet under the physician's hands.

Richard Evans—Aged 79 years; lived on Fort street; was set upon by the mob in a most brutal manner.[243] His aged wife and himself were all that were at home. Some entered, and others fired the house. A villain drew a pistol and directed it at his head, and discharged the contents in his face. The ball took effect, tearing the flesh to the bone, and the old gentleman fell to the floor exclaiming, "you are now satisfied—you have done the deed, and shot me!' The conclusion was that he was dead and they left him, after plundering the house of something over a thousand dollars, from the different members of that distressed family.

Father Clark—Eighty odd years of age, was at the cooper shop of Mr. Reynolds, and was badly beaten. His head was cut in several places, and his body so bruised up, that the marks will follow him to his grave.

All this affliction fell upon the people without the slightest pretext whatever. If Faulkner had been colored, and really had seduced the girls, we have no apology to offer for crime, but he was sentenced for life to the Penitentiary; so that there was no cause for the mob.

---

243. In the 1860 Census, age 69, Black, born in Louisiana. Detroit City, 3rd Ward, 179.

Mr. Bloss, officer Sullivan and others really exposed their own lives in their efforts to save the distressed, for which they will be blessed.

Lewis Pearce—I was at the cooper shop and when the mob attacked us, and while we stayed in there the mob did not dare to come in, but commenced with great fury on the dwelling-house. We then went there to defend the women and children. As soon as we left the shop they set it on fire.

All the while they were throwing stones and other missiles. I was knocked down by a stone in the yard while the house was burning, and when I came to myself enough to know anything, I found the flames so intense that I would soon be burned to death, unless I had some shelter; so I drew a wheelbarrow over me, that fortunately was just there. I was unable to walk, and there I lay till a couple of policemen came to me and dragged me out, and took me outside of the lot, and turned me loose. I then staggered over to Mrs. Jones', being weak from the blows and loss of blood. I had not been there but a few moments before they came and said to me: "Get out of there." It was, as I suppose, the same two men who took me out from under the wheelbarrow. I found it impossible to get away; so I got out into the privy to conceal myself, and soon a couple of fellows—one a man in soldier's clothes, and the other a man who sold in the market, named Dollar—came to me and brought me out on St. Antoine street, beating me all the way along, the mob behind me throwing at me, and some pelting me with stones and sticks till they got me to Croghan street; and there they fell on me, and with kicks and clubs, beat me till they thought life was extinct, and then went off and left me for dead! My head was bruised so that for weeks my head and ears run with corruption. My knee cap was broke right in two by a stroke from some weapon. My body was so bruised that for two days I vomited nothing but pure blood; but, through the mercy of the Lord, I am now getting better, but never shall overcome the effects of the injuries I have received.

Statement of Frederick Wilson—I reside on the corner of Fort and Beaubien streets, and about half past four or five o'clock on Friday, March the 6th, 1863, I was aroused by the cry of "A mob! a mob!" On hastening to the door, I saw thousands of men and boys coming down Beaubien street, yelling in a most hideous manner, as if all Pandemonium were turned loose. They let loose a perfect volley of all kinds of missiles at Mr. Buckner's dwelling, on the corner of Beaubien and Croghan streets.

From this they came on down to Mr. W. Reynolds' residence and cooper shop. Here they made a general halt, as if determined to make a total destruction of every thing.

The several parts of the house and shop were attacked with indescribable fury! Doors, windows, and every part were under a shower of missiles. Axes, spades, clubs and stones, and whatever they could lay hands on to do mischief with, were freely used. It was heart appalling to see the fury with which they made their attack. No warning was given to the men engaged in their lawful avocations in the shop, till they were set upon in that murderous assault.

The workmen in the shop seemed to defend it from within; as I could see the mob falling back from the door, when they rushed as if they were going to enter. A single shot from a gun seemed to make all retreat. A short time after, I saw the flames rising from the shop. Some wretch had set it on fire!

Here I was compelled to pause, in wild astonishment, and ask myself the question: "What is the meaning of all this? What nation of barbarians do those families live in!"

But it was but a few moments, and I was called from my vision of the wrongs of my friends to witness my own outrages.

Having completed the work of destruction at the last named place, they came on to Mr. Morton's, who was a huckster in the market. It seemed as if they took great pleasure in doing all they could to such men as were about there doing business for themselves. And soon his house was in flames. They then let loose on my residence, and smashed in some windows and passed on.

I gathered up my family and part of my things, and a friend of mine went with them to go over to Canada. When the two draymen got down to the ferry, they made my friend pay them; and when I came down they demanded of me full pay again. It is plain to any honest man that the great purpose of the mob was to rob and plunder; so I had to give it or subject myself to the cruel treatment of many others who were suffering innocently as I could possibly be! I hope never to see another such a scene.

Statement of Thomas Holton—I reside on Fort street, between Beaubien and St. Antoine streets, and have a wife and one small child. We were aroused by the yells of the mob, and, on going to the street, heard windows smashing and hammering against doors, with dreadful curses of "Kill the N--."

A crowd rushed up to my residence, and commenced their work of destruction in every possible way, with bricks, stones and other destructive missiles, and the torch was soon set to our house. Myself and wife, with one child, now had to make the best of our efforts to escape with our lives.

They rushed after us with demoniac rage, and their curses and yells were terrifying. We would, most certainly, have fallen a prey to them, had not the hands in the Morocco Factory, just in the rear of our lot, called to us to run through there. We took it as a great favor, for no one could tell in what direction to go—all the streets seemed to be filled with the mob.

Without a moment's time, to even put on cloak, bonnet, or shawl, we started and wandered out to find a friend's house in the suburbs of the city, but losing our way, we found, on inquiry, way in the night, that we had been three miles and a half from the city. Being now at Cork Town, I feared to let them know who we were, for they might be a part of the number who had driven us from our homes.

We wandered all that night in the woods, with nothing to eat, nor covering from the cold, till morning light. With frosted feet and all our property destroyed, did the morning sun rise upon us, as destitute as when we came into the world, with the exception of what we had on, and without a friend to offer us protection, so far as we could learn. Oh, Detroit! Detroit, how hast thou fallen! No power in noonday to defend the helpless women and children from outlaws, till they have fully glutted their hellish appetites on the weak and defenseless. Humanity, where is thy blush!

Statement of Benjamin Singleton—I lived at the corner of Fort and Beaubien streets, and have been sick for the last two years. I am so afflicted with blindness, that while I stand right up to you I can't discern the eyes in your head. All I could hear or understand were the yells and curses of, "Kill the N--s," &c. A shower of stones, &c. made me understand that I was not to escape. They set fire to my house, and I was not able to get out; but some white ladies came to my relief. They broke a board off my fence, and came through the back way and dragged me out, or I should have been burned up with my house and all that I had.

I had a horse hitched at my door, and some of the mob came to cut his throat, because he belonged to a "n--." And it was only by a white man coming up and declaring the horse was his, that they were deterred from their brutal act.

Here I was, blind, sick and helpless in the midst, as I had always supposed, of a civilized, yea, christianized people; and to find my property destroyed in broad day light seemed almost impossible. But it was a dread reality.

Mary Mathews, whose husband is insane and in the Lunatic Asylum; her house was fired, and all its contents destroyed. But before the destruction, they took the pains to go through all parts of the house and first carried off what they saw fit, and the balance they brought out and burned in the streets.

Joseph Boyd, a young man, and an excellent mechanic, was knocked in the head with an axe. After this he was unconscious, and was dragged out of the way of being destroyed by the flames. Officer Sullivan, who appeared the only authorized officer of peace that discharged his duty in the face of the mob, as was known as such. He gave poor Boyd some aid, and after having him taken to a saloon, the mob found out that the innocent victim was there, and they made a rush and dragged him out, though he was unconscious! His head gaping wide from the wounds by the axe, which were sufficient to kill him; and enough was the affliction inflicted upon him to have satisfied the most savage of a heathen tribe, even had he been guilty of some crime! But astonishing to tell, Dutch and Irish fell on him with hellish fury, and with all kinds of missiles; they beat and dragged him back as if determined to end his suffering in the flames, but came to a halt, as if their rage was abated, when they saw no stroke moved him. They considered him dead.

He lived unconscious some thirty odd hours, and died a mangled child of sorrow to appear in the judgement against the inhabitants of this city, whose blood will be required at their hands. And though no Court or Council here may do justice to the sufferers, that Council and tribunal to which we all shall appear, will give to all their due reward!

The wonder to us all is, that no more of us were murdered; and as fully shows the hand of God over us, as the case of Israel when pursued by Pharoah.

Oppressors should take warning from the past, for in the history of the world it always has been, and ever will be, for the mouth of God hath spoken it—"As you do to others shall it be done to you. And he that leadeth into captivity shall go into captivity." And already do we see in this giant rebellion, of which this mob was an offspring, (first trying its hand upon the unfortunate blacks, and if the [sic] could see their way clear, to fall, in its weighty influence, on all the black man's friends); and it may be well for the Republicans to bear in mind, as well as the Abolitionist, that they are all placed on the same category in the estimation of the party that mobs the "n--" North, and is killing the Union soldiers South. Don't stand with hands in pocket and say, ye men for the Union, "it is only the unfortunate blacks that are to suffer." Joseph's brethren looked on his tears unmoved when he cried "why they sold him to the Ishmaelites;" but poor Joseph was a long time after that, by Divine arrangements, permitted to look on his brethren in as deep distress as ever they saw him in.

Mary Jones—Resided on Fort street, and her house was set on fire, but she rushed in through the mob several times, and they throwing at her even to her own "smoothing irons," with as much venom as if she was a rattlesnake approaching their dwellings, for her attempting to take her wearing apparel out of the flames.

It was taking something from them that some of those villains anticipated having to sell and buy whisky with, to prepare them for another day's work of destruction. Wonderful to say, she escaped unhurt, except some severe bruises.

And indeed we have to defer till the final day of settlement, for an entire disclosure of what our people suffered on that occasion.

Robert Burley—The mob approached my residence, No. 37 Lafayette street, and before night they commenced breaking in the doors and windows. I left the house for personal safety with my family.

At night they returned and robbed the house of all the valuables, and the balance they broke up, leaving me entirely destitute of everything but what we had on our backs.

Mr. Horace Brown—Resided in the same building, and he shared the same fate.

C. Fletcher's house was burned with all its contents, and the mob, on entering, plundered, ravaged and knocked him down, and threw him out of the second story window—as they supposed dead! but he escaped with far less injury than could have been expected.

William Jones—I reside in Canada, and just had entered into the city of Detroit. In passing Mr. Reynold's house I was spoken to by Mrs. Dale. I then went in; and when I went in, I saw nor heard anything to cause me any fear of danger.

The people were then at the jail as I heard. A few minutes after I got in, I was sitting in the room, and the first intimations I had, was some one yelled out: "Here is the coopershop"; and at that moment a shower of clubs and stones came through the windows.

The attack seemed to be general on all the house and shop in rapid succession.

After the assault was made on the shop, the men left the shop and came into the dwelling where the women and children of the three families were.

While we were in the house, a white man came and pointed a pistol in the window and fired in our midst, but, astonishing to relate, no one was shot.

In a short time, we saw the shop was on fire, and the flames soon ascended to the dwelling. The women screaming and almost distracted to get out of the house; the flames rolling in sheets nearer and nearer, and the mob all around the entire premises, with every kind of missiles, knocking and throwing to keep them in and burn up; the women crying for mercy's sake to let them out, for already a part of the roof of the house had fallen; but no entreaty, no appeal for sympathy, moved the mob. They seemed to be as deaf as the adder, and vile as the rattlesnake, determined to burn them all up.

We then made an attempt to force our way out of the house, from the back door, but was met by United States soldiers and others, with stones, bricks and billets of wood! I then rushed to the front door, and was met in a similar manner. With all the fury of demons did they fall on me, but through it all, I made my way through them, several times being knocked down upon my knees, inflicting severe wounds on my head, shoulder and side, and one stab in the neck.

I was still pursued by the mob, till I got to Ingersoll's Machine shop, crying: "Kill the n--;" "kill the n--." On arriving at the back part of the shop, Mr. Ingersoll told me to go into his shop in the upper story, where two others were.

It was to the humanity of Mr. and Mrs. Ingersoll, through the mercy of God, that my life was spared. She rushed into the mob saying: "You scoundrels are you going to kill that man!"

I heard one fellow say: "She ought to be shot for protecting the n--." Finding a shelter, stayed there till dark before I could get to the dwelling house, where he sent after Dr. Gorton, who dressed my wounds; and in the morning they gave me breakfast, and desired me to stay longer, but I came over home. May the blessing of heaven rest upon those generous hearted persons who protected us.

The Robberies Aggravating.

Another feature of this mob was, the robbing that was perpetrated during its progress. It has been stated in Mr. Reynolds' case of his wife having dragged the trunk, with his most valuable clothes and twelve hundred dollars in it, up to Mrs. Clark's, where they all had to escape for their lives, and leave it to the mob.

The mob entered the house and broke open the trunk, and took its contents, with all such valuable things as they could find. At other places they went in and took out the best of the things and carried them off; and to make a cloak for their villainy, they would bring out the rough things and set them on fire. Well might they bring out such things as they could not conceal in carrying off, when they would, by that means, secure themselves from the charge of robbing of all they might take.

The loss to the colored people, in this outrage, will not fall short of from fifteen to twenty thousand dollars—saying nothing of the physical sufferings, and loss of time, from the support of their wives and children, occasioned by the same.

* * *

Only nine months prior, William Dollarson had come home from exposure to the violence and brutality of war. He is not mentioned among those who suffered directly in the Detroit riot, but his family fell within the ambit of those injured. Traumatic effects from this racial violence were hard to escape.

The event "was the largest race-related riot to occur in the Midwest during the Civil War years."[244] It attached a blot on the escutcheon that represented the Wolverine State's noble response to the call to defend Union, Constitution, and liberty. It would become the province of Michiganders of color to erase that mar.

---

244. Taylor, *"Old Slow Town,"* 103.

Part Four

The 1st Michigan Colored Regiment

To Lay Us Down for Freedom's Sake

In 1863, no one could require any one of them to step forward, to leave home, to undergo the rigors of training as a soldier, to put aside a hard-won liberty, to face an enemy whose government did not recognize and would not treat you as a fully human being. No matter what dangers one had experienced under slavery or freedom, nothing could prepare for the sounds, the smells, the sights of a battlefield, the grinding of the immense and terrible machinery of mayhem and death.

A scurrilous meme developed in Civil War historiography that slaves were freed "without any effort of their own. … The war that freed them was a war against their masters; their freedom came as an incident of that conflict."[245] Participation by free Blacks also failed to be noted by mainstream historians for many years.[246] Evidence that Michiganders of color sought immediately to participate in defense of the Union has long been available from official sources.

When the Civil War was officially declared over in 1866, the death toll for African American soldiers demonstrated powerfully the patriotism of those who donned the uniform of the U.S. Army. Some 40,000 had perished.[247] Such a two-year toll far exceeded the losses experienced by U.S. Military Personnel in the Revolutionary

---

245. W.E. Woodward, *Meet General Grant* (New York: Literary Guild of America, 1928), 372.
246. Cornish, x-xii.
247. Sharon A. Roger Hepburn ed., *Private No More: The Civil War Letters of John Lovejoy Murray, 102nd United States Colored Infantry* (Athens: University of Georgia Press, 2023), 1.

War, 1775-1783 (4,435), War of 1812-1815 (2,260), and Mexican-American War, 1846-1848 (13,283).[248]

A total of 1,673 men served in the 1st Michigan Colored Volunteers, according to the official roster. A handful were officers, a position reserved at this stage for those of European descent. Nearly all in the ranks volunteered. A few were drafted; some went as substitutes for other draftees.[249] Regardless of the avenue by which they were mustered in, they served. Doing so was the culmination of a long-sought effort to demonstrate fitness for the fight that others with different heritage had undertaken.

The actual deed of emancipation issued forth on January 1, 1863, and a meeting convened five days later at the Second Baptist Church in order to give expression to the reactions of supporters. A series of resolutions unanimously passed, including this vow:

> Resolved, That in this hour of the Nation's peril, we are ready when called up on to buckle on our armor in defence of the Liberty which has been given to our Southern Brethren, and if in the fort on the field, on shipboard or meeting the enemies of constitutional right in the deadly conflict, we will prove that we are not traitors, but willing to defend the land of our birth.[250]

The *Detroit Advertiser and Tribune* soon weighed in on the issue, and favorably:

> It is a matter of authentic history that Negroes make brave and efficient soldiers. Andrew Jackson, the hero of New Orleans,

---

248. Congressional Research Service, *American War and Military Operations Casualties: Lists and Statistics*, RL32492, version 32 (2020), 1-2.
249. The Enrollment Act of 1863 made "all able-bodied male citizens of the United States ... liable to perform military duty in the service of the United States when called out by the President for that purpose." 12 Stat. 731, *supra*.
250. McRae, 27-29.

has given unequivocal testimony upon this point. No one doubts the loyalty of the Negro population of Michigan, nor will anybody question their courage and determination to act in an issue such as is now pending between the North and the South. The bare announcement of the fact that the government is discussing the expediency of introducing such an element in its military organization creates the most lively satisfaction among the Negro population of our city, and the greatest eagerness is manifested by them that immediate measures be adopted for enlistment ...[251]

In April, the paper continued agitating for Michigan to gain approval to launch recruiting. "[G]ive the colored men of Michigan," it editorialized, "the chance they have been so long wishing for."[252] That Spring, not content to limit duties to support roles, Governor Blair and Senator Chandler jointly applied to the War Department for authority to raise a regiment of colored infantry.[253] The role played by Michiganders of color in securing this approval from Washington has not yet been documented. On the heels of the March riot, however, the securing of this major event in recognizing the equality of people of color, and the mustering in of the regiment early the next year, powerfully demonstrate the fortitude of Black Michiganders.

Dollarson had gone to war as a civilian, skirting the ban on Blacks. Other African Americans of the Great Lakes State also refused to wait until the U.S. War Department gave approval for it to form a Black regiment. Among the rosters of Michigan volunteers in the Civil War is a volume, the 46th, purporting to contain a complete list of that unit's members.[254] Rosters of men in 14 other units are included.

251. Jan. 29, 1863, quoted id. 31-32.
252. McRae, 37.
253. *Detroit Free Press*, Apr. 22, 1863, 2. Blair had called for arming of Blacks and service in the Union army as early as Summer 1862. *Detroit Advertiser and Tribune*, Aug. 7, 1862.
254. The title page is simply "Record of Service of Michigan Volunteers in the Civil War 1861-1865." The cover bears the inscription "Record/First Michigan

Missing, however, are the names of some 70 soldiers from Michigan who served in the 54th Massachusetts Volunteer Infantry, the first full unit of Black soldiers to be raised in the North. Eleven of them hailed from Lenawee County, of whom four were wounded in the assault on Fort Wagner.[255] Portrayed in the 1989 award-winning motion picture *Glory*, the regiment is likely the best known of all the "Colored" units called into service.[256]

Other Union regiments mustered in Michiganders of color, and the regiment from the Great Lakes State included residents of others and of Canada.[257] Even before official sanction came down, a few of African antecedent had managed to enlist in White units.[258] Nick Biddle of Pottsville, Pennsylvania, served as an orderly to a Captain of

---

Colored Infantry/Civil War/1861-1865" with an image of the State Seal. Lobbying by veterans resulted in passage of a law, Public Act 147 of 1903, to print "an alphabetical regimental history of all soldiers and sailors who enlisted from and were credited to this state during the war of the rebellion."

255. Appreciation to historian David C. Ingall of Monroe County for this information.

256. Starring Morgan Freeman and Denzel Washington, and Matthew Broderick as the regiment's Colonel, Robert Gould Shaw. For a book acclaimed as "the real story behind the movie," see Joseph T. Glatthaar, *Forged in Battle: The Civil War Alliance of Black Soldiers and White Officers* (New York: Meridian, 1991). Also see Russell Duncan ed., *Blue-Eyed Child of Fortune: The Civil War Letters of Colonel Robert Gould Shaw* (Athens: University of Georgia Press, 1999).

257. See Hepburn, *supra*. As an example, the regimental chaplain, William Waring, hailed from Oberlin, Ohio. His Michigan connections included marrying in Cass County in 1855 and ordination as a minister in Kalamazoo in 1860; a son, born in Niles, became "the most distinguished" of this family branch. *Record of Service*, Vol. 46, 104; *The Negro History Bulletin*, Vol. XI, No. 5, Feb. 1948, 99-106; Findagrave #49333784. See Noah Andre Trudeau, *Like Men of War: Black Troops in the Civil War, 1862-1865* (Boston: Little, Brown & Co., 1998), 333. An 1865 letter by Waring is in Edwin S. Redkey ed., *A Grand Army of Black Men: Letters from African American Soldiers in the Union Army, 1861-1865* (Cambridge: Cambridge University Press, 1992), 71-77.

258. Donald Yacovone ed., *Freedom's Journey: African American Voices of the Civil War* (Chicago: Lawrence Hill Books, 2004), 7-8; Henry Louis Gates Jr., *Life Upon These Shores: Looking at African American History, 1513-2008* (New York: Alfred A. Knopf, 2011), 123. Perhaps because they "passed for white." McRae, 23.

the Washington Artillery assigned to the 25th Pennsylvania Infantry for a 3-month term.[259] William H. Johnson, born free in 1833, was refused entry into a Connecticut regiment but was allowed to accompany the unit to Washington, D.C.[260] It is possible that a few Black Michiganders did the same.

Because it was likely that Massachusetts could not furnish the entire 1,000-man roster to staff the 54th, Governor John A. Andrew set up mechanisms "to recruit beyond the borders of the Bay State." Major efforts were launched in New York, Ohio, and Pennsylvania. Frederick Douglass personally engaged in recruiting and wrote for publication a "1,100-word manifesto" entitled "Men of Color, to Arms." One who volunteered was James Caldwell, grandson of Sojourner Truth. When fully staffed, only 13 percent were 1861 residents of Massachusetts, with the remainder having residence in 15 Northern States and other locales.[261]

On May 1, 1863, the *New York Tribune* gave voice to what it described was "the great majority" of "Loyal Whites," who had "no faith" that Blacks would make good soldiers and fight. Other than the fear of Blacks "taking what were viewed as white jobs, no issue generated more political or racial controversy."[262] When the 54th Massachusetts assaulted Fort Wagner in the defenses of Charleston Harbor on July 18, it suffered grievous losses. Its performance was not a failure: "in a broader sense it was a significant triumph" for "black troops had proved once again their courage, determination, and willingness to die." Had the regiment faltered, the *Tribune* warned, the remaining thousands of Black troops "for whom it was a pioneer would never have been put into the field, or would not have been put

---

259. Gates, 123; https://www.loc.gov/resource/cph.3c26417/#
260. Yacovone, 90-91.
261. Douglas R. Egerton, *Thunder at the Gates: The Black Civil War Regiments That Redeemed America* (New York, 2016), 70-82. The book's coverage is of three regiments, all credited to Massachusetts.
262. Taylor, *"Old Slow Town,"* 71.

in for another year."²⁶³ The men from Michigan deserve credit along with their Bay State comrades for refusing to falter.

Publicly expressed sentiment in favor of Black soldiering was not limited to the one Detroit daily. In May 1863, from the birthplace of the Republican Party, came this editorial:

> The prejudice and hostility to the blacks that was alleged to exist among our soldiers, is all bosh. The white soldiers are anxious to receive all the aid the blacks can render them in crushing the rebellion. They take a practical, common sense view of the whole matter. They want the rebellion put down, the Union saved, and peace restored as quickly as possible. … Black men can stop rebel bullets, as well as white men. … The army has entered upon serious warfare. All romancing is laid aside. The scabbard is thrown away, and he is counted a friend, be his complexion of whatever hue, who steps in to the ranks and shoulders a loaded musket and shares the hardships of the march and the perils of the battle field.²⁶⁴

In Detroit, meetings were held at Second Baptist to discuss whether to encourage enlistment in the 54th Massachusetts, since Michigan had no Black regiment to be joined. George DeBaptiste spoke in favor, while another community leader opposed the idea. That viewpoint, however, was based on the policy of restricting the opportunities for Blacks to serve:

> John D. Richards, better known as "Boss" Richards, but really the most respectable member of the congregation, was opposed to leaving the land of his birth, the home of his wife and five children, to fight for thirteen dollars a month, unless

---

263. James M. McPherson, *The Negro's Civil War: How American Blacks Felt and Acted During the War for the Union* (New York: Vintage Books, 2003), 187, 195.
264. *Jackson Weekly Citizen*, May 6, 1863, quoted in Dunn, 14.

Old Abe would remove the obstacle that prevents "colored" men from becoming officers well as privates. The speaker considered it degrading for him to fight under "pale-faced" officers, when there were n----s who were perfectly competent to lead their black brethren to "victory or death." He advised his hearers to hold on a little longer; the rebels were whipping the federal soldiers as fast as possible, and it would be but a short time before it would be necessary to call upon the blacks for succor. Then the President would make them the equals of white men, and they could fight with the consciousness that it was for their own freedom they were struggling. The "Boss" wouldn't fight under any other circumstances, and he urged upon all other n---s the importance of following his example.[265]

On May 22, 1863, the War Department issued General Orders No. 143, establishing in the Adjutant General's Office a Bureau for "matters relating to the organization of Colored Troops." The directive also provided that "No persons shall be allowed to recruit for colored troops except specially authorized by the War Department."[266] The first (and only) Michigan regiment "of colored troops" arose from authorization on July 24, 1863, in a letter from Secretary of War Edwin M. Stanton to Blair. More details came from the Adjutant-General's office the next day.[267] The recipient was Henry Barnes, the editor of the newspaper that had consistently advocated for Blacks to be able to enlist. Within just a couple of weeks, Adjutant General Robertson, under instructions from the Governor, wrote to authorize Barnes to begin enrollment in the first Michigan regiment of persons of color. The choice of a newspaperman to lead the effort, and his

---

265. *Detroit Free Press*, May 8, 1863, 1. The language employed in this front-page piece is an exemplar of the editorial policy of the newspaper.
266. U.S. War Department, *General Orders, Adjutant General's Office, for 1863* (Washington: Government Printing Office, 1864).
267. *Michigan in the War*, 488-489.

commissioning as Colonel of the regiment, meant that someone with no military experience would initially lead the contingent.

This activity flew in the face of an edict from the Congress of the Confederate States of America about the treatment of African American POWs and their officers. The death penalty could be imposed upon the latter, and the former could be enslaved even if never previously so. Lincoln responded with General Orders No. 252, issued July 31, 1863:

> The government of the United States will give the same protection to all its soldiers, and if the enemy shall sell or enslave anyone because of his color, the offense shall be punished by retaliation upon the enemy's prisoners in our possession.[268]

Recruitment launched on August 12. Achieving the requisite strength to qualify for mustering in the regiment was slower than advocates thought. The pool of candidates had been reduced by early volunteers who joined the units of other States, such as Massachusetts. An additional factor were the bounties offered in other jurisdictions; the War Department authorization expressly stated that "no bounties will be paid" to volunteers in this regiment.[269] To prevent undermining of Michigan's efforts, the Legislature acted to prohibit recruiting of Michigan men by out-of-state interlopers.[270] Efforts were aided by the role played by prominent Black Detroiters, such as George DeBaptiste and John D. Richards.[271]

A signal event transpired in November. The great equal rights advocate Sojourner Truth "brought many gifts and food from the people of Battle Creek" to the soldiers of the regiment during a visit

---

268. Moore, 578-579; *Collected Works of Abraham Lincoln* (Springfield: Abraham Lincoln Association, 1953), Vol. VI, 357.
269. Id. 488.
270. Smith, *The First Michigan Colored Regiment*, 52.
271. Katzman, 15. Both men went with the regiment to South Carolina, serving as sutlers for six months. Id.

to Camp Ward. She arrived on Friday the 20th and stayed through worship on Sunday. Her words included a reminder of the duties they were assuming.[272] According to her memoir, it was a "gala day":

> The Colonel ordered the regiment into line 'in their best' for the presentation, which was made by Sojourner, accompanied by a speech glowing with patriotism, exhortation, and good wishes, which was responded to by rounds of enthusiastic cheers. At the close of the ceremony, Sojourner spent an hour or two among the soldiers in motherly conversation, and assisting in opening the boxes and distributing their contents, which the recipients disposed of with hearty good-will.[273]

Truth composed a song to honor the Regiment.[274]

Late in 1863, the regimental leadership and band made a tour of the southern Michigan counties, stopping in Ypsilanti, Ann Arbor, Jackson, Niles, Cassopolis, Marshall and Kalamazoo. Traveling the circuit paid off, doubling the number of enlistments in just a few weeks. The contingent "marched down the main street and received the plaudits of the crowd" in Ypsilanti; in Ann Arbor, they marched from the depot down Detroit Street to Ann Street and on to Main Street.[275] Governor Blair greeted them in his hometown on December 9. It was an unprecedented occasion: the Chief Executive addressing a military unit representing the State of Michigan comprised of persons of African heritage. The people of Jackson turned out in droves to witness the event as men of the 1st Michigan Colored Infantry left their breakfast station, formed up, and with military bearing stepped off:

> About 9 1/2 o'clock they took up a line of march to his residence, the streets along the entire way being densely packed

---

272. McRae, 53-54.
273. *Narrative of Sojourner Truth* (Battle Creek: Review & Herald, 1884), 173.
274. Id. 126.
275. McRae, 55.

with human beings, by whom the boys were greeted with loud and prolonged cheering. In fact it was a perfect oration. The men, for their soldierly bearing, neat and clean appearance, were highly complimented. I did not hear a single reproachful or disparaging remark made in reference to them. Arriving at the Governor's residence, the battalion was marched into an open lot near by, where they were put through a series of military movements, in presence of Gov. Blair, Col. Loomis, Capt. Barry, the Provost Marshal, Dr. Blaker, of the 21st Infantry, and a large concourse of people, a great proportion of whom were ladies. After performing various evolutions, the battalion was formed into a hollow square, when they were introduced to the Governor by Lieut. Col. Bennett, in a few appropriate remarks.

Then, it was Blair's turn to speak. He began by mentioning a sensibility not often uttered previously regarding those in uniform before him:

> I find my position in your square somewhat new. It is the first time that I ever saw a battalion of colored soldiers together, and I, together with the vast concourse you see surrounding you, feel proud of your general bearing. ... They are proud to see colored soldiers banded together to fight for a country that has heretofore promised much, but never accomplished a great deal for the colored race. It has done much for everybody but you. That feeling is fast being dispelled, and the time will come when the world shall recognize that the Constitution of our country means what it says, that every man shall enjoy life, liberty and pursuit of happiness. [Prolonged applause.]

The Governor had experience in giving speeches and reviewing Michigan regiments. He had been to the front; he had looked into the faces of the volunteers; he had read the casualty lists and sought to provide elements of care for those wounded, and killed, and their survivors. Now, he turned to that subject, expressing the same kind of concern for these men:

> We have committed to your care the flag of our country. That you will fight for it no one doubts, and if perchance any of you should fall, there will be a consolation that you will find honorable graves. It is my earnest wish you may escape unharmed, and that you may be able to return to your families. Such shall be my prayers, as well as of all those who love their Country. Hoping to see you again ere you depart for the seat of war, I bid you good bye.[276]

Leaving Jackson, the regiment's representatives "were cheered and lionized" at "every whistle stop" until arriving at Kalamazoo. At Marshall, the mayor and dignitaries "escorted them through the town." Lieutenant-Governor Charles S. May reviewed them in Kalamazoo. At Niles, they were greeted by the Mayor and honored with a 34-gun salute, followed by a two-night fete:

> That night proved to be a gala occasion. The streets were illuminated by torches and bonfires. According to the correspondent attached to the regiment, there were more Negro citizens present than white in the crowd which escorted the men of this regiment to Killoy Hall where they spent the night. The following evening there was a war meeting in Niles. After the meeting, the colored people of Niles gave a dance in honor of the regiment.

More ceremony followed:

> When the regiment left Niles, the men marched to Cassopolis, a distance of 16 miles. Farmers along the way wished them

---

276. *Detroit Advertiser and Tribune*, Dec. 10, 1863.

well and gave them fruit. When the troops arrived in Cassopolis, the residents were surprised. Like the kind-hearted hostess who is confronted with unexpected guest, the good people of Cassopolis scurried about to make them welcome. For many of the men in this regiment Cassopolis and Cass County were home.

The Reverend Mr. Sherwood invited the men to worship at the Presbyterian Church in the town. Afterwards, there was a dress parade at the fair grounds, where the regiment performed several intricate maneuvers.

Newspapers in Kalamazoo and Niles extolled the discipline and appearance of the Black soldiers in blue.[277] Nine individuals enlisted from Lansing.[278]

If these ceremonies had ended the year, it would have done well. But the training site for the regiment did not do Michigan proud.

Camp Ward was the location on the near east side of Detroit where volunteers for the regiment were inspected and enrolled into the service. Traditionally, that area of the city had been the primary home for most Detroiters of color.[279] On December 22, 1863, the Medical Director for the Department of the North acted on a request from Lieutenant-Colonel Bennett H. Hill, the commander of the District of Michigan, to look into conditions at Camp Ward. When Dr. Charles Stuart Tripler made his inspection, he found matters less than satisfactory:

> The Army surgeon recommended that the sides [of barracks] be repaired with tar paper and also the roofs and then covered with sand; more windows; planed boards for the floor; brick flues for the stove pipes; decent bunks instead of bed sacks;

---

277. McRae, 55-56.
278. Matthew J. Vanacker, *Lansing and the Civil War* (Charleston: The History Press, 2023), 119-122, 162.
279. Katzman, 25-26.

two blankets per man because one blanket was not sufficient in this climate; and a mess room so that men will not have to eat and cook where they sleep.

The War Department responded by ordering improvements.[280]

On January 5, the regiment was honored by the Colored Ladies' Soldier's Aid Society:

> They presented the First Michigan a banner with its regimental colors. During the ceremony, the regiment was drawn up into its hollow square formation. John D. Richards presented the colors to the regiment in behalf of the ladies. Miss Betty Martin assisted in conveying the colors to the color guard. Chaplain Waring made a brief speech. Another part of the ceremony dealt with the presentation of a gift. One hundred thirty non-commissioned officers and privates of the regiment presented Lieutenant Colonel W. T. Bennett with a sword and sash.

Richards's remarks were reported by the pro-abolition newspaper in town:

> It is a glorious thing to be an American soldier, but thrice glorious when you know that every blow you strike will help to unrivet the chains which centuries of prejudice have bound us. You have hoped and prayed for the day when, under the good old flag of the Union, you could take up arms in its defense, and prove to the oppressors of our race, that although they have wronged us, still we could forgive—that although they have brutalized us as far as human agencies could accomplish

---

280. McRae, 48, 58-59; Smith, "Raising a Black Regiment," 509, 515 n.26. Tripler's role, and other evidence of the shoddy conditions, is referenced in Hepburn, 9, and *His Sword a Scalpel*, 147-148.

it, we still had sufficient of manhood and love of liberty left to strike, when by striking we could be free …[281]

Wayne County nominally held claim to being the jurisdiction with the most Blacks in the 1860 Census. That Cass County alone furnished 99 volunteers for the 1st Michigan Colored should, then, be noted. Several would die of disease while in service; several would be discharged on account of disability; and one soldier, John Russell of Pokagon Township, was discharged for wounds on June 8, 1865.[282]

In *Glory*, the character played by Morgan Freeman (Sergeant Major John Rawlins) appears to be the oldest in the regiment. One eminent source specifies: "Army regulations set the minimum age at 18 and the maximum at 35, raised to 45 by the enrollment act of 1863."[283] How did the 1st Michigan Colored match up? George York of Ypsilanti enlisted on October 20, 1863, at Ypsilanti; he was 15 years of age. Six soldiers were 16: Henry A. Brown, enlisted at Adrian; Eugene Charris, Walton; Andrew Gillam, Cassopolis; Cyrus F. Martin; and Daniel Starks, Detroit, who enlisted as Musician, and William Sterling, Detroit, as "Drummer." Twenty-one were given as age 17.[284] One, George Washington, enlisted at Detroit on November 21, 1863, age 49. Four gave their age as 48, one as 47, and three as 46.[285] Volunteering for military service at ages outside of legal parameters demonstrated another level of commitment.

After the war, the Michigan Adjutant-General published statistics

---

281. *Detroit Advertiser and Tribune*, Jan. 6, 1864, as quoted in Dunn, 32.
282. L.H. Glover ed., *A Twentieth Century History of Cass County, Michigan* (Chicago: Lewis Pub. Co., 1906), 326-327. Russell's wounds were "received in action at Deveaux Neck, S.C., Dec. 9, 1864." *Record of Service*, Vol. 46, 85.
283. https://www.civilwarmed.org/surgeons-call/exams/
284. For insight as to one of these volunteers, see Jesse Lasorda, "Orrin Edgar Wilson: The Life of an African American Civil War Veteran" in *Chronicle*, Vol. 35, No. 3, Fall 2012, 24-25.
285. *Record of Service*, Vol. 46, 16, 19, 22, 37, 38, 63, 66, 76, 88, 93, 94, 96, 104, 114, 119.

on the "nativity"—i.e., birthplace—of the more than 90,000 troops credited to the State. For those of African heritage, the figures were:

Free States	Colored 217
Slave States	Colored 956
Canada	Colored 441
Miscellaneous	Colored 47
Total Colored	1,661

Well more than half, therefore, had been born to enslaved mothers. Their willingness to go south of the Mason-Dixon line is remarkable. Four in 10 had been born free; twice as many were free-born across the international boundary as within the State's borders.[286] Neither of those demographics needed to leave the safety of their homes—but they did.

On February 17, 1864, the 1st Michigan Colored Regiment mustered, 895 strong, and marched down Woodward Avenue to the approbation of onlookers.[287] Not until March 14, however, were orders issued by the War Department for the regiment to leave Michigan. Special Orders No. 117 assigned the unit to the IX Corps of the Army of the Potomac, commanded by Major-General Ambrose E. Burnside, and ordered it "to the depot of said Corps."[288]

When news reached the men of the regiment on March 27 that they were to leave for the front on the morrow, the response was dramatic:

> The enthusiasm displayed by the men on hearing that they were going exceeded all bounds. Cheer after cheer was given, hats waved, and everybody was merry and happy. The

---
286. *Michigan in the War*, 69.
287. George S. May, *Michigan and the Civil War Years, 1860-1866: A Wartime Chronicle*, 2d Ed. (Lansing: Michigan Civil War Centennial Observance Commission, 1966), 56.
288. McRae, 64-65.

eagerness of the men to fight for their country gives abundant reason to believe that they will show themselves gallant men on the battlefield.[289]

On March 28, the regiment embarked for Annapolis and further organization and training. The *Free Press* hailed its departure as a signal for the return of "peace and tranquility of our city." Its hostility to the service of African Americans continued for, among other things, it was "raised under abolition auspices."[290] Barnes resigned as Colonel effective April 12, his mission to deploy Black soldiers from Michigan in the field having been accomplished.[291] Detroiter Henry L. Chipman, an officer of high regard, was promoted to command of the regiment.

Much has understandably been made about the officer of European ancestry who commanded what has become the most famous Black regiment, the 54th Massachusetts. Robert Gould Shaw was 25 years old, of a distinguished Boston family, and of the right qualifications as set by the Governor of the State for field officers: "young men of military experience, of firm antislavery principles, ambitious, superior to a vulgar contempt for color, and having faith in the capacity of colored men for military service."[292] Because of the stakes for this first-ever regiment of African American soldiers, the unit's leader would have to be of first-rate stuff. Shaw met the challenge; he trained and then led the men into battle in South Carolina, and their sacrifice hallowed the memory of the 54th down through the decades. In 1989, the Academy Award best picture designation went to *Glory* for its depiction of the story of the regiment and Shaw.

Henry Laurens Chipman was in every way Shaw's equal. That he

---

289. *Detroit Advertiser and Tribune*, Mar. 29, 1864, as quoted in Dunn, 58.
290. Mar. 29, 1864, 2.
291. Barnes met a tragic end in 1871. He is credited as key for being "a tireless advocate in the fight to gain a black regiment for Michigan." Harlan B. Hargrove, "Their Greatest Battle Was Getting Into The Fight: The 1st Michigan Colored Infantry Goes to War" in *Michigan History*, Vol. 75, No. 1, Jan./Feb. 1991, 26.
292. Luis F. Emilio, *History of the Fifty-Fourth Regiment of Massachusetts Volunteer Infantry, 1863-1865*, 2d ed. (Boston: Boston Book Co., 1894), 3.

was chosen to command the 1st Michigan Colored speaks volumes about the significance of the regiment for the State, nation, and cause.

Henry Laurens Chipman came from a line every bit as distinguished as Bostonian Robert Gould Shaw. One source asserts the "Chipman family was established in this country in 1630."[293] Another puts the date in 1631.[294] The first immigrant, John Chipman, married a daughter of an original 1620 Pilgrim to Massachusetts Colony.[295] Their grandson graduated from Harvard College in 1711.[296] Descendant Nathaniel Chipman (1752-1843) was a Yale graduate, veteran of the Continental Army (including Valley Forge), member of the Vermont House of Representatives, member of the Supreme Court of Vermont, appointee of President George Washington as first judge of the U.S. District Court for the District of Vermont, U.S. Senator, and professor of law at Middlebury College. He had six children with Sarah Hill (1762–1831), including oldest son Henry C., born in Vermont in 1784.[297]

Henry C. Chipman graduated from Middlebury College in 1803. He began the study of law and was admitted to the Vermont bar in 1806. Recuperation from illness relocated him to Jamaica, and in returning to the U.S. he settled in South Carolina and worked in the office of Charles C. Pinckney, one of the delegates to the Constitutional Convention of 1787. During the War of 1812, Chipman served as adjutant with the South Carolina Regiment and was stationed at Beaufort, protecting Hilton Head Island against British invasion. He had married Martha Mary Logan in 1812, and their union yielded six children: four daughters and two sons. "Having a disgust for slavery which his wife, though a planter's daughter, shared" they moved to Detroit in 1823-1824. He continued to practice law and also worked for *The Morning Herald*, "at the time the most popular journal of the West." He was appointed Chief Justice

---

293. George I. Reed ed., *Bench and Bar of Michigan: A Volume of History and Biography* (Chicago: Century Pub., 1897), 398.
294. R. Manning Chipman, *The Chipman Lineage, Particularly as in Essex County, Mass.* (Salem: Salem Press, 1872), 12-13.
295. Id. 20-21.
296. Id. 25.
297. https://bioguide.congress.gov/search/bio/C000369 ; https://www.fjc.gov/history/judges/chipman-nathaniel

of the Wayne County Court. In 1827, to fill a vacancy, Chipman was appointed to the Supreme Court of the Territory of Michigan. President John Quincy Adams reappointed him, and Chipman served until 1832. He joined the Whig Party with its anti-slavery leanings until it was subsumed into the Republican Party in 1854. He identified with the Episcopal Church and was, during a large part of the time, either a member of the vestry of St. Paul's or a trustee of the Mariner's Church. Judge Chipman died in 1867, Martha Chipman in 1868. The graves of both are in Elmwood Cemetery.[298]

In the prior generation, the second son of Nathaniel and Sarah was Jeffrey Chipman, born in Vermont in 1789. He was Magistrate, Commissioner of Deeds, and School Commissioner in Canandigua, New York, before moving to Michigan and becoming Judge of the Kalamazoo County Court. He had married Lucy Baker in Vermont in 1814; they had six children.[299] He died December 1, 1849, age 60, and was buried in Mountain Home Cemetery, Kalamazoo County, Lot B, Sec. 40, Grave 2. Lucy lived until 1895; her grave is number 1.[300]

One of their children, Henry Laurens Chipman, was born on February 1, 1823, in Canandaigua, Ontario County, New York, and thereafter moved to Michigan with his family—he had married a native of Walterboro, South Carolina, in January 1848. In 1860, he and wife Laura were living with Judge (and uncle) Henry C. Chipman in his home in the 6th Ward in Detroit. Henry L.'s age was given as 34, Laura's as 40.[301]

At the inception of Michigan's involvement in the Civil War,

---

298. *American Biographical History of Eminent and Self-Made Men, Michigan Volume* (Cincinnati: Western Biographical Publishing Co., 1878), 31-32; 168; Bert L. Chipman, *The Chipman Family, a Genealogy of the Chipmans in America, 1631-1920* (Winston-Salem: Bert L. Chipman, 1920), 105; Michigan Historical Commission, *Michigan Biographies*, Vol. I (Lansing: 1924), 168; *Detroit Free Press*, Apr. 4, 1867, 1; Boatner, 154; https://www.micourthistory.org/justices/henry-chipman/ Their oldest son, Henry Logan Chipman, became a Lieutenant in the U.S. Navy and died at age 32. Another, John Logan Chipman, "a man of eloquence and recognized power," was a member of the Detroit bar.
299. *The Chipman Family*, 106.
300. Findagrave #30753722, #30753723.
301. 1860 Census, Detroit City, 3rd Ward, 25.

Governor Austin Blair came to Detroit on April 16, 1861, to lead its immediate response to the President's call for volunteers. One of his activities was to meet with a coterie of prominent military men. These "magnificent 7" included Alpheus S. Williams, John Robertson, William D. Wilkins, Orlando B. Willcox, Henry M. Whittlesey, James E. Pittman, and Henry L. Chipman,[302] who was the second Captain of the Detroit Light Guard, the leader of Company B. James Pittman commanded Company A.[303]

Chipman entered service in the 2nd Michigan Volunteer Infantry at its organization, commissioned as Lieutenant Colonel on April 25, 1861, for 3 years, age 38. His commander, temporarily, was Israel B. Richardson. He was mustered May 25, 1861, and discharged on June 24, 1861, to accept appointment as Captain, 11th U.S. Infantry, effective May 14, 1861. He received a Brevet promotion to Major as of May 3, 1863, for gallant and meritorious services in the Battle of Chancellorsville. Another, to Brevet Lieutenant-Colonel effective July 2, 1863, came for gallant and meritorious service in the Battle of Gettysburg.

He was appointed Colonel of the 1st Michigan Colored Infantry on April 15, 1864, and served in this capacity until being mustered out at Charleston, S.C., on September 30, 1865. Holding his commission in the Regular Army, Chipman was transferred from the 11th to the 29th U.S. Infantry on September 21, 1866. He transferred back to the 11th U.S. Infantry on April 25, 1869, and received promotion to Major, 3rd Infantry, on October 29, 1873. He received a promotion to Lieutenant-Colonel of the 7th U.S. Infantry on May 19, 1881. On February 1, 1887, he retired. His final promotion for Civil War conduct was to Brevet Brigadier-General of Volunteers as of March 13, 1865, for gallant and meritorious services during the war.[304]

Mrs. H.L. Chipman served as a Vice-President of the Michigan Soldiers' Aid Society commencing in 1864.[305]

In 1880, the couple lived at Fort Logan in Montana Territory; he

---

302. Walter F. Clowes, *The Detroit Light Guard: A Complete Record of this Organization from its Foundation to the Present Day* (Detroit: John F. Eby & Co., 1900), 32.
303. Id. 413, 529.
304. *Record of Service*, Vol. 2, 47; Heitman, 299.
305. *Michigan in the War*, 127.

was Major, 3rd U.S. Infantry, while she kept house.[306] In the 1910 Census, "Uncle" Henry lived with Edward L. and Emma Chipman in their home at 679 Trumbull Avenue in Detroit. He was a "Retired Officer," widower, age 88.[307]

General Chipman died on October 27, 1910, age 87, and was buried in Elmwood, Section A, Lot 166, next to his predeceased spouse. She died February 27, 1896, age 78.[308]

---

306. County of Meagher, Enumeration District 21, 8.
307. Supervisor's District 1, Enumeration District 118, 10B.
308. Findagrave #54471641, #99988558.

The unit received orders on April 12 and was transported to Hilton Head Island, South Carolina, on April 15, removing it from the IX Corps.[309] On May 23, was redesignated as the 102nd United States Colored Troops in accordance with War Department requirements.

The men of the regiment had truly fulfilled the sentiment expressed in verse:

> We are coming, Father Abraham, three hundred thousand more!
> You have called us, and we're coming by Richmond's bloody tide,
> To lay us down for freedom's sake, our brothers' bones beside ...[310]

An insightful source of information on activities of the 102nd is a diary housed at Michigan State University of one of its commissioned officers. Wilbur Nelson of Arcadia Township in Clinton County had

---

309. For photographs of the Island during the War, see Robert Carse, *Department of the South: Hilton Head Island in the Civil War* (Hilton Head Island: Heritage Library Foundation, 2002).
310. Words of a poem attributed to James S. Gibbons and set to music composed by L.O. Emerson.

served in the 8th Michigan Infantry from 1861 to 1863 when he was wounded in action and resigned. In March 1864, he accepted a commission as Captain in the 102nd. He recorded the departure from Michigan:

> Mon Mar 28—We marched this morning, at 10 o'clock we took the cars for Toledo. We got there about noon. We remained in Toledo today. Marched up through town. Some of the men were rather unruly.
> Tues Mar 29—We started at two o'clock and ran to Dunkirk by midnight where we changed cars.
> Wed Mar 30—We reached Elmira about noon. There we drew rations and changed cars for Baltimore. We got started about dark.
> Thurs Mar 31—We passed Harrisburg after dark and went on to Baltimore.
> Fri Apr 1—We reached Baltimore at sunrise. Took breakfast at the Soldiers' Relief and went aboard the steam boat George for Annapolis. Got to Annapolis about five o'clock and marched out to our camp three miles from town. It was one o'clock before we got to camp.
> Sat Apr 2—Last night was a stormy, rough night and the boys had a rather rough time without their tents and oil blankets. It snowed quite fast this morning and snowed and rained today. We drew our tents and put them up. I got small tents for the men and wall tents for the officers.
> Sun Apr 3—Simon and Alec Wurtz[311] came to see men and I went over to the camp of the 8th Mich in the evening and had a good visit.
> Mon Apr 4—Took breakfast with Capt Smith and Lt. Doane

---

311. Alexander Wurtz. Gratiot County. Enlisted in Company C, 8th Michigan Infantry, Aug. 19, 1861, at Sumner, for 3 years, age 24. Re-enlisted Dec. 29, 1863. Taken prisoner Sept. 1, 1864. Discharged July 6, 1865. *Record of Service*, Vol. 8, 147.

(Co C 8th Mich) then returned to camp. Drilled the company in the forenoon. It rained after noon, there was no drill.
Tues Apr 5—It rained today. In the afternoon I went to Annapolis with Sime McLaughlin (an old friend of the 8th Mich)[312] and made some purchases.
Wed Apr 6—Lt D___ T___ went down town on a detail today. I remained in camp. We did not drill today but had dress parade. It did not storm today as usual but was quite cold.
Thurs Apr 7—We had battalion drill in the afternoon. Major drilled the regiment. It was quite warm.
Fri Apr 8—I was officer of the day; things run rather loose. The guard do not know their duty very well and some of the officers are very slack.
Sat Apr 9—It rained in the afternoon. I did not drill today. I wrote all day on company business; I got up some orders to govern Company "I."
Sun Apr 10—I went down and visited Lt. Doane of the 8th Mich in the afternoon. In the evening Capt. Smith and Lt. Hovey (?) came up to see me. It was warm and pleasant today.
Mon Apr 11—We had battalion drill in the afternoon. Major Clark[313] drilled the regiment. It was very warm and pleasant.
Tues Apr 12—Drew clothing and shoes for the men. I wrote a letter to William in the morning then drilled the company one hour before noon. After noon we had battalion drill by Col. Bennet.[314] It was quite warm in the forenoon but got cold after noon and rained tonight.

The rather mundane schedule changed dramatically. The regiment had the honor of being inspected by two notable commanders:

---

312. Simon McLaughlin.
313. Newcom Clark, Clarkston.
314. William T. Bennett, Charleston, S.C.

Wed Apr 13—Gen. Grant reviewed us about one today. He was accompanied by Gen. Burnside. I hear he spoke well of the regiment.[315] Gen. Grant is not so impressive in appearance but he looks as though he knows something.

Thurs Apr 14—We got orders to be ready to embark for Hilton Head tomorrow morning at 7 o'clock. I received a letter from Nathan Church and answered it.

Fri Apr 15—We embarked today on board the steamer North Point for the South. Our boat got under way about night. Three companies got on the North Point, Companies "I," "C," and "D."

Sat Apr 16—We passed Fortress Monroe this morning about nine o'clock. The bay is very smooth; when we get in the Atlantic ocean it will be rougher. We reach Cape Hatteras about Sunday.

Sun Apr 17—This morning was clear but the wind blew quite hard and it was very rough. The Captain says we are 25 or 30 miles from Cape Hatteras. The sea is so rough and the wind is so hard we make about 6 miles an hour. I slept most of the forenoon. After noon I went on deck and amused myself with pop (?) and a cigar (?). Four weeks ago today I was sleigh riding in Gratiot; times have changed.

Mon Apr 18—The sea was smooth this morning when I first got up but the wind soon __ up from the south. Today we passed the blockading fleet off Charleston about four in the afternoon. At nine o'clock we are not in sight of Hilton Head.

Tues Apr 19—We arrived in sight of Hilton Head about noon and took a pilot aboard. We got in about 2 o'clock and marched out a mile and camped. Hilton Head has improved since I was here two years ago; it is quite a town now.

Wed Apr 20—I'm detailed officer of the day. Col. Chipman is

---

315. The *Detroit Advertiser and Tribune* of Apr. 20, 1864, reported that Grant regarded the regiment's appearance as "splendid." McRae, 65.

coming as commander of the regiment. He reported for duty just before we left Annapolis. He is a regular officer and seems to be a good man. We laid out our camp and pitched tents. I was very busy today.[316]

It must be acknowledged how much difficulty the assignment to this duty station brought to the regiment. The men of the unit were "alien to the South." They were not familiar with its geography or topography, and the heat, humidity, and hostile insect life proved significant challenges.[317] In one sense, the deployment to this coastline could be seen as a lack of confidence in the Black soldiers. But they also were green, i.e., inexperienced, and the Union's ability to substitute these new soldiers for experienced veterans who could be brought directly into battle made a huge contribution to successfully concluding the war.[318] If that was all that they contributed, it would have validated their service in and of itself.

Another kind of validation involved pay. White soldiers received $13 per month as their wage, with an additional $3 provided for a clothing allowance. The War Department had authorized formation of the Colored regiment based on a monthly pay of $10 per month. Ostensibly, the reasons for the difference lay with the compensation specified for persons of African descent in the Militia Act of July 17, 1862—$10. The Department implemented that law by issuing an order decreeing monthly pay at $10, minus a $3 clothing allowance.[319]

April 27th was payday. Nelson recorded: "Most of the men in Company 'I' refused to sign their names for Ten dollars a month. I advised them to take what they could get but they appeared set in their determination." Two days later, the paymaster paid off the

---

316. Wilbur Nelson Diary 1864, Michigan State University. Archives and Historical Collections. Question marks are in the transcriptions: https://d.lib.msu.edu/cwc-wnelson/1 ; https://d.lib.msu.edu/cwc-wnelson/2
317. Dobak, 86-87. On June 20, the thermometer recorded 100 degrees.
318. Dobak, 61.
319. *OR*, series III, III, 250-252 (General Orders No. 163, § VI, June 4, 1863).

company, but many of the men would not accept their pay because it was only $7 per month. They were joined by other Black soldiers, and that resistance to discrimination resulted in June by Congress setting their pay at $13 (under certain circumstances). Soon, pay for all Union soldiers was raised to $16 per month regardless of race.[320]

At some point, the soldiers of the regiment learned of events associated with the Confederate capture of Fort Pillow, a Union fortification along the Mississippi River north of Memphis, Tennessee, on April 12. The Union garrison included African American soldiers of two artillery regiments. Outnumbered, but declining surrender, the fort's defenders put up a heroic defense until overwhelmed by superior forces under command of Major-General Nathan Bedford Forrest. During the taking of the fort and the attempt by Union soldiers to make their escape, numerous men in blue were shot down without mercy. The Joint Committee on the Conduct of the War issued a report that concluded many Union soldiers were killed after offering to give up their arms: "The rebels commenced an indiscriminate slaughter, sparing neither age nor sex, white or black, soldier or civilian."[321] On April 19, the *Free Press* republished an article from the *Cairo News* of four days prior, with this subhead: "Slaughter of Negro Troops After the Surrender." It recounted how "every man fought like a hero, feeling well assured that no quarter would be given" since Forrest had demanded unconditional surrender. Scenes of "indiscriminate slaughter" resulted, "negroes were driven into houses, when the buildings were set on fire," and "the most revolting spectacle presented itself" after the atrocities had concluded.[322] Confederates argued the charges were false and trumped up. Most recent examination of the evidence, including by an eminent Civil War historian from Michigan, supports the conclusion "that a massacre took place" and that Confederates "tried to cover it up."[323]

---

320. *OR*, series III, IV, 445-448;
321. *Report No. 65*, 38th Congress, 1st Session, May 6, 1864, 4.
322. *Detroit Free Press*, Apr. 19, 1864, 4. Nelson's Diary held no mention.
323. John Cimprich, "The Fort Pillow Massacre: Assessing the Evidence" in

On the 30th, "some cannonading today to the west of us" was heard by the men of the regiment. As of May 3, the men had yet to receive mail. Soon, however, the regular supply chain via water brought letters from home as well as supplies and armaments. On May 6, Companies C and K were ordered to Fort Welles as part of the garrison.[324]

Detachments of the regiment were employed on picket duty on St. Helena and Jenkins Islands, and at Seabrook and Spanish Wells, on Hilton Head Island during their first month. Such an assignment was typical with USCTs, rather than front-line service. Three companies were involved, leaving four in camp and, during battalion drill, presenting a "very small" looking contingent.[325] On June 14, the War Department issued a new policy directive, which seemingly put an end to the non-combat emphasis:

> The incorporation into the Army of the United States of colored troops renders it necessary that they should be brought as speedily as possible to the highest state of discipline. Accordingly the practice which has hitherto prevailed, no doubt from necessity, of requiring these troops to perform most of the labor on fortifications and the labor and fatigue duties of permanent stations and camps will cease, and they will only be required to take their fair share of fatigue duty with the white troops. This is necessary to prepare them for the higher duties of conflict with the enemy. Commanders of colored troops in cases where the troops under their commands are

---

John D. Smith ed., *Black Soldiers in Blue: African American Troops in the Civil War Era* (Chapel Hill: University of North Carolina Press, 2002), 150-165. The eminent Michigan historian, Albert Castel, published his conclusions in 1958 in "The Fort Pillow Massacre: A Fresh Examination of the Evidence," *Civil War History* 4 (Mar. 1958), 45, 48-50.

324. Nelson Diary 1864. The facility was originally Fort Walker, erected in May 1861 by Confederate forces and named for the Secretary of War, LeRoy Pope Walker. It was captured by the Union expeditionary force in November 1861.

325. Id.

required to perform an excess of labor above white troops in the same command will represent the case to the common superior through the regular channels.[326]

Striking their tents during the evening of the 15th of June, the regiment moved to Beaufort, on Port Royal Island, where it was employed in camp and fatigue duty, as provost guard, and for a portion of the time as garrison until the 1st of August. Embarking on that date, the regiment proceeded to Jacksonville, Florida, where it arrived on the 3rd.

In Florida, the role of the 102nd was to reinforce Union forces in the District of Florida commanded by Brigadier-General John P. Hatch.[327] It was also part of a bigger strategic picture: supporting efforts to erect a loyalist State government was significant, as well the military goal of reducing food supplies to Confederate armies.[328] On the following day the regiment marched inland to Baldwin, a railroad junction 21 miles from Jacksonville of the Cedar Keys and Gulf Railroad and the Florida Central Railroad, where it engaged in picket duty and in destroying railroad track. Captain Nelson recorded that they had drawn new guns for the expedition and had "celebrated the anniversary of the liberation of the slaves in the West Indies." The march inland through a low, swampy country had been hard with the Florida heat, plus: "Alligators are thick."

The regiment tore up three miles of track on the 7th. That effort drew a response when on the 10th of the month it saw its first action. Upon moving out six miles to rip up rails, the regiment was attacked by a force of Rebel cavalry seeking to prevent further depredations and take back the rail junction. Nelson recorded that "a party of rebels fired into the left of our regiment from the woods. We deployed skirmishers and went after them but they had gone on when they heard us." Hatch reported:

---

326. *OR*, series III, IV, 431.
327. *OR*, XXXV, pt. I, 36. For biographical information on Hatch, see *infra*.
328. Dobak, 61.

On the 10th instant there was some little skirmishing between the enemy's cavalry and the One hundred and second U.S. Colored Troops, which was engaged in destroying the railroad in front of Baldwin.

On the 12th, the enemy advanced with two companies of cavalry and a piece of artillery. The One hundred and second U.S. Colored Troops was engaged in destroying the track about 3 miles in front of Baldwin. A small force of the Seventy-fifth Ohio in their front charged, and 2 men passing through the line were cut off and taken prisoners. Colonel Beecher fell back slowly, skirmishing with the enemy, and reported the case by messenger. I was in Baldwin and detached 100 cavalry and two pieces of artillery to his assistance. They drove the enemy back to the Saint Mary's, but took no prisoners. We lost all together 1 man killed and 4 taken prisoners.[329]

Understated was the fact that the 102nd had made an incursion deeper along the railroad west of Baldwin. The regiment had its first opportunity in armed conflict—it "saw the elephant"—and by "its splendid conduct on that occasion fully convinced its officers of the reliable and gallant fighting qualities of their men" in repulsing and scattering the enemy.[330]

A strategic purpose prompted the effort to take control of portions of Florida. President Lincoln sought to aid efforts "to reconstruct a loyal state government in Florida."[331] The campaign, then, had among its goals the assistance of efforts for the speedy restoration of the State to loyal status. Additionally, the expedition sought to cut off a source of Confederate supply and to obtain recruits for Colored regiments.[332]

---

329. *OR*, XXXV, pt. I, 426.
330. *Michigan in the War*, 490.
331. *Collected Works*, Vol. VII, 126.
332. These were the general goals of Major-General Quincy A. Gillmore, Department of the South. See Mark F. Boyd, "The Federal Campaign of 1864 in East Florida" in *Florida Historical Quarterly*, Vol. 29, No. 1 (Jul. 1950), 3-5.

A convention by loyalists was held within Union lines in Jacksonville in May for the purpose of selecting delegates to the national Union convention to be held in Baltimore on June 7-8.

The regiment's first successful encounter was followed up on August 15 with a march of 20 miles "through a low, swampy country" until reaching Milton Station on the Florida Key West Railroad. A march of 15 miles followed on the second day, then 18 miles during the next two. On August 19, the men reached their destination at Magnolia on the St. Johns River north of Jacksonville.[333] The five days required a many-mile trek through northeast Florida, tearing up track and destroying rolling stock. They also freed some 60 enslaved persons.[334] Their route passed the battleground at Olustee where, just months earlier, a Union force had been defeated. If accounts of that conflict were accurate, casualties in the Black troops had included post-battle hostilities. Having been relieved by another unit, the 102nd sailed back to Beaufort on the 29th and arrived at Beaufort on August 31. It resumed picketing at Coosa, Lady's, and Port Royal Islands. Rebel skirmishers were encountered and driven off.[335]

On September 8, the men heard that Sherman had taken Atlanta. Indeed, the capture of the major rail town on the 2nd constituted a major Union victory that aided mightily in the reelection of the President. They also heard of the death of Confederate cavalry raider John Hunt Morgan, which occurred on September 4 in Ohio. Back in Detroit on the 8th, the friendly daily published a list of soldiers who had died—all of disease—since May 18. As the names were discovered in the homes of the deceased, hearts that had yearned for their return began to break.[336]

In October, an unspecified illness that brought fever beset the regiment. On the 16th, four Rebels in a boat came near shore and were fired upon by pickets. Three were taken prisoner; when the fourth

---

333. *OR*, XXXV, pt. I, 429-431; *Michigan in the War*, 490.
334. Nelson Diary 1864.
335. *Michigan in the War*, 490.
336. McRae, 71.

tried escaping, he was shot and killed. On November 2, an escaping slave tried to swim the river at the ferry but "drowned in the attempt just before he got to our side." Inspections repeatedly resulted in compliments for Company C, a change from its early appearance.[337] Taking stock, its first eight months of service had not lacked action or moment, though the scale of hostilities was limited. That state of affairs was soon to end.

337. Nelson Diary 1864.

Battle of Honey Hill
300 Strong

Thanksgiving Day 1864 fell on November 24. The residents of Beaufort had little to be thankful about if they hoped for Confederate success, since such prospects remained tenuous. For those in the uniform of the United States, the mood was considerably more positive. The Union League Club of New York City sought to provide dinner to every soldier and sailor on that Thursday, and solicited donations from the people of the North. The Club arranged for shipments of food to as many Army regiments and Navy vessels possible.[338] As for those in the Port Royal region, the day meant another in a long series of strictly defensive operations.[339] On the 25th, that posture changed. Foster acknowledged a confidential letter from the War Department and began to put together an offensive plan.[340]

The legendary "March to the Sea" had been underway for about a week. From Atlanta, William T. Sherman set off for Savannah, Georgia, hoping to reach and capture the city by end of year. On November 11, he had telegraphed Washington with news that arrangements for the "grand raid" were complete on his end. In what he thought would be his last telegraphic communication until the objective was obtained, Sherman requested a coordination of forces such that he would not be the only Federal force to be reckoned with. He requested the main

---

338. The 1864 hurricane season was the third consecutive without a U.S. landfall. In 1865, two came ashore, and one paralleled the coastline of the Carolinas. https://www.aoml.noaa.gov/hrd/hurdat/All_U.S._Hurricanes.html
339. *OR*, XLIV, 506, 516, 525.
340. Id. 547.

rail link between Savannah and its South Carolina counterpart be pressured:

> I would like to have General Foster to break the Savannah and Charleston road about Pocotaligo about December 1. All other preparations are to my entire satisfaction.[341]

The General of the Armies must have immediately received a copy of Sherman's telegram. On the 12th, Grant telegraphed Chief of Staff Henry W. Halleck:

> I presume you have sent instructions to General Foster in accordance with General Sherman's request. I think it will have a good effect to make the attempt to get into Pocotaligo even if it should not succeed entirely. If the troops cannot get through, they can keep the enemy off General Sherman a little, as Derby held the editor of the San Diego Herald, or as Sturgis kept Forrest off our communications in Middle Tennessee.[342]

Halleck's instructions to Foster did not completely track with these missives. He advised that Sherman "wishes you, *if possible*, to cut the Savannah and Charleston Railroad near Pocotaligo" (emphasis added). Then came the real message: "At all events a demonstration on that road will be of advantage."[343] Unlike an assault, Halleck sought "a show of force by which no advance against an enemy is made," the object being to deceive.[344]

From the vantage point of an office in Washington, the task seemed easy enough. The Broad River could serve as a thoroughfare to

---

341. *OR*, XXXIX, pt. III, 740.
342. Id. 750.
343. *OR*, XXXV, pt. II, 328.
344. Boatner, 233. As distinguished from a "feint," involving an attack by a small component, since "no actual attack is made." Id. 276-277.

carry a shipborne contingent inland to where the railroad crossed on its route between Charleston and Savannah, near Coosawatchie. The Rebel defense could be anticipated as light; no troops could possibly be stationed there. True, the rails would enable speedy reinforcements, but surprise and swiftness should prove practicable. Least of all was the possibility that a prepared set of entrenchments would create a formidable obstacle to such a raid, serving as a bulwark against a hostile incursion.

That unexpected disadvantage was exactly what the Confederate high command had contemplated. On the heels of an unsuccessful attempt to defend western Virginia from Union advances in mid-1861, Robert E. Lee was ordered to the defense of the South Carolina/Georgia coast. President Jefferson Davis regarded it as so important to the Confederacy that he assigned Lee, a graduate of West Point in engineering, to bolster Rebel preparedness. Lee traveled to Charleston and then to Coosawhatchie on the C&S Railroad, "the station nearest Port Royal Sound." He established his headquarters there, acting as commander of the Department from November 8, 1861, to March 3, 1862. A review of geography and terrain, along with a sense of the Confederacy's resources, led him to a plan. It involved construction of a deep interior line protecting the communication/supply line, drawn so that a defender could concentrate and hold it with available troops while compelling the enemy to fight where guns of warships could not be employed. In a real sense, it was the son following the lesson of the Revolutionary War father—Light Horse Harry Lee—of withdrawing beyond the reach of shielding naval firepower. Further, he designed it deep enough into the country that it could be held by a small force until the arrival of reinforcements via the railroad.[345]

At evening on November 28, a force of 5,000 soldiers and 500 sailors and marines boarded federal gunboats at Hilton Head Island.[346] The waterborne arm also furnished the protecting cover of six gunboats:

---

345. Douglas S. Freeman, *R.E. Lee*, Vol. I (New York: Charles Scribner's Sons, 1934), 608-609, 613-615, 629; *OR*, VI, 309, 323.
346. *OR*, XLIV, 420.

Mingoe, Pawnee, Pontiac, Sonoma, Winona, and *Wissahickon.* Their destination was Boyd's Landing up and on the southern shore of the Broad River, and their expected arrival at daybreak would have stolen a march on the enemy. This deep water landing on Boyd Creek provided a hospitable spot to bring the force ashore. It could involve a march of only a few miles to cut the rails at Grahamville.[347] Among this expeditionary force was a detachment of the 102nd regiment, consisting of 12 officers and 300 men. The detachment was commanded by Captain Calvin S. Montague, Colonel Chipman being in brigade command.[348] Montague, of Kalamazoo, had enlisted as Sergeant in the 2nd Infantry on May 10, 1861, age 22. He was commissioned 2nd Lieutenant February 24, 1863, and was wounded in action during the Vicksburg Campaign on July 1, 1863, at Jackson, Mississippi. He accepted a commission as Captain in the 102nd effective March 11, 1864.[349]

Unfortunately, atmospheric conditions did not cooperate with Washington's strategy. The night sky was clear when the signal rocket was fired to mark at 2:00 a.m. on November 29 the departure of the Union expedition.[350] A "dense" fog moved in and covered the river. Several vessels grounded, while others followed the wrong route or dropped anchor to avoid such problems. Some had to retrace their route. Altogether, the complications meant that the deboarding did not commence until 11:00 a.m. the next day. Advantage might yet have been achieved had the right route to Grahamville been followed, and beyond,[351] but the lead elements went "in a direction opposite to the route we were to march." The force counter-marched and went into bivouac early in the morning of the 30th at Bolan's Church. At

---

347. Id. 420-421. The town in modern times of Ridgeland on the opposite side of I-95 dominates the area.
348. *Michigan in the War*, 490.
349. *Record of Service*, Vol. 2, 123.
350. William H. Bragg, "Victory at Honey Hill: 'A Mere Flicker of Light'" in *Civil War Times Illustrated*, Vol. XXII, No. 9, Jan. 1984, 12.
351. The line passed a mile west since villagers had objected to locating the station there. https://www.hmdb.org/m.asp?m=6210

that hour, a Confederate force arrived in Savannah from Macon, the alarm having been sounded by Confederate watching posts. Their lead reinforcements arrived at Grahamville at 8:00 a.m. via rail, underscoring the importance of the transportation link to the Confederacy.[352] The failure to reach the station on the 29th would prove critical.

When the Federals managed to set out in the right direction, leaving behind "swamps and rice fields,"[353] they were delayed by enemy cavalry and artillery, the latter shelling the column from ahead on the narrow country road. The Union infantry deployed in force, only to be met with a field of broom grass fired by the Rebels, dispensing "clouds of smoke and ashes" toward the Federals,[354] followed by the discovery of enemy entrenchments ahead. They discovered the Confederates were defending "a strong earth work that nobody knew anything about"[355] that occupied "a low ridge about thirty feet in elevation." The ground over which the Federals advanced was hardly favorable:

> About 100 yards in front of the ridge was a tangled swamp, 20 yards wide, where dense vegetation clustered around tall water oaks and gum trees. A nameless creek, not more than two feet deep, wandered sluggishly through the swamp, roughly paralleling the Rebel line.[356]

After the Confederate skirmish line was forced back, Union regimental commanders began to make uncoordinated and mostly unsupported attacks on the works. These assaults continued into the afternoon, each failing as the Rebels were able to concentrate their fire on each separate advance. When the Union 2nd Brigade under Colonel Alfred S. Hartwell arrived, which included the Michiganders, it was

---

352. Emilio, 239.
353. Bragg, 16.
354. Id.
355. Dobak, 78.
356. Bragg, 16, 18.

put into position behind the front line rather than used in a flanking movement. After some misdirection,[357] Hartwell moved his other men rapidly to the front upon hearing heavy firing. Would it be a case where "the Michigan colored soldiers would again miss the action"?[358]

Not so. Taking fire from Confederate artillery and sharpshooters, a section of the Union guns was forced to abandon three of its pieces. To keep them out of the hands of the Rebels, a force of infantry would have to advance under fire.

> A detail of a company of the One Hundred and Second, under the command of Captain A.E. Lindsay, was ordered to bring off the guns. At the head of his company, Captain Lindsay rushed into the storm of shot and shell, but was killed before reaching the field pieces. The only other officer, Lieutenant H.H. Alvord, was wounded first by a minnie [sic] ball in the right ear, and then by grapeshot which struck the ring and hook of his sword forcing it five inches into his flesh. The command of the company now devolved upon Sergeant J.W. Madry. The sergeant, unaware of the reason for the company's advance, and finding himself under deadly fire by which the two officers and eight or ten enlisted men had been stricken down, fled to the right and brought his men off in good order. The severity of the fire was shown by the fact that during the retreat Lieutenant H.H. Alvord received a third wound when he was struck in the back of the head by a musket ball.[359]

Despite the lack of success, and the position of the guns within 150 yards of the enemy and 100 yards beyond the Union lines, another effort was ordered. A detail of 30 men of the 102nd under command of Lieutenant O.W. Bennett went out to retrieve the guns. The

---

357. Charles B. Fox, *Record of Service of 55th Regiment of Massachusetts Volunteer Infantry* (Cambridge: John Wilson & Son, 1868), 41-42.
358. Dunn, 95.
359. Id. 95-96 (footnotes omitted).

advance was coolly led and gallantly performed; the three guns were brought off the field and back into Union Army possession.[360] The men of the Regiment then covered the withdrawal of the Union force back toward the landing point. Not until 7:30 p.m. did they join the retreat.[361] The Federals had not succeeded in fulfilling Sherman's wish, but they had shown their mettle—and it would be only a matter of several months before the coastal railroad would be put out of business. "Grahamville would burn, and Charleston would fall."[362]

A diary by a medical officer in a companion regiment provides a contemporary account of the affair and gives a sense of the attitudes of the soldiers themselves. The expedition to Honey Hill was regarded by the officers as "of some importance" since Sherman was within 30 miles of Savannah and the foray was escorted by gunboats, an uncommon aspect. In addition to the very deep fog after midnight on November 29, the vessels also had to deal with low tide. Included was a report on the combat in which his regiment and the men of the 102nd were involved:

> Wednesday we arose an hour before daylight and at dawn started inland toward the railroad. Gen. Hatch was with Potter's brigade in advance; our regiment was the first of the four comprising Hartwell's brigade. There was some firing nearly all the way, for the confederates kept a brass field piece in the narrow road along which we had to move in a narrow column; much of the way there were thick woods on both sides. About the middle of the forenoon our regiment halted in the midst of a field for about an hour, and then, firing having commenced in front, we advanced in that direction where the other brigade was already engaged. The spot selected for the first reception of the wounded was about an eighth of a mile from the fighting line and so I can describe only what was

---

360. *OR*, XLIV, 423, 434.
361. Id. 434.
362. Bragg, 19.

told me of the fight itself. It seems that when the head of the column reached a sharp turn in the road it was confronted by a rebel earthwork mounting several guns. No serious effort to take this was made till Hartwell volunteered to lead a charge. The order to advance seems to have reached only four of our companies. The way was further blocked by a slough with logs in it. The woods at the side of the road were filled with rebels. In a very short time we lost 120 killed and wounded. Co. B alone lost 30. Hartwell was shot in the hand but kept on till his horse was killed and fell on him. Lt. Ellsworth dragged him from beneath the animal at the risk of his own life, for the colonel was wounded twice more, tho not dangerously. Capt. Crane and Lt. Boynton were killed; Capt. Woodward and Lt. Jewett were wounded, and Capt. Soule slightly, but he is on duty. The charge was unsuccessful, but the artillery and most of the infantry remained in action till dark when they were gradually withdrawn.[363]

Several days later, the 102nd performed an important holding action:

Thursday, 6th, 3:00 P.M. There was no firing last night but we did not feel very safe because, in order to send a large force on an expedition up the river, the Naval Brigade on our left was replaced by the 102nd U.S., and other troops were withdrawn from our right leaving our brigade of two regiments to hold the entire line. Our regiment now extends half a mile from the road at the edge of the woods so that the men are six feet or more apart; if the confederates know our weakness and are not themselves too much occupied with Sherman they may make trouble for us.[364]

---

363. Richard M. Reid ed., *Practicing Medicine in a Black Regiment: The Civil War Diary of Burt G. Wilder, 55th Massachusetts* (Amherst: University of Massachusetts Press, 2010), 198-200 (footnotes omitted).
364. Id. 202.

The official Michigan war history noted the regiment's performance: "At the points named the officers and men referred to, most gallantly engaged a superior force of the enemy, sustaining an aggregate loss in these affairs of sixty-five in killed and wounded; Captain A.E. Lindsay being among the killed and Lieutenant H.H. Alvord among the severely wounded."[365] It also republished a report from "a correspondent," who recalled that "derision" had met the regiment at organization. Now, however, "its praises are on every one's lips" for its heroism:

> On one side of our little detail of 300 men the 54th Massachusetts (colored) was drawn up, on the other a white regiment, the 127th New York. Here our forces sustained a charge from the enemy, and charged in turn. In this affair the 102d covered themselves with glory. It is acknowledged without stint on all hands that our regiment maintained the steadiest line of battle and fought with the greatest determination of any troops on the ground. Many who were wounded quite severely refused to go to the rear, but kept on fighting, while the blood was flowing from their wounds. But the enemy's position was found too strong to be taken, and our forces were withdrawn. The enemy's fire having been very severe upon our artillery, and so many horses having been killed, they were obliged to abandon two pieces of artillery on the field, and while all were falling back, and after the retreat had been sounded, two companies of the 102d hauled off the two pieces of artillery by hand.[366]

The day ended with the Union troops retiring back to the crossroads that led to Boyd's Landing. They did not evacuate; instead, the position served as a launching point for raids, or demonstrations, in the direction of the railroad in order to keep up pressure at this point in

---

365. *Michigan in the War*, 490.
366. Id. 490-491.

the Confederate defense system and thus aid Sherman's advance on Savannah.[367]

At Port Royal, where the Union military protected the community of escapees and White Northern civilians who had come to help bolster their fortunes, news of the affair caused consternation—for a time. On December 1, a visitor from Beaufort brought news of a "twice repulsed" advance. Two days later, rumors were "various and contradictory, but the impression seems to be that we have been whipped, but hold on and have entrenched at Grahamville." Anxiety reigned, and "it makes our hearts sink to hear the guns as we do. Pray God we may succeed this time and Sherman may come through."[368]

The 102nd was also engaged at Tillifinny on December 7 and at Devaux Neck on the 9th.[369] Again, the objective was to cut the railroad, this time over the Coosawatchie River.[370] Again, their performance under fire drew commendations:

> For several days fighting and skirmishing were kept up quite briskly near the same place, during which time the 102d not only maintained their credit, but were constantly gathering new laurels. The white regiment which fought next to ours held our men in the highest estimation, and expressed their preference to fight beside our regiment rather than any other regiment in the department.

---

367. *OR*, XLIV, 420. Some aspects of this battle account are drawn from: Emilio, *supra*; William A. Courtenay, "Fragments of War History Relating to the Coast Defence of South Carolina, 1861-'65, and the Hasty Preparations for the Battle of Honey Hill, November 30, 1864" in *Southern Historical Society Papers*, Vol. 26 (1898), 62ff; Lowell D. Hamilton, *The Battle of Honey Hill, South Carolina Wednesday, 30 November 1864*, available at http://www.fireandfury.com/rffscenarios/HoneyHillHistoricalCommentary.pdf
368. Elizabeth Ware Pearson ed., *Letters from Port Royal Written at the Time of the Civil War* (Boston: W.B. Clarke Co., 1906), 289.
369. *Michigan in the War*, 491.
370. *OR*, XLIV, 421.

After the expedition withdrew to Bull's Neck, further skirmishes occurred. The "102d fought as well as any troops ever fought, no other Michigan regiment excepted." Fortitude was on display:

> There were men in my company who were shot through and through the fleshy part of the arm who have not gone to the hospital, but after having their wounds dressed have come to their company quarters, remained there, and seemed scarcely to notice their wounds.

In fact, the veteran "correspondent" of nearly the entire war regarded "such bravery I never saw before … I never before saw men exhibit such unyielding bravery in battle."[371] The conduct of the men reflected well on the regimental commander. It was circulated that Colonel Chipman was recommended for a promotion to Brigadier-General.[372]

Black troops had demonstrated their mettle at the Battles of Port Hudson, the Crater, New Market Road (or Heights), and Nashville,[373] and they would do so in the Appomattox Campaign that wound up the war in Virginia in April 1865. That the 102nd did not fight in such a contest ought not to detract from their reputation. They faced the enemy for many a month, risking life and limb. The account of one of their officers, William Sleight of Bath, Michigan, reveals that fact in first-person detail.[374] By one count, "African American troops took part in some 449 separate engagements; only an encyclopedia could have covered all of them."[375] Unlike for soldiers of European descent "there were few, if any, advantages for black soldiers, nationally or locally."[376]

On December 22, from Savannah via Fort Monroe in Virginia,

---

371. *Michigan in the War*, 491.
372. Id.
373. Long & Long, 359, 548, 575, 610-612.
374. See Appendix.
375. Trudeau, xix, 466.
376. Smith, *The First Michigan Colored Infantry*, 135.

Sherman sent a telegram to "His Excellency President Lincoln." It contained one sentence:

> I beg to present you, as a Christmas gift, the city of Savannah, with 150 heavy guns and plenty of ammunition, and also about 25,000 bales of cotton.[377]

A rumor had reached Port Royal on December 11 of this achievement, prematurely.[378] The President now replied with "[m]any, many thanks for your Christmas gift, the capture of Savannah." He had been anxious when Sherman began his campaign from Atlanta, "if not fearful." The undertaking had proved to be a success, and "the honor is all yours," he told his General. It had brought those who had "sat in darkness to see a great light." Please, he abjured, to "make my grateful acknowledgments to your whole army, officers and men."[379] Although not directly credited, the men of the 102nd could take pride in their contributions to retaking Georgia for the Union.

The turn of the calendar page saw the Regiment continue its work along the Southeast Coast. It skirmished with Confederate cavalry, tore up rails, built fortifications, and then marched toward Charleston in late February as part of another effort to aid Sherman, this time during his Carolinas Campaign.[380] The war had commenced in that city's harbor in April 1861, and now a unit full of African Americans was participating in the campaign to effectuate its surrender, which took place on February 18. On that day, its Hospital Steward wrote his wife back in Michigan. James Curtis of Howell had mustered into the unit in February 1864 and accompanied it until the effects of dysentery sent him on an extended furlough. Although his correspondence initially revealed both an anti-slavery bent with a less than positive attitude toward Blacks, this letter, sent upon rejoining the

---

377. *OR*, XLIV, 783.
378. Pearson, 290.
379. *OR*, XLIV, 809.
380. Trudeau, 354-356.

Regiment in the field, reflected its performance and reputation after recent martial activity: "I can assure you that to belong to the 102d is a great honor & here every mouth is full of praise for them." He added that "the men are in great Spirits."[381]

The 102nd continued to fulfill its duty, and on March 9 it was ordered to Savannah. The entirety of the Regiment arrived via transports by March 16.[382] On the 28th, five of its companies moved to Georgetown in anticipation of another campaign. In April, men of the 102nd undertook another effort to aid Sherman's progress through the Carolinas and eliminate Confederate ability to provide sustenance to the forces opposing his advance.[383] It involved "a most hazardous and daring expedition from Charleston, S.C., to join General Potter on the Santee river, striking it at Nelson's Ferry, distant about seventy miles" and marching through enemy country.[384] On the 7th, the five companies destroyed a bridge while under fire. On April 18, elements of the Regiment met the enemy in force at Boykins Mill, eight miles from Camden, flanked the Rebels, "attacking them with much spirit and gallantry" and driving them "in great disorder." That "the rebels at once gave way" was attributed to the maneuver effected by the 102nd.[385] More specifically, they crossed over a swamp "on a log." The remainder, under Chipman, had taken a circuitous route through the country, "skirmishing all the way," until they joined the main expedition.[386] The next day involved more of the same: "a successful flank

---

381. Robert Beasecker ed., *This is a War for the Utter Extinction of Slavery: The Civil War Letters of James Benjamin Franklin Curtis, Hospital Steward, 1st Michigan Colored Infantry* (Grand Valley State University, 2020), 93. Books and Contributions to Books. 24. https://scholarworks.gvsu.edu/library_books/24 [This free online work is book-length (some 100,000 words).]; *Record of Service*, Vol. 46, 28.
382. Dunn, 110.
383. Trudeau, 375.
384. *Michigan in the War*, 492.
385. *OR*, XLVII, pt. I, 1026.
386. Id. 1030, 1037. A marker erected in 1967 on SC-261 for the Battle of Boykin's Mill keeps faith with the Lost Cause by stating: "Here on April 18, in one of the last engagements of the war, a small force of Confederate regulars and

movement was made by the regiment, which resulted, after a most gallant brush, in forcing him to abandon a strong position and in routing him most thoroughly."[387] The presence of "armed Negroes" struck dread into the Rebels to an even greater extent than Sherman during his March to the Sea.[388]

When Chipman wrote up his report of the two weeks of operations from April 11-25, he did so from Georgetown, South Carolina, evidence of how Federal forces had been able to extend their reach. His account was straightforward, demonstrating how his men had achieved a fitness and level of experience that placed them fully within the veteran status of the Union's infantry without regard to make-up.[389] They had marched into camp only after, "on the 21st, the enemy sent in a flag of truce, with dispatches from General Beauregard stating that Generals Sherman and Johnston had ceased hostilities."[390] The war appeared to be almost over.

Nelson recorded the events of that period:

Friday, April 21st.
We marched this morning at sunrise and marched about twenty miles. At noon we heard by flag of truce that peace has been concluded. We discharged our guns over the news, which I hope will prove true.

Saturday, April 22nd.
We marched about 20 miles today, past Wright's Bluff on the Santee River, and camped near Murrin's Ferry (?).

Sunday, April 23rd.
  We marched somewhat over 20 miles. Heard the sad news of Lincoln's assassination.

---

local Home Guard fought a defensive action which delayed their advance for a day." "Their" refers to a Union force of "2700 white and Negro Union troops."
387. *Michigan in the War*, 492.
388. Trudeau, 377.
389. *OR*, XLVII, pt. I, 1039-1040.
390. *Michigan in the War*, 492.

The 21st had brought communications to the Department from higher up. One told the mournful news of Lincoln's death. The other reported on the "convention" entered into by Sherman to end the war. Accordingly, all hostile actions were put on hold, pending the ushering in of peace.[391] One veteran looked back on the year's work of "the most agreeable army" in which the troops worked "in perfect harmony" with "a unity of feeling." In addition to their direct military efforts, the expeditionary force had "been instrumental in liberating about six thousand slaves."[392]

Nelson made an observation about the post-slavery South in his entry for Friday, June 2, 1865:

> The people are somewhat disposed to make the best of matters. They are freeing their slaves and making bargains with them to work for pay.[393] The south is well-beat.

On July 4, he recorded that the Regiment had a "first-rate" review. It was at Winnsboro on August 8; on August 11, the men "received orders to prepare to muster out at once." On September 2: "We had a review today by General Chipman. In the evening some of the officers visited the editor of the paper here and advised him not to publish pieces against negro troops." On September 8, they marched back toward Orangeburg, passing through Columbia where Sherman's force had contributed to the decimation of the downtown in retribution for the State's role in launching the war.

Eventually, the 102nd returned to Charleston. It was mustered out of service there on September 30 and proceeded to Michigan. Evans recorded their final voyage:

Monday, October 9th.

---

391. *OR*, XLVII, pt. III, 272-274.
392. Trudeau, 395.
393. Nelson was over-optimistic, as Reconstruction would prove.

We went on board the Steamer "Edward Everett" this evening, but did not sail. We lay in the harbor all night.

Tuesday, October 10th.
We sailed today for New York. The sea was smooth and pleasant.

Wednesday, October 11, 1865.
We passed Hattaras lighthouse just at sundown today. The sea is smooth.

Thursday, October 12th.
A heavy gale sprang up in the afternoon and we had to run into a Delaware breakwater at night.

Friday, October 13th.
We run up to New York Harbor in the evening, but did not go inside.

Saturday, October 14th.
We landed at New York this morning, crossed over to Jersey City, and took the cars about three o'clock.

Sunday, October 15, '65.
We passed thru Elmira today about noon. Took dinner at Hornellsville

Monday, October 16.
We changed cars at Dunkirk last night. Took breakfast at Erie this morning, dinner at Cleveland, and took the Steamer "Cleveland City" for Detroit in the evening.

Tuesday, October 17th.
We had a pleasant trip last night and arrived in Detroit this

morning. We ---- with a good breakfast at the Michigan Central depot. Then marched up to the barracks and went into camp.

At Detroit, it was paid off and disbanded.[394] The war had ended months before, and people were returning to their everyday lives, resulting in less than a total turn-out of the city to honor their return. Nonetheless, they did receive a formal welcome home:

> They arrived a little earlier than was anticipated, yet the committee was promptly on hand, and dealt out to them a hospitable reception, consisting of a good warm meal and hearty congratulations at their safe return from the tented-field and from a service of labor for the preservation of the government.

Since the arrival consisted of only part of the Regiment, plans were made for a future event:

> The balance of the regiment, five companies, are expected here tomorrow morning, and as soon thereafter as possible at no distant day, it is intended to give General Chipman and his officers and men a public reception. Some of our best speakers will be in attendance and will address the regiment on Campus Martius. Our citizens will then have an opportunity of seeing for themselves what the regiment can do in a military line.

Because of weather, the public reception on October 26 had to be canceled.[395]

Evans's on-the-ground account did not mention a major effect on

---

394. *Michigan in the War*, 492.
395. *Detroit Advertiser and Tribune*, Oct. 18, 1865, as quoted in Dunn, 122-123.

the Confederacy from the mustering in of Black troops into Union blue. The service of the 102nd and its companion units had led the military and political leadership of the Confederate States to examine and then address the issue of enabling African Americans to serve in its armies. The influx of some 200,000 Blacks into Union arms compounded the manpower problem of the Rebel forces, which suffered from battle losses, disease, and desertion as the war became more relentless. If slaves were to be armed, though, and if they "will make good soldiers our whole theory of slavery is wrong," candidly admitted one politician. The whole proposal "went against fundamental Confederate theory." Initially proposed by an officer dubbed "the Stonewall Jackson of the West" in January 1864, it finally passed the Confederate Congress and became law in March 1865—"too late" to "bring practical benefits."[396]

Who was there to hail the Michigan Regiment's deeds?[397] What sacred ground could interested observers visit to find the scenes of its heroism? Honey Hill had been an important battle historically because it was the first large-scale combat engagement by a majority African American force against Confederate forces. Four courageous soldiers received the Medal of Honor. The site was added to the National Register of Historic Places many decades later—in July 2004. The nomination form supported its significance by stating (in part):

> the site of an important operation of the Civil War on the southeastern coast, one launched in direct support of Gen.

---

396. *OR*, LII, pt. II, 586-592 (Major-General Patrick R. Cleburne, with other signatories); Bruce Catton, *Never Call Retreat, The Centennial History of the Civil War, Volume Three* (Garden City: Doubleday & Co., 1965), 424-430; see generally Bruce C. Levine, *Confederate Emancipation: Southern Plans to Free and Arm Slaves During the Civil War* (New York: Oxford University Press, 2006). For African American militancy against the Confederacy in the South, see David S. Cecelski, *The Fire of Freedom: Abraham Galloway & the Slaves' Civil War* (Chapel Hill: University of North Carolina Press, 2012).

397. See Appendix for the Regiment's list of engagements.

William T. Sherman's epic march from Atlanta to Savannah. The Battle of Honey Hill was one of the three largest Civil War battles fought in South Carolina, and was one of the most notable Civil War engagements involving African American troops. ... The 1864 road net is substantially intact, and extensive Civil War earthworks are extant and well-preserved on the property.[398]

But the land was not held by a public entity. It would take another set of years before the prospect began to emerge of access to the battleground. A Battlefield Historic Preservation Grant received just a few years ago may enable visitors to understand the courage exhibited by African American soldiers on that unfortunate day. There is no substitute for going over the ground to comprehend the nature of the service performed by soldiers in the War of the Rebellion.

---

398. http://www.nationalregister.sc.gov/jasper/S10817727007/S10817727007.pdf

The Women's Work

Without the roles played by the women of America, the Civil War would not have the dimensions it reached. With their husbands, sons, fathers away, many women progressed into the primary responsibility for managing their family's welfare. In rural communities such as Cass County, women had to assume greater responsibility for farm labor, managing family accounts, and taking on the work that male family members had done in peacetime.

The documentary record is fairly sparse concerning the specific roles played by females of the Midwest during the Civil War.[399] Just within recent years has the first study appeared that seeks to tell their story. It reports that "as individuals as well as through female and mixed-sex anti-slavery societies, the women of Ohio, Indiana, Illinois, Michigan and Wisconsin forged an important space for themselves in the antislavery movement."[400] The record is even more sketchy regarding the lives of women of color.[401] Several of prominence, however, can be noted with some detail. Equally, if not more, important is the role played by those who shall forever remain less known:

---

399. Jack Dempsey ed., *When Slavery and Rebellion Are Destroyed: A Michigan Woman's Civil War Journal* (Athens: University of Georgia Press, 2023), 20.
400. Robertson, *Hearts Beating for Liberty*, 2.
401. A recently published article attempts to remedy this issue: Margaret Washington, "'I Am Going Straight to Canada': Women Underground Railroad Activists in the Detroit River Border Zone" in *A Fluid Frontier*. See Jennifer R. Harbour, *Organizing Freedom: Black Emancipation Activism in the Civil War Midwest* (Carbondale: Southern Illinois University Press, 2020); Jeffrey, 8.

Families, and the larger community, were critical supporters of the war effort, and numerous war propagandists agreed. African American women, more specifically, received frequent public praise from a racially diverse group of northerners for their prominent role in getting able-bodied men to enlist. For instance, Pennsylvanian Congressman William D. Kelley proclaimed that African American mothers, such as Elizabeth Powell and Sarah Potts, and wives, such as Elizabeth Rothwell, were vital to the war effort. The *Weekly Anglo-African* (published in New York City) printed similar statements in widely circulated newspaper articles.[402]

Black women contributed to the Union war effort through various efforts:

> Many stayed home and raised families alone, while their husbands and sons enlisted in the Union army. Free black women's organizations in the North raised funds and collected supplies for black regiments and the contraband camps in the South. Some assisted Union regiments as nurses, cooks, laundresses, teachers, and in other ways.[403]

They particularly broke barriers "by serving as nurses and aides in caring for the sick and wounded."[404]

An antebellum exemplar of a Midwest Black woman who sought equal free status is Elizabeth Denison Forth. She was involved in "Michigan's Own Dred Scott Case" as the daughter of Peter Denison, who sought legal freedom for his children in an 1807 case.[405] Peter and

---

402. Pinheiro, *supra*.
403. Roy E Finkenbine, *Sources of the African American Past: Primary Sources in American History* (New York: Longman Publishers, 1997), 77.
404. Joe H. Mays, *Black Americans and Their Contributions Toward Union Victory in the American Civil War, 1861-1865* (Lanham: University Press of America, 1984), 75.
405. *In re Elizabeth Denison*, 1 St Ct Terr Mich 63 (1807).

wife Hannah were held in enslavement by William Tucker, whose will provided for their freedom upon his death but continued "ownership" of their children by his heirs. Territorial Judge Augustus Woodward ruled, first, that the state of law, involving treaties with Great Britain, meant continued enslavement. He then decided that the absence of treaty language regarding the return to the United States from Canada of fugitive slaves meant they could not be remitted again into bondage. The Denisons "slipped across the border to Canada" and later returned to the Detroit area—now free. On September 25, 1827, Elizabeth Denison married Scipio Forth at St. Paul's church in Detroit, a union that ended with his death three years later. Elizabeth lived a frugal life and accumulated a significant estate while working over the next 30 years. She became the first Black to own property in Pontiac and left a bequest that funded construction of St. James Episcopal Chapel on Grosse Ile. Two State historical markers commemorate her life.[406]

It should be no surprise that Michigan women played an important role in the Underground Railroad. It is not too much to say that the network to freedom could not have functioned in Michigan (or elsewhere) without the participation of women of color. One example is Mary Bibb, who with her husband, Henry, established the first successful African American newspaper to support the abolitionist cause.[407] A key to successful resistance was "the concerted efforts of black communities" in Michigan and elsewhere, "urban and rural,"[408] male and female. Black women served as conductors and did the "unsung work" of "feeding, sheltering, and nursing fugitives."[409]

---

406. Reginald R. Larrie, *Makin' free: African Americans in the Northwest Territory* (Detroit: Blaine Ethridge Books, 1981), 8; Edward J. Littlejohn, "Slaves, Judge Woodward, and the Supreme Court of the Michigan Territory" in *Michigan Bar Journal*, Vol. 94, July 2015, 22ff; Ashlee, 337, 499.
407. Afua Cooper, "The *Voice of the Fugitive*: A Transnational Abolitionist Organ" in *A Fluid Frontier*.
408. R.J.M. Blackett, *The Captive's Quest for Freedom: Fugitive Slaves, the 1850 Fugitive Slave Law, and the Politics of Slavery* (New York: Cambridge University Press, 2018).
409. Bordewich, 369.

Given that prominent White female abolitionists like Laura Smith Haviland a decade ago were spoken of as having "been largely overlooked," the paucity of historical literature on Black females might not surprise. Efforts to adequately explore her activities would reveal that when Haviland traveled in support of her anti-slavery work, it was "often alone or in the company of black men and women."[410]

Black women of the North came together in the antebellum years to form associations of common interest. Among these were Boston's Afric-American Female Intelligence Society, New York's African Dorcas Society, and Philadelphia's Female Literary Association. Michigan featured "the Detroit Female Benevolent Association, a Black organization." Beyond such organizations, free Black women worked in unofficially recognized groups and as individuals to support the abolitionist movement. Their participation "was an important feature of abolition," and they can be said to have "laid much groundwork for a distinct pattern of black female activism that would become important" in the modern Civil Rights movement. Given both gender and cultural frameworks, the work of Black women on behalf of universal human freedom served up a "complex experience" involving "multilayered" roles.[411] And Detroit was a place "where black feminist thought developed."[412]

In some families, female Blacks were not encouraged to work for abolitionism; hence, the banding together gave them reinforcement lacking at home. An example is a Detroit boarding house resident named Kingsbury, who found her sympathies shared by only one other boarder. Her husband did not support her getting involved in the struggle, a position that was a great trial for her. Women raised

---

410. Miles, 1, 17.
411. Shirley J. Yee, *Black Women Abolitionists: A Study in Activism, 1828-1860* (Knoxville: University of Tennessee Press, 1992), 2-3, 62-63, 75-76, 113, 156.
412. Melba Joyce Boyd, *Discarded Legacy: Politics and Poetics in the Life of Frances E.W. Harper* (Detroit: Wayne State University Press, 1994), 216.

monetary support for antislavery efforts through canvassing for donations, fairs, and levees. One was held in Detroit in 1852.[413]

One prominent Black female abolitionist was Frances Ellen Watkins Harper of Baltimore. Instructor and teacher and an "articulate, dignified, and composed" public speaker, she traveled through New England, Pennsylvania, and the Midwest giving lectures on the evils of slavery during the 1850s. She spoke on at least two occasions in Detroit, one documented in September 1858 at Second Baptist Church. She was described as "the greatest female speaker ever was here."[414] On July 20, 2023, the National Park Service added the Frances Harper Inn, 307 Horton Street in Detroit, to the National Register of Historic Places. In the first half of the 20th century, the inn was operated by the Christian Industrial Club, a Black women's club, as a rooming house and place of refuge. Originally a home built in 1893, the facility was "[n]amed after Black abolitionist and educator Frances Ellen Watkins Harper."[415]

Black churches in antebellum Detroit—Second Baptist and the "Bethel Church," an African Methodist Episcopal congregation, and St. Matthew's—had drawn strength from their female members. These churches featured a "female benevolent society."[416] Women may not have led these congregations, but their involvement was crucial to viability and virtue and to the activities on behalf of liberation both before and during the Civil War.

Then there is the case of Isabel Baumfree, or Hardenbergh—more well known as Sojourner Truth. In the late 1850s she moved to the

---

413. Jeffrey, 34, 85, 183,257 n.77.
414. Id. 45.
415. Karren Yurgalite, "The Frances Harper Inn: A Home for Black Women" in *Chronicle*, Vol. 46, No. 2, Summer 2023, 22ff; *Detroit News*, Aug. 27, 2023; Jeffrey, 204-208. She co-founded the National Association of Colored Women's Clubs. At the corner of Ferry and Brush Streets in Detroit is the National Registry-listed 1941 Detroit Association of Colored Women's Clubs headquarters.
416. Katzman, 19-22. The Bethel A.M.E. congregation organized in 1841 and met from 1847-1889 in a structure at Lafayette and Fort Streets. https://www.bethelamechurchdetroit.org/our-history ; Hargrove, "Their Greatest Battle," 26.

Battle Creek area, making it home for the rest of her life. That span had begun in 1797 in an enslaved condition in New York State.

Her life in Michigan began in October 1856 when she spoke in Battle Creek at the annual meeting of the Michigan Progressive Friends. Several members, including Frances Titus, became friends, leading her to acquire a lot in Harmonia on July 28, 1857, and build a home there.[417] Living in Harmonia provided Truth with greater accessibility to the audiences of the Midwest for her remarks, speeches, and lectures. In the 1860 census, Truth's home in Harmonia included her daughter Elizabeth Banks and grandsons James Caldwell and Sammy Banks. The village never thrived, and destruction left by a tornado on August 4, 1862, signaled its virtual demise. Truth moved to 38 College Street in Battle Creek, her home when she died on May 23, 1883. Her gravesite is in Oak Hill Cemetery, Battle Creek.

Her greatest impact on the issue of equal rights came from speaking engagements before the Civil War. She celebrated the Emancipation Proclamation, and she welcomed the opportunity for Blacks to enlist in the Union army. Her grandson James Caldwell became one of the volunteers in the first all-Black regiment, the 54th Massachusetts. When Michigan was organizing its Black regiment, she decided to collect donations for a Thanksgiving dinner for them from Battle Creek area contributors. She brought the food and money gathered to the soldiers at Camp Ward that November. Colonel Barnes ordered the men into formation, and she delivered a patriotic speech. Her fame was such that she attracted a wider audience for another set of remarks, then stayed in Detroit until February.[418]

In summer 1864, she embarked on an epic trip. She was back in Detroit in July, then in August stayed in Boston where she met Harriet Tubman for the first time. In September, she appeared in New Jersey and delivered remarks supportive of Lincoln's reelection. Reaching Washington, she began to work among the escapees from bondage

---

417. Carleton Mabee & Susan Mabee Newhouse, *Sojourner Truth: Slave, Prophet, Legend* (New York: New York University Press, 1993), 95-96.
418. Id. 116-117.

who had flocked into the nation's capital. It can be confirmed, from her own correspondence, that the site was on Mason's Island, today known as Theodore Roosevelt Island in the Potomac River between the District of Columbia and the Virginia shore. Because of the great influx, a former military encampment was converted to a place for refugees to live and from which to find employment in the District. Even so, this camp soon was overcrowded. The Association of Friends for the Aid and Elevation of Freedmen, a Quaker organization created to assist the conditions of newly freed persons, contributed personnel (via at least one woman leader, Louisa J. Roberts) and other necessary aid.[419] Truth also helped, as witnessed by this letter:

Mason's Island, Virginia, November 3d, 1864
And here I am in the midst of the freedmen, women, and children—and I am in a comfortable place here at the house of Rev. D.B. Nichols, Superintendent of Freedmen and am treated very kindly indeed. I do not know but what I shall stay here on the island all winter and go around among the freedmen's camps. They are all delighted to hear me talk. I think I am doing good. I am needed here, I see that the people here (white) are only here for the loaves and fishes while the freedmen get the scales and crusts, and Mr. Nichols sees it too.

I have had … opportunity to talk with Mr. Nichols and his wife and they have told me things that would render [*sic*] a heart of stone. And to hear what Mr. Nichols and wife have gone through in trying to elevate these folks, it is awful. These office seekers tries to root every one out that try to elevate these people and make them know they are free. …

---

419. Ira Berlin et al. eds., *Freedom: A Documentary History of Emancipation, 1861–1867*, Series I, Vol. II (New York: Cambridge University Press, 2012); *First Annual Report of the Board of Managers of the Association of Friends for the Aid and Elevation of the Freedmen* (Philadelphia: Merrihew & Sons, 1865), 8-9.

I am going around among the colored folks and find out who it is sells the clothing to them that is sent to them from the North. They will tell me for they think a good deal of me. ...

Sammie[420] and I are perfectly well and he is delighted with the place. He thinks he can be useful.

I don't calculate to ask the government for any thing, only what I have to eat, for the colored people must be raised out of bondage.

I have been to see the President and was there three hours. Mrs. Coleman[421] was with me all the forenoon from eight in the morning until twelve at noon. He put his name in my book and invited come again. ... I calculate to go and see President Lincoln again. I hope all will do all they can in putting him in as President again. ...

I have had two meetings in Wash. and two here at Mason's Island. Those in Wash. were for the benefit of the Freedmen's Aid Society. They took twenty-five cents at the door from everyone and gave me some of the money. ...

Sojourner Truth [422]

Her visit to the President on October 29 was significant: it was likely the first time a Black Michigander had visited the White House to see the Chief Executive.

Truth also aided efforts to improve conditions of the newly freed at the Freedmen's Village in Arlington, Virginia. As with her earlier work, it provided evidence that she—without any presidential or other official commission—had sought to elevate those who, like herself, had once suffered the great wrong of human bondage.[423]

No doubt other females of similar ethnicity did similar work. The

---

420. Grandson Samuel Banks.
421. Lucy Colman of Rochester, New York.
422. Mabee, 119.
423. Mabee, 120, 128.

increase of knowledge about women's roles in the Civil War has accelerated in recent years. More research, for example, may uncover support for a historian's view that "Northern African American women made U.S. Army camp visits routine occurrences."[424]

---

424. Pinheiro, *supra*. See Leslie M. Harris & Daina Ramey Berry, "Researching Nineteenth-Century African American History" in *The Journal of the Civil War Era*, Vol. 12, No. 4, Dec. 2022, 429ff.

Aftermath

At 10:00 a.m. on April 7, 1870, the firing of a cannon signaled the start of a parade in downtown Detroit in which 1,500 people formed the procession. The occasion was ratification of the 15th Amendment to the U.S. Constitution, guaranteeing citizens of the United States the right to vote regardless of race, color, or previous condition of servitude. Michigan had been the sixth State to approve the amendment, acting on March 8, 1869, and the requisite number for effectiveness had been reached on February 3rd. It was a joyous day in Detroit, and the parade was an inter-racial event. School boys, bands, Colored Masons, and individual citizens marched together until arriving at the Opera House. One group especially stood out:

> And then came the pride of the black citizenry: fifty members of the 102nd United States Colored Infantry. Fully armed and equipped, they were reunited under their old regiment flag.

Governor Henry Baldwin attended, as did other dignitaries. The address of the day was delivered by John D. Richards, "recently appointed customs inspector and leading black politician." A feeling of good will and fellowship reigned this Thursday as Michiganders and special guests celebrated progress in racial equity that in large part was "a product of the North's victory in the Civil War."[425]

In the Spring of 1865, as that fratricidal conflict drew to a close with the prospect of imminent Union success, the Congress of the

---

425. Katzman, 3-5.

United States proposed to the States a far different 13th amendment. The 1861 version had been ratified by only five States, and two had rescinded their ratification. The newly proposed amendment embodied precisely the opposite purpose from its failed predecessor:

> Section 1. Neither slavery nor involuntary servitude, except as a punishment for crime whereof the party shall have been duly convicted, shall exist within the United States, or any place subject to their jurisdiction.
> Section 2. Congress shall have power to enforce this article by appropriate legislation.

Involved in authoring this text was Jacob M. Howard, the junior U.S. Senator from Michigan. The antecedent of this language in the Northwest Ordinance can be clearly seen.

Sequential surrender of Confederate armies in April, May, and June of 1865 brought organized armed conflict to an end. The quest to bring forth a new nation founded on human bondage had failed. By end of the year, with the 13th amendment ratified and officially added to the U.S. Constitution, slavery within the United States of America was legally and constitutionally dead. Much work remained to realize a true brotherhood from sea to shining sea and to see the day when every flaw would be mended.

A sober reminder of the power of prejudice reared its ugliness in August 1866. John Taylor, a Black perhaps all of 20 years of age, had worked as a farmhand for Ingham County farmer John Buck. After a dispute over pay, Taylor moved on to another Delhi Township farm. On the evening of August 23, he returned to the Buck farm to collect the pay due to him. The farmer was away, and when Taylor came upon his wife, daughter, and mother-in-law in the dark, he struck at them with an axe and fled. It was reported that Taylor had killed the daughter in an attempt to murder all three women. He was caught and housed in the Ingham County Jail in Mason to await trial.

The murders, and the trial, never occurred. Buck's wife Mariah died in 1884; daughter Martha died in 1897; and mother-in-law Mary Fisher died in 1890. A State Historical Marker relates what happened to the accused killer:

> Reacting to inaccurate news reports of a supposed triple-murder attempt, a mob seized teenaged John Taylor from his jail cell on August 27, 1866, and brutally lynched him near the railroad depot in Mason. Several local papers criticized the lynching's "inhumanity and lawlessness," but others excused the event by declaring the law would have been too lenient. The citizens of Mason passed a resolution to condemn the killing and formally "disclaim any participation in the horrible crime." A mob leader was tried but acquitted.

The incident was a shocking case of people almost within sight of the finial atop the spire above the State Capitol dome "playing the role of judge and jury."[426]

A grand jury was convened in January 1867 and brought indictments against five local men for Taylor's murder. Only one was tried, but a jury refused to convict him. Former Governor Blair served in the case as an assistant prosecutor to County Prosecutor Rollin Dart. One of the reasons for his role may be attributed to Taylor's conduct on behalf of Michigan during the Civil War.

On August 9, 1864, as a 17-year old, Taylor enlisted in Company G of the 1st Michigan Colored Infantry for a 3-year term. His volunteering came as a substitute for an Oakland County draftee. He joined the regiment at Beaufort, S.C., on October 4 and served until his discharge at Charleston, within sight of the immortal bastion defending its harbor, on September 30, 1865. He was born into slavery in Kentucky, gained his freedom when Union troops advanced into the State in Fall 1861, and moved to Michigan. After work as a servant

---

426. Vanacker, 121.

in Hillsdale, he moved to Jackson where, once allowed, he joined the ranks of the Army that had enabled his escape from slavery.

The Marker was erected in the Fall of 2019 in John Taylor Memorial Park by Delhi Township. The dedication ceremony included a military salute by several organizations that commemorate the service of Michigan's Civil War soldiers. It serves as "a lasting monument to a long-forgotten man who met a gruesome fate" that he had escaped during his 14 months in the uniform of the U.S. Army.[427]

It also serves as a reminder of the work to come in terms of a fundamental change of law wrought by the War, that of extending and enforcing equal rights to all Americans. The gruesomeness of the episode is a measure of that work: a Union veteran who had been arrested for an alleged crime was meted out an uncivilized form of "justice" in one of the States that had remained loyal. Ironically, the crimes against Blacks committed in the South had motivated Congress to enact the first Civil Rights Act—over a presidential veto. The proposed 14th Amendment had emerged from Congress in June to enshrine protections in the Constitution; it would be ratified in 1868. Even with these changes in public policy, more was needed in human hearts and minds.

Although veneration of the Underground Railroad has revived, it took until the 21st century for a comprehensive work to demonstrate adequately that Michiganders "played a vital role" in these deeds of liberation.[428] Still, the 19th century did not close before one magisterial study of the network's history was published. This seminal work identified Michigan participants by name: "At Detroit there were several colored agents; among them George de Baptiste and George Dolarson."[429] The stated source for Dollarson's involvement was a

---

427. Id.; Jacob McCormick, "Reckoning With a Troubled Past: The John Taylor Lynching" in *Chronicle*, Vol. 44, No. 1 (Spring 2021), 17-19; *Record of Service*, Vol. 46, 97; https://www.hmdb.org/m.asp?m=182170
428. Mull, 1.
429. Wilbur H. Siebert, *The Underground Railroad from Slavery to Freedom* (New York: MacMillan & Co, 1898), 70; cited in W.E. Burghardt Du Bois ed., *Economic Co-operation among Negro Americans* (Atlanta: Atlanta University Press, 1907), 28.

"[c]onversation with Judge J.W. Finney, Detroit, Mich., July 27, 1897."[430] Jared W. Finney actually filled the position of U.S. Commissioner, an officer of the United States District Court for the Eastern District of Michigan, serving from 1908 onward. He had been Assistant U.S. Attorney in 1870 and U.S. Attorney in 1884 and 1896. Given his reputation before the bar, he ably carried the Finney name into the second generation as "a highly respected and thoroughly honored one."[431] The fame of Seymour, his father, derived from upholding a higher law.

More than three decades had elapsed since the Civil War when this account appeared. The passage of time may have confused "George" for "William" Dollarson, and it appears likely that the former was the name of a son. George W. "Dolarson" had been recorded as "colored, baker, 167 Russell" in the 1861 city directory, at an address adjacent to William and "Mrs." Dollarson. And, perhaps, the name—George—derived from the one that the escaping young man had purchased aboard his steamboat of freedom: "Jomer." The Dollarsons' home in the "border city, a main escape route for fleeing slaves, and with a Negro population, small though it was, that had shown itself militant in behalf of the fugitives," put them in a key position to be "conductors" at the end of the line.[432]

Edward Cahill, 1st Lieutenant, Company C, of the 1st Michigan Colored Infantry, became one of seven Michigan Supreme Court justices with Civil War connections. He was only 20 when he accepted a commission on January 19, 1864, at Detroit to become one of the officers of the Regiment. Hailing from St. Johns, he was promoted to Captain on January 16, 1865, serving until mustering out at

---
430. Siebert, 70 n.5.
431. *Successful Men of Michigan: A Compilation of Useful Biographical Sketches of Prominent Men* (Si. U. Collins, 1914), 194-195.
432. Katherine DuPre Lumpkin, "'The General Plan Was Freedom': A Negro Secret Order on the Underground Railroad" in *Phylon,* Vol. 28, No. 1 (1st Qtr. 1967), 63, 65. See Roy Finkenbine, "A Community Militant and Organized: The Colored Vigilant Committee of Detroit" in *A Fluid Frontier,* 154ff.

Charleston, S.C., on September 30.[433] He served on the Ionia County Commission and as prosecuting attorney for Ingham County. He was appointed to the Michigan Supreme Court by Governor Cyrus Luce and took office on April 5, 1890. His term was brief, ending on December 31 when he did not succeed in the Fall election for the seat. Although his tenure was not lengthy, one of the decisions he joined had more enduring meaning. In *Ferguson v Gies*, 82 Mich 358, decided October 10, 1890, the Justices ruled that providing separate accommodations based on racial identity was in violation of a statute requiring equal treatment. The plaintiff in the case had a family history of advocating for equal rights.[434]

A year earlier, William Dollarson had died on May 9. He was recorded as being 81 years of age.[435] His service as a civilian volunteer with the U.S. military would remain hidden for decades.

So, too, would be the service by persons of African descent alongside Whites in some Michigan regiments. An example is Acquilla Lett. The official record states that he enlisted in the 13th Michigan Volunteer Infantry at Lafayette for a one-year term on September 1, 1864. With a residence in Paw Paw, the 35-year-old farmer was mustered the same day and served until June 8, 1865, when he received at Washington, D.C. his discharge. He died February 20, 1902, and was buried at Hicks, Michigan. An online death certificate reveals vital statistics: he was born on January 12, 1828, in Ohio (meaning his age at enlistment was 36); he died at home, a widower, in Broomfield Township, Isabella County, age 74. And one more: for "Color," the undertaker wrote "Mulatto." His gravestone lists his service in Company K. The cemetery is located in Lawrence, Van Buren County.[436]

---

433. *Record of Service*, Vol. 46, 3, 20.
434. See Appendix. Three of the five justices were Union veterans. Vanacker, 121.
435. Michigan Pioneer and Historical Society, *Historical Collections*, Vol. XIV, 2d. ed. (Lansing: Wynkoop, Hallenbeck, Crawford Co., 1908), 193.
436. *Record of Service*, Vol. 13, 91; Findagrave #140541103; Juanita Patience Moss, *Forgotten Black Soldiers Who Served in White Regiments During the Civil War*, Vol. II (Berwyn Heights: Heritage Books, 2014), 23-24.

So far as it goes, the Lett story is a rich one. But it goes deeper. Private Lett married Sarah Jane Caliman, daughter of Benjamin Caliman on March 4, 1856. She was born in Virginia on April 8, 1833, and died on August 28, 1897, in the town of Bangor in Van Buren County. She was buried there in Arlington Hill Cemetery.[437] In the 1880 Census, they were living on their farm in Arlington Township. The enumerator listed both of them as "Mu" in the race column: for mulatto.[438] Sarah, then, was likely born into slavery. Acquilla had been born free, as had his father, Samuel, and grandfather, also named Acquilla. The grandfather's mother was Jemima (Banneker) Lett, sister of the famous astronomer who participated in the original survey of the District of Columbia.[439]

Other similarly "forgotten" Michigan soldiers include 4th Michigan Infantry volunteer Debraire Miller, who enlisted in Sumpter Township on September 12, 1864. His record lists him as "Colored Cook." He served until August 5, 1865, when he was discharged at New Orleans.[440]

History continues to make discoveries, and thus it is unconscionable when such heritage is threatened. When the City of Detroit was looking to get rid of the storied Grand Army of the Republic building on Grand River Avenue in the downtown area, it ran into a vigorous defender. Celestine Hollings, whose grandfather, Jacob Allen, was a Civil War veteran of a U.S. Colored Troops regiment, resurrected the local chapter of the Daughters of Union Veterans of the Civil War. Learning that the Sarah M. W. Sterling Tent #3 had met in the GAR building, Ms. Hollings became determined to save the structure. According to a special *Detroit Free Press* supplement on November 14,

---

437. Findagrave #12815014.
438. E.D. 206, 2. The Letts likely owned their own farm because others were listed as "works on farm."
439. Rachel Jamison Webster, *Benjamin Banneker and Us: Eleven Generations of an American Family* (New York: Henry Holt & Co., 2023),18-19, 33.
440. *Record of Service*, Vol. 4, 171; https://nativeamericansofdelawarestate.com/MilitaryService/Deborix_MILLER.htm; Moss, 24-25, 76, which lists several others.

2007, she attended Detroit City Council meetings, "wrote a letter to her pastor," and took other actions all "in an effort to retrieve artifacts from the building." Finally, "as president of the national Daughters of Union Veterans (and the first African American president of the predominantly white organization), she led the group to successfully sue the city and obtained a consent judgment to preserve certain historical parts of the building." Her son, Robert A. Mitchell, now a member of the Sons of Union Veterans of the Civil War, joined in the fight. The building was saved, renovated, and today stands proudly renewed.

A modern monument denotes Detroit's signal place on the Underground Railroad. At the foot of Woodward, along the river, "The Gateway to Freedom" provides one-half of an international commemoration of the network. The complementary monument rises on the Windsor riverfront.[441] A plaque adorning the Detroit sculpture reads, in part:

> At first, Michigan was a destination for freedom seekers, but Canada became a safer sanctuary after slavery was abolished there in 1834. With passage of the Fugitive Slave Act in 1850, many runaways left their homes in Detroit and crossed the river to Canada to remain free. Some returned after Emancipation in 1863. The successful operation of Detroit's Underground Railroad was due to the effort and cooperation of diverse groups of people, including people of African descent, Whites, and North American Indians. This legacy of freedom is a vital part of Detroit and its history.[442]

---

441. The sculptor for both was Edward Joseph Dwight Jr.
442. The first of August was the day the Slavery Abolition Act of 1833 ended slavery in the British Empire as of 1834. The date has been commemorated in Canada (and in other British-associated territories) as "Emancipation Day." An "act to prevent the further introduction of Slaves, and to limit the Term of contracts for Servitude within this Province" passed on July 9, 1793, in the legislature of Upper Canada, the part of British North America that became Ontario, but did not receive similar commemoration. On the 45th anniversary of the 1833 enactment, a monument to the memory of abolitionist Jonathan

Battle Creek is home to another monument commemorating the role played by Michiganders in the network to freedom.[443]

Michigan's legacy includes its proud African American regiment, and it should not overlook the service and sacrifice of others who served elsewhere. Among the Michiganders in the 54th Massachusetts who were casualties at Fort Wagner, South Carolina, or the preceding Battle of Grimball's Landing on July 16, were:

- Corporal Charles Augustus, a married man, age 30, from Ypsilanti, missing in action after the battle on July 18
- Private William Fowler, 25, single, a cook by trade, home at Battle Creek, wounded at Fort Wagner, discharged for disability, May 10, 1864
- Private William Henry Harrison, named after the 9th U.S. President, a 22-year old teamster, also from Battle Creek, killed in action at Fort Wagner
- Private John Leatherman, single, a Great Lakes seaman, enlisted at Ypsilanti on April 21, 1863, wounded and captured on July 16, 1863, at James Island, S.C., made prisoner of war, exchanged on March 4, 1865, at Goldsboro, N.C.

The case of Sergeant James Munroe from the Kalamazoo area is further significant. Wounded on July 18, 1863, in the assault on Fort Wagner, he finally was discharged for disability on June 3, 1865, at Charleston, S.C. At that juncture, the city had surrendered to U.S. authorities as the Confederacy collapsed. Munroe appears to have been incarcerated at Charleston, for other prisoner exchanges occurred at the sites where Confederate prisons existed. A fellow prisoner, a White officer in a New York regiment, reported on the conditions in that jail:

Walker was dedicated by an assemblage of 6,000 in Muskegon's Evergreen Cemetery. See Bordewich, 268, 434; Nye, 260; Jack Dempsey, "The Man with the Branded Hand" in *Michigan History*, Vol. 99, No. 1, Jan./Feb. 2015, 49ff.
443.   Located on the grounds of the W.K. Kellogg House, which is on Monroe Street; it is also a work by sculptor Dwight.

There were twenty-one negro soldiers, most of them belonging to Colonel Shaw's Fifty-fourth Mass. regiment of immortal memory, among the number. They were never to be exchanged, but were to be reduced to slavery. They were all that were left of the colored troops captured at Wagner. The rest were bayoneted and shot after they surrendered. Their rations were bread and water; still they would sing Union songs, pouring their melody through their prison bars for the entertainment of the Union officers in the prison and below.[444]

The rosters of more regiments would need to be combed to find Michiganders of color who volunteered to serve the Union cause. Enumerating every one of these soldiers is a worthy goal. According to the State's immediate official report on the Civil War, likely source for the marker text, a total of 1,446 officers and men were carried on the regimental rolls. The casualty figures reveal 140 total losses: 2 officers, 4 men killed in action; 5 men died of wounds; 1 officer and 128 men died of disease.[445] One in ten of these volunteers, according to this tally, never returned to Michigan alive.

According to Volume 46, the enrollment in the First Michigan Colored Regiment actually totaled 1,673 individuals. Casualty data were also different from the 1882 compilation: 5 killed in action; 7 men died of wounds; 116 men died of disease; and 114 were discharged "for disability (wounds and disease)." Based on these data, the regiment's casualty ratio was one in seven, over fourteen percent, if those who likely returned home incapacitated for military service are included.[446] Another aspect of the lives of these volunteers is their post-war experience, some of which included returning to the lands of their enslavement.[447]

---

444. Emilio, 415.
445. *Michigan in the War*, 493.
446. *Record of Service*, 4.
447. Matt H. Wallace, "Bittersweet: Black Virginians in Blue at the Battle of

Despite racial stereotyping—the "myth" that those of African descent were better able to withstand the vicissitudes of the Southern climate, geography, and environment—the reality was that ethnicity gave no individual a leg up. In the case of units assigned to the "epidemiologically deadly" posts along the coasts of Florida, Georgia, and the Carolinas, Blacks suffered disproportionately to White soldiers. In general, Black Union soldiers served "in conditions of considerably more distress."[448]

Ironically, the 1st Michigan Colored regiment was the first Civil War unit to be commemorated in the modern Michigan historical marker program launched by legislative action in 1955. The program for the unveiling ceremony on May 19, 1968, also signified how Michigan political leadership treated the event with importance. In addition to remarks by Governor George Romney, Detroit Mayor Jerome P. Cavanaugh, Detroit Historical Commission President Leonard N. Simons, Michigan Historical Commission President Dr. Lewis Vander Velde, Superintendent of Detroit Public Schools Dr. Norman Drachler, and officers of the Michigan National Guard, the invocation was delivered by Rev. A.A. Banks of the Second Baptist Church, the benediction by Rev. Maurice J. Higginbothan, and the entire affair conducted under Master of Ceremonies John Roundtree, Vice-President of the Detroit Branch of the A.S.N.L.H. Having the unveiling and dedication on that Sunday afternoon enabled the event to fall within Michigan Week 1968.[449] Although the Civil War

---

Honey Hill and Beyond," John L. Nau Center for Civil War History, University of Virginia, available at: https://naucenter.as.virginia.edu/blog-page/936

448. Andrew K. Black, "In the Service of the United States: Comparative Mortality among African American and White Troops in the Union Army" in *The Journal of Negro History*, Vol. 79, No. 4, Autumn 1994 (University of Chicago Press), 317, 318, 325, 328-332.

449. Marker file, Michigan History Center, Lansing, Michigan; *Souvenir Program, Marker Unveiling Ceremonies, Memorial to First Michigan Colored Regiment, 102nd United States Colored Troops, Army Infantry Volunteers, Duffield School Ground, Sunday, May 19, 1968—4:30 P.M.*

Centennial had officially closed, commemoration of its victorious warriors had not.[450]

Thirty years after the Michigan marker was unveiled in Detroit, the African American Civil War Memorial in Washington, D.C., had its dedication in July 1998. Located in a plaza on the southeast corner of U Street NW and Vermont Avenue, the "Spirit of Freedom" bronze statue portrayed several Black soldiers and sailors surrounded by half-walls on which are inscribed the names of individual service members.[451] It represented the military experience of some 200,000 men of African descent who took up arms to defend the Union. The inscribed names at the Memorial include 1,387 associated with Michigan.[452]

To those who wore Union blue, or served those who had, the conquest of slavery was their achievement. The great Union armies of the Republic had been composed of millions of citizen volunteers and comparatively few professionally trained warriors. These civilian individuals had left office jobs in cities, merchant shops in towns, farms in the countryside, in order to marshal arms together and place themselves in harm's way. Although these soldiers had fought in Pennsylvania and Ohio, nearly all of their service had been south of the Mason-Dixon line and below the Ohio and Missouri rivers, in a vast country with impeding waterways, mountains difficult to penetrate, and a frequently hostile population. Hundreds of thousands of them never returned home to enjoy again the embrace of family and friends. Their remains hallowed the soil on hundreds of battlefields, thousands of picket posts, all throughout the South.

Among those loyal defenders were hundreds of thousands of persons of African descent. Some had been born free; some had secured their freedom; some had fled oppression to achieve it. All

---

450. For further information on the Centennial and Sesquicentennial commemorations, see Appendix.
451. The sculptor, Edward Norton Hamilton Jr., was artist for the Joe Louis sculpture inside the convention center at 1 Washington Boulevard in downtown Detroit.
452. According to the relevant website: https://www.nps.gov/afam/index.htm

were possessed of a distinctiveness that put their lives even more at risk than their counterparts of European or native descent. Their skin color in a Union uniform marked them as a direct repudiation of racial supremacy. They were men; they sought to protect their human rights, and those of all peoples; their kin and kinfolk cheered them on in equal measure with every other warrior. In the words of the great poet, "American earth is richer for your bones."[453]

For far too long, a school of history equalized the exploits of those on opposing sides during this conflict. For even longer, the heroism of those who placed their lives at this extra risk faced neglect. A more thorough historiography in the early years of the 21st century has sought to discover and reveal all of the depth of the numerous stories that remain to be told of the service and sacrifice of those who went to the front to contend with disunion, disloyalty, and destruction. Two decades into that century, Americans continue their quest to form a more perfect Union.

William Dollarson's contributions to the liberation of other Americans appear to have ended with the close of the Civil War. He had been a faithful conductor on the Underground Railroad, helping numerous other self-liberators in their escape from bondage. He bought and moved onto a farm near Royal Oak "in order to encourage the colored people of Detroit to become landholders." Back in the early months of the War, he went to the front when persons of African descent were not officially permitted. He was in harm's way with the Union army in the slave States of Maryland and Virginia. When the Union and emancipation emerged victorious, no doubt the Dollarsons rejoiced. They witnessed passage of the 13th, 14th, and 15th Amendments, designed to secure rights for all Americans irrespective of race. Upon the death in 1878 of the General on whose staff he had served, Dollarson went to the Christmas Eve funeral, then followed on foot despite the severe cold in the procession to the graveyard. In 1883, he gave a newspaper interview that revealed

---

453. Randall, *supra*.

many otherwise hidden details of the Dollarsons' life stories. Each overflowed with pathos. "Born a slave," it began, he was "three times sold, many times whipped." The Dollarsons had 20 children, "but all are now dead, and he and his aged wife are left to finish the journey of life alone." In 1889, he passed from this life; two years later, Maria was also gone. "A man of most honorable character," had concluded the brief biography; a man—a patriot—whose life, it said, reflected honor upon all his fellow citizens, and whose memory they should ever cherish.

Credit: *Mary A. Lewison of Ann Arbor*

Appendix[454]

I. List of Engagements of 1st Michigan Colored Volunteers/102nd U.S.C.T.

- Baldwin, Fla., August 8, 1864
- Honey Hill, S.C., November 30, 1864
- Tullifinny, S.C., December 7, 1864
- Devaux Neck, S.C., December 9, 1864
- Cuckwold's Creek Bridge, February 8, 1865
- Sumterville, S.C., April 8, 1865
- Spring Hill, S.C., April 15, 1865
- Swift Creek, S.C., April 17, 1865
- Boykin's, S.C., April 18, 1865
- Singleton's Plantation, S.C., April 19, 1865[455]

II. Record of 1st Michigan Colored Volunteers/102nd U.S.C.T.

Organized May 23, 1864, from 1st Michigan Colored Infantry. Attached to District of Hilton Head, S.C., Dept. of the South and District of Beaufort, S.C., Dept. of the South, to August, 1864. District of Florida, Dept. of the South, to October, 1864. 2nd Separate Brigade, Dept. of the South, to November, 1864. 2nd Brigade, Coast Division, Dept. of the South, to February, 1865. 2nd Separate Brigade, Dept. of the South, to March, 1865. 1st Separate Brigade and Dept. of the South to September, 1865.

---

454. This format follows that established in the Series.
455. *Michigan in the War*, 493.

Service. Garrison at Port Royal, S.C., till June 15. Moved to Beaufort, S.C., and garrison duty there till August 1. Moved to Jacksonville, Fla., August 1-3. Picket duty at Baldwin till August 15. Attack on Baldwin August 11-12. Raid on Florida Central Railroad August 15-19. At Magnolia till August 29. Moved to Beaufort, S.C., August 29-31, and duty there till January, 1865, engaged in outpost and picket duty on Port Royal, Lady and Coosa Islands. (A Detachment at Honey Hill November 30, 1864. Demonstration on Charleston & Savannah Railroad December 6-9. Deveaux's Neck, Tillifinny River, December 6 and 9.) Detachment at Beaufort; rejoined other Detachment at Deveaux's Neck, S.C., January 24, 1865. Moved to Pocotaligo February 28. Advance on Charleston February 7-23. Skirmish at Cuckwold Creek February 8 (Cos. "B," "E" and "I"). Duty at Charleston Neck till March 9. Moved to Savannah, Ga., March 9-16. Moved to Georgetown March 28-April 1. (Right wing of Regiment, under Chipman, moved to Charleston April 7-9, thence march to join Potter at Nelson's Ferry April 11-18.) Potter's Expedition from Georgetown to Camden April 5-29. Statesburg April 15. Occupation of Camden April 17. Boykin's Mills April 18. Bradford Springs April 18 (right wing). Dingle's Mills April 19. Singleton's Plantation April 19. Beech Creek, near Statesburg, April 19. Moved to Charleston April 29, thence to Summerville May 7-8; to Branchville May 18; to Orangeburg May 25, and provost duty there till July 28. March to Winsboro July 28-August 3, and duty there till September. Moved to Charleston and muster out September 30, 1865.[456]

III. Union Order of Battle, Honey Hill, S.C., Nov. 30, 1864

Brigadier-General John P. Hatch, commanding[457]

---

456. Frederick H. Dyer, *A Compendium of the War of the Rebellion* (Des Moines: Dyer Pub. Co., 1908), 1738.
457. Born in 1822, Hatch graduated 17th of 41 in the West Point Class of 1845. A Mexican-American War veteran, he was commissioned Brigadier-General in September 1861, served in both cavalry and infantry commands,

1st Brigade, Brigadier-General Edward E. Potter[458]
    25th Ohio Infantry
    32nd U.S. Colored Troops
    34th U.S. Colored Troops
    35th U.S. Colored Troops
    56th New York Infantry
    127th New York Infantry
    144th New York Infantry
    157th New York Volunteer Infantry Regiment
2nd Brigade, Colonel Alfred S. Hartwell
    54th Massachusetts Colored Volunteer Infantry
    55th Massachusetts Colored Volunteer Infantry
    102nd U.S. Colored Troops
Naval Brigade, Commander George H. Preble
    Sailor Battalion of Infantry
    U.S.M.C. Battalion of Infantry
Artillery Brigade, Lieutenant-Colonel William Ames
    Battery A, 3rd Rhode Island Heavy Artillery (section)
    Battery B, 3rd New York Light Artillery (4 12-pounders)
    Company F, 3rd New York Artillery (4 12-pounders)
Cavalry, Captain George Hurlbut
    1st Regiment Massachusetts Volunteer Cavalry (2 companies)[459]

---

was wounded in action at Turner's Gap on September 14, 1862, for which he received the Medal of Honor, and died in 1901. *Cullum's Register*, Vol. II, 225-227. According to one historian, "Hatch hardly seemed one to inspire troops in combat. He had performed poorly as a cavalry commander" early in the War and would be "shuffled from one administrative job to another." Peter Cozzens, "Smokescreen at Honey Hill" in *Civil War Times Illustrated*, Vol. XXXVIII, No. 7, Feb. 2000, 32, 24. Before Honey Hill, Hatch "had yet to reveal any real talent for combat." Trudeau, 315. One historian characterized Honey Hill as an "ill-planned and badly executed" battle. Cornish, 287.

458.   Before Honey Hill, Potter "had never led troops in battle. For most of the war, he had served as an administrator ..." Cozzens, 34. The Union commanders carried out a "feckless" operation here. Id. 35.

459.   *OR*, XLIV, 421; Emilio, 236-237.

IV. Regimental Casualties at Honey Hill

Alvord, Henry H. Bay City. Commissioned 1st Lieutenant May 4, 1864. Wounded in action.[460] Mustered out at Charleston, S.C., Sept. 30, 1865.

Buckner, John. Enlisted in Company D, Nov. 13, 1863, at Detroit, for 3 years, age 26. Discharged at David's Island, N.Y., Apr. 28, 1865, from wounds received in action.[461]

Estes, James. Enlisted in Company C, as Corporal, Oct. 21, 1863, at Detroit, for 3 years, age 22. Wounded in action.[462] Mustered out at Charleston, S.C., Sept. 30, 1865.

Ford, Jerry. Enlisted in Company C, Sept. 2, 1864, at Jackson, for 1 year, age 23. Substitute. Wounded in action. Mustered out at Charleston, S.C., Sept. 30, 1865.

Goodman, Daniel. Enlisted in Company D, Nov. 23, 1863, at Detroit, for 3 years, age 26. Wounded in action.[463] Mustered out at Charleston, S.C., Sept. 30, 1865.

Gray, John E. Enlisted in Company C, Feb. 10, 1864, at Ypsilanti, for 3 years, age 22. Discharged at Beaufort, S.C., June 8, 1865, from wounds received in action.[464]

Harris, Henry S. Enlisted in Company D, Nov. 12, 1863, at Detroit, for 3 years, age 22. Wounded in action.[465] Died at Charleston, S.C., Feb. 28, 1865.

Harrison, Henry. Enlisted in Company E, Jan. 4, 1864, at Detroit, for 3 years, age 21. Wounded in action.[466] Mustered out at Charleston, S.C., Sept. 30, 1865.

Horton, Isaac. Enlisted in Company K, Aug. 27, 1864, at

---

460. Wound said to be: "thigh." *The Palmetto Herald*, Port Royal, S.C., Vol. L, No. 41 (Dec. 8, 1864). Same source for all, *infra*.
461. Wound: "thigh, badly."
462. "face, slight."
463. "contusion, foot."
464. "right leg, severely."
465. "side, slightly."
466. "side, slight."

Kalamazoo, for 1 year, age 19. Wounded in action.[467] Discharged for disability at Detroit, May 20, 1865.

Johnson, Isaac. Enlisted in Company A, Feb. 3, 1864, at Detroit, for 3 years, age 29. Wounded in action.[468] Deserted at Orangeburg, S.C., July 4, 1865.

Lindsay, Arad E. Ionia. Entered service as Captain, commissioned Jan. 8, 1864. Killed in action.

Marshall, Joseph. Enlisted in Company D, Aug. 15, 1864, at Pontiac, for 3 years, age 22. Substitute. Died at Beaufort, S.C., Dec. 22, 1864, on account of wounds received.[469] Buried at Beaufort.

Morgan, Joseph H. Enlisted in Company E, Dec. 10, 1863, at Ypsilanti, for 3 years, age 21. Wounded in action.[470] Corporal, July 1, 1865. Mustered out at Charleston, S.C., Sept. 30, 1865.

Powell, Thomas H. Enlisted in Company H, Aug. 30, 1864, at Jackson, for 1 year, age 34. Wounded in action. Mustered out at Charleston, S.C., Sept. 30, 1865.

Smith, Jacob. Enlisted in Company B, Oct. 8, 1864, at Detroit, for 3 years, age 22. Wounded in action.[471] Mustered out at Charleston, S.C., Sept. 30, 1865.

Strother, David. Enlisted in Company H, Dec. 29, 1863, at Battle Creek, for 3 years, age 22. Wounded in action.[472] Discharged for disability at Detroit, June 7, 1865.

Thompson, Ezekiel. Enlisted in Company C, Nov. 3, 1864, at Detroit, for 3 years, age 45. Discharged May 29, 1865, at Beaufort, S.C., from wounds received in action.[473]

Wade, John. Enlisted in Company H, Jan. 4, 1864, at Detroit, for 3 years, age 18. Killed in action.

Washington, George. Enlisted in Company H, Dec. 18, 1863,

---

467. "left arm, badly."
468. "fingers shot off."
469. "back of neck."
470. "right arm badly."
471. "slight in face."
472. "fingers and head, slightly."
473. "right arm, badly."

at Detroit, for 3 years, age 24. Wounded in action. Mustered out at Charleston, S.C., Sept. 30, 1865.

White, Phillip. Enlisted in Company D, as Corporal, Nov. 17, 1863, at Detroit, for 3 years, age 20. Discharged at Indianapolis, Ind., May 24, 1865, from wounds received in action.[474]

V. Honey Hill Battlefield Historic Preservation

On February 14, 2019, the National Park Service awarded to the South Carolina Department of Archives and History (SCDAH) a Hurricanes Harvey, Irma, and Maria Emergency Supplemental Historic Preservation Fund grant for $1,946,485 (HIM ESHPF grant, CFDA No. 15.957, Federal Award Identification Number P19AP00015) to assist with the repair to historic properties damaged by Hurricane Irma. SCDAH awarded a grant of $57,500 to the Town of Ridgeland for earthworks stabilization. Hurricane winds in 2017 knocked over 23 trees near the Confederate earthworks at the battlefield site, which were to be removed with only minimal further damage to the earthworks and archaeological resources. Any artifacts recovered during the tree removal were to be documented and placed on loan at the Morris Center for Lowcountry Heritage in Ridgeland for use in an exhibit about the Honey Hill battlefield.[475]

The National Register listing contained information supportive of modern-day interpretative opportunities:

> Those portions of the battlefield within the boundary selected are generally very well preserved, and some areas appear virtually unchanged since the Civil War. The uplands on the property include mixed pine and hardwood forest and pine savannah, with scattered bird hunting fields and wildlife fodder fields. Wetland areas exhibit ditches and dikes remaining

---

474. "right leg, flesh wound." *Record of Service*, Vol. 46, 7, 18, 33, 35, 38, 39, 43, 44, 50, 55, 63, 66, 71, 79, 91, 96, 99, 103, 105, 108.
475. South Carolina Department of Archives and History information sheet, 2 of 5, undated.

from antebellum use as rice fields, but are now densely overgrown in hardwood forest. Extensive Civil War earthworks are extant, and the modern road net is nearly the same as that used during the campaign; these factors allow the placement of historic events on the modern landscape with a high degree of confidence.

Contributing Resources

The following properties contribute to the historic character and significance of the Honey Hill/Boyd's Neck Battlefield:

1. Confederate Earthworks, Honey Hill
2. Confederate Earthworks, Partridge Hill
3. Federal Earthworks
4. Federal Earthworks (Unfinished Battery), Boyd's Neck
5. Boyd's Landing (Salvesbarg Landing) and Boyd House Site
6. Boyd's Landing Road
7. Euhaw Road
8. Grahamville Road
9. Wood Road
10. Rice Dike Used as a Defensive Position during the Battle of Honey Hill

… The Boyd House was a Federal headquarters, and was fortified as the innermost, last-ditch defensive position of the Federal enclave left on Boyd's Neck after the Battle of Honey Hill …

VI. Sleight's Account

In May 1861, 21-year-old William E. Sleight from Bath, Michigan, volunteered for service in the 65th New York Infantry Regiment. He was badly wounded in May 1863 and convalesced in a Washington hospital that received a personal visit from the President. Once well enough, Sleight returned to Ann Arbor for a 30-day furlough, then reported to St. Mary's Hospital in Detroit. On January 20, 1864, he was commissioned 2nd Lieutenant in Michigan's regiment of color. On May 6, he received a commission as 1st Lieutenant. His account of War service, written in 1917, spends much until reaching 1864 and his commissioning. He did not participate at Honey Hill but was in charge of Company D of the 102nd in the aftermath and ordered to Deveaux Neck. The memoir from that point records:

> We joined the balance of our Regiment brigade. Here we remained a few days issuing clothing, shoes, rations and ammunition. And then commenced our march upon Sheridan [uncertain] right up the coast to Charleston. I was in command of the Company and we had some light skirmishing upon one [our] route; we had orders to clean up everything as we proceeded. I was detailed with my company to burn and destroy completely a long tested [trestle] work and the bridge across the Santee River that was owned by the rail road that ran from Savannah to Charleston. We worked one day with one company and completely destroyed the draw bridge across the river and also the rail road works for nearly one mile across a marsh. After finishing up our work our regiment continued burning and tearing up and destroying this rail road until within a few miles of Charleston when the enemy evacuated Charleston and our brigade was the first to march in the city.
>
> While upon this march we lost several men killed and wounded and among them, our Quartermaster, Wm. McDowhlan of Detroit, who was killed and robbed of his boots, clothing, watch and saber. His body was recovered and sent home to his family at Detroit.[476]

---

476. Likely Patrick McLaughlin, listed as Quartermaster of the 1st Michigan at organization, *Record of Service*, Vol. 46, 3, and "Killed in action at Salkehatchie, S.C., Feb. 8, 1865," *Record of Service*, Vol. 16, 106; grave at Mount Elliott

After marching to Charleston we remained there a few days and rested up a little while and issued rations and clothing. We again received orders to hold our companies in readiness to move in a moment's notice. We remained about 24 hours when Coln. Chipman received orders to march his regiment to Charleston to be transported at once to Wilmington, South Carolina. We moved to the dock at Charleston and upon our arrival, there, were not transports enough to receive our whole regiment and only the left wing of the regiment went away with the expedition that day. We remained here three days before our transports showed up to take us upon board. We were then taken upon board of a large steamer and arrived at Wilmington three days after the other division and our five companies alone. Orders from the Commander of the Expedition for Coln. Chipman to follow with his company as soon as he arrived were received and there was no other way than obey this order but we were three days behind the army and had to march through the enemy's country unprotected and only five companies.

This was a desperate undertaking as the country where we had to march through was well guarded by rebel cavalry, but the order was given and must be obeyed. Coln. Chipman commenced the march to join the command as ordered. The first day we march until noon and was not interfered with but at noon while laying at a halt making our coffee and resting a squad of rebel cavalry sneaked upon us out of a piece of woods and before we knew they were there they poured a volley in upon us but wounded only one man. This, of course, put us upon our nerve and from that on we were ready for battle. We formed a skirmish line upon both flanks and an advance and rear squads. I was ordered to guard the left of the company. That afternoon we had several skirmishes with the rebels but none wounded. That night we arrived at the Santee River where we were to be met by a small gun boat and transported up the river about five miles, but when we arrived there this boat was not at the landing and had to remain at the river over night. I was detailed with my company to do picket duty that night and moved back and around the camps about one-half mile. During the night we could hear the rebels moving artillery and cavalry all around us and expected to be attacked any moment but they seemed to be afraid of us for they did not attack us until noon the next day when the companies undertook to move up the river one mile to the gun boat that was to carry us up the Santee river several miles and land us upon the other side of the river where we were to continue our march and join General Potter's expedition.

As soon as our regiment had received orders to move up to the gun boat and Coln. Chipman had sent orders for me to call in my pickets, and I had done so, the rebels seemed to know just what move we were about to make for they moved down upon my Company as soon as I drew in my pickets and as my men in retreating across a creek would have to walk over the creek upon the stringers of a bridge that had been destroyed by the rebels it would be a desperate place to be caught in if we were not upon our guard as the rebels evidently intended to attack us when we started to cross the creek. I, seeing their plans, at once ordered the orderly sergeant of my company to detail ten of the best men of our company to remain with me and then ordered the Sergeant to move the balance of the company down the road and cross the creek upon the stringers of same.

As soon as he moved down the road the rebel cavalry came down the road and commenced firing upon them; they held their fire and I with my ten men moved out of the road over the fence and got located in a heavy underbrush where the rebels could not see us. We waited there until the rebel cavalry came down the road just opposite us and then we opened upon them. We shot several of them out of their saddles and our surprise to them caused a regular stampede with their men and as soon as they could get their horses turned around they all retreated as fast as possible and we had killed several of them and their horses. We lost no time in retreating across the creek and moving up to the gun boat where we found our regiment being loaded upon boat. We were all landed aboard gun boat about four o'clock in the afternoon and started up the Santee River.

We had not gotten fairly started up the river when the Commander of the Gun Boat came to me and told me that about two miles up the river there was a high bluff when without doubt the rebels would be located in a heavy force and attack us as we passed that bluff and as he said we were so heavily loaded with men that they could not use their naval guns. I got my men in good shape for battle when we reached the bluff. They were very liable to cause a stampede among our men and was liable to upset our boat, as she was overloaded and then kill all of us. I was then in command of the advance guard and could command all of the men. I at once arranged all of my company along the railing of the bow of the boat; the first rank knelt down on their knees and the second rank stood up and I instructed them to see that all of their muskets were loaded. This done, we were nearing the bluff and everything in readiness for battle, and none too soon as when we came in gun shot of the bluff we could very plainly see that there were lots of rebels lying there awaiting us.

As we turned around a sharp curve in the river the rebels all raised to their feet; as they did that I commanded the men to open fire upon them and it was done at once and the battle was on.

At once they poured the shot thick all around us and battered the pilot house of the boat, that was covered with steel plate, full of dents from thick bullets but as they were 25 or 30 feet above our boat they fired over our men on lower deck and we had but one wounded. We fought for about 30 minutes and the smoke from our and their guns was so dense that we could not see what effect our guns were having but after we got past the bluff the Commander of the boat came to me and told me that from the pilot house he could see what effect our guns had and he said that we killed and wounded lots of them. After the battle we were near where we were to land in about an hour and when we landed it was dark and we went into camp for the night—all of us pretty well worn out from the effect of the work and excitement.

Soon after we had landed and had gone in camp for the night the Colonel sent an orderly to my tent with an order for me to report to his quarters at once. The order startled me somewhat as the Colonel had given orders to me while upon this expedition not to fire the first shot upon the rebels and I, of course, did order my men to open fire upon the rebels just as soon as I saw what they were about to do, but I reported to the Coln.'s quarters as ordered and when I was in his tent the Coln. said to me, "Lieut., who fired the first shot," I said to him, "I did, Sir." The colonel said, "That's all Sir," and I expected from the way he acted that he might have me dismissed for disobeying his orders but some of the line officers knew what orders he had given me and they knew that I had disobeyed his orders and they knew that to obey his orders at that time might have meant death to every man aboard that boat and some of the officers came to me to know what the colonel said and I told them and they said, "let him dare to attempt to have you dismissed and we will report him to the Commanding General," but I never heard anything more about who fired the first shot.

We laid in camp upon the bank of this river all of the next day under cover of this gun boat. The next day we commenced our march to join General Potter's army, then 40 or 50 miles from us. I was commanded to act as rear guard that forenoon. About noon an old negro came to the Colonel and told him that there were about 1,000 cavalry awaiting us just around a bend in the road in the timber. This caused a halt and this old negro told the colonel of a by-road that we could take and go around these cavalry men. So after halting here about one-half hour we took a by-road. I was in command of rear guard but we moved on all the afternoon and was not attacked by the rebels and at night our company went in camp upon a hill in the woods and I with my company did the picket duty that night. We expected to be attacked every moment but was not.

In the morning I was ordered to come in with my company and take the advance. I moved my company to the front, halted and saw that each man had his musket loaded and fixes bayonets and had the company numbered off in squads so as to be ready for a skirmish as soon as possible as I knew that we would not move that morning many rods before we would have another fight. When all was in readiness I ordered forward march. We moved on about one hundred rods when the rebel pickets opened upon us. We at once deployed as skirmishers and pushed right on after them. We soon came out in an open field where the rebels could see every man and they made the grass and dirt fly with their bullets. They came so close to my head that they would go by with a hiss. I looked up the hill and saw that they had built a barricade across the road with rails and logs and there seemed to be 500 or more cavalry behind them well armed. I at once sent one of my men and told the Coln. that it would take more men to drive them out of their position and the colonel sent reinforcement and they turned their left flank and we charged and drove them out and only had one man killed and one or two wounded. We then moved on for a number of miles without any more trouble. We marched until in the afternoon and had only once in a while a rebel picket fire upon us but the rebels had been planning to draw us in a death trap just ahead of us upon the road that we had to pass; there was a dense swamp, one that it would be impossible to get through outside of the main road. This swamp was full of water about knee deep and our only way to cross the swamp was by a narrow crossway about fifteen rods long and the water was about eighteen inches deep upon this crossway. The rebels had placed upon the opposite side of this swamp two pieces of twenty four pounds that covered this crossing completely and as they knew that we would have to call in our skirmish line and form companies and then march through the swamp in four ranks and through this water eighteen inches deep they thought that they had us sure.

As we neared this death trap of theirs they commenced to crowd our rear guard and when I had assembled my company and just got started across this swamp the rebels attacked our rear guard and just as they attacked our rear guard I heard a terrible confusion in front of us upon the other side of the swamp and what caused this confusion was this: The evening before this the colonel was about to detail some officer to go through the rebel lines and report to Gen. Potter and have him send us reinforcements. Lieut. Barrel volunteered to go and he was given a detail of two cavalry men and was mounted himself and after dark he started out upon his very dangerous expedition. He succeeded in getting through himself that night but lost both of his cavalry men and horses and his horse and when he got through was all tattered and torn from the effect of crawling through the briar and bramble bushes that night.

He reported to Gen. Potter our whereabouts and he made a detail of cavalry and placed Lieut. Barrell in command and he returned just in time to this swamp where we were just in the act of crossing in the rebels' death trap when he charged upon their two gun batteries and captured same and without a doubt was the means of saving nearly all of my company's lives as they had this battery so arranged that they covered this road completely and as we were crossing this narrow space in four ranks they certainly would have made things lively for us before we could have gotten across the swamp but Lieut. Barrell saved us just in time.

After this battery was captured Lieutenant Barrell took the advance with the detail of cavalry and we had no more fighting that day and joined General Potter's command that night.

The next day we had but little fighting. I was detailed to command the rear guard but had no trouble with the rebels but we then had with us thousands of contrabands, negros of all description, from children to old decrepit negro women and old slaves that looked as though they might be one hundred years old. They were loaded down with all kinds of old blankets and rags of all description, corn meal and bacon. It was a sight to see this lot of old, decrepit people straggling along trying to keep up with our army.

The next day we struck the rebels and had some skirmishing with them and the contrabands of war disappeared; the next day we received a truce of peace that notified our general that there had been thirty days' armistice declared and orders to cease fighting, this was glad tidings to us all and we were ordered to discharge our muskets and we did so at once and the war was nearly over.

This army while upon this expedition was getting their rations from foraging but now as the orders had been given not to do any more foraging we were out of rations and we had a day's marching to do before we would reach Wilmington, S.C., we had to have something so our foraging party had quite a quantity of corn on hand that they could issue to the men. They issued a number of ears of corn to each man and we returned from the expedition living upon corn on the ear as rations and the war then at a close. But to sadden all this glory this same day while upon our way to Wilmington, S.C., we received the dreadful news of the Assassination of our Hon. President Lincoln. This news we would hardly believe at first but it proved to be true and then a gloom seemed to come over our whole army.

We moved back to Wilmington S.C., and was transported back to Charleston, S.C., and our regiment was then detailed to do Private Duty at Brandeville, Orangeburg, Winslow, S.C., I with my company was located at Winslow as private guard. While upon private guard duty at Winslow, S.C., there came to my tent a young negro, seemingly about 18 or 20 years old. He said to me, "Master, would you please take this chain off of my neck, dat my Master put on long ago?" I told him I would and when I came to examine it I found what we would call an old fashioned long linked train chain; this was placed around his neck under his clothes and the end link passed through another line and a small pad-lock locking same around his neck. Then, the chain was passed down on his left side under his clothes down his left leg to his ankle where his chain was fastened to a small strip that was fastened around his ankle. There were raw sores around his neck and ankle where this chain had cut him. I took this off and I never have forgotten the thankful look this young negro gave me when I had taken same off. I asked him why his master put this on and he said, "cause I tried to run away to you Yankees."

We remained at this duty until Sept. 30th, 1865, when our regiment was mustered out of the Service and returned to Detroit where we were paid off and disbanded. Thus ended a long term of four years and seven months in active service and nearly two years of my time was served as Commissioned Officer in a Colored Regiment and although I have had people say to me you only had a Commission in a n--- regiment,

I was not and am not ashamed to have anyone know that I held a commission in what these people call a n--- regiment for in the first place every officer that received a commission in this United States Colored Regiment had to pass an examination before a Board of Regular Army Officers before they could receive a Commission and they had to be men that had seen active service in the field and then they had to have some grit to accept a position in one of these Regiments for the reason that the Confederate President, Jeff Davis, when informed that our Government was going to organize Colored Troops and Officer them with white officers issued an order to his army never to show an officer of these colored troops any respect but shoot or hang every one taken prisoner. Consequently the man who accepted a Commission in one of these regiments knew his fate if captured. It was no place for cowards and then our colored regiment fought as well when in battle as any troops, always brave and ready to go anywhere ordered and no troops could have done more than they.

This was a cruel war forced upon this northern people and right against the Lord's wishes. The Lord designed that this country should be a free country where people could become educated and become enlightened so as to know good from evil and advance his cause and this war was forced upon the North to extend slavery and ignorance all over United States and block completely the Lord's plan for the betterment of the whole world and it was an honor to have had a hand in such a war. It was not a way for territory or to uphold kingdom. And I thank the Lord that I was permitted to have the honor of assisting in putting down such ungodly principles and also that the Lord has spared life and health until the present time so that I could see the good results of that war.

I enlisted as a private and served through all of the grades of promotion to Lieutenant and when mustered out the Government offered me a Captain's Commission in the regular army but I did not accept it as I was sick of War and Military duty.

W.E. Sleight, Late 1st Lieutenant.

Company D. 102nd U.S. Colored Troops.

Written

March 16th, 1917.[477]

VII. The *Ferguson* Cases

As mentioned in the text, the Michigan Supreme Court ruled October 10, 1890, in *Ferguson v Gies*, 82 Mich 358, that segregating public accommodations based on racial identity violated Michigan law in the form of an 1885 civil rights bill. The presence on the Court of Civil War veterans plausibly contributed to the result. Ironically, the U.S. Supreme Court only six years later in *Plessy v Ferguson*, 163 U.S. 537 (1896), approved the opposite outcome. Another interesting aspect of the Michigan case is the identity of the plaintiff.

William Webb Ferguson and a friend on August 15, 1887, had entered the European Hotel Restaurant in Detroit. They were required to sit in the saloon side of the eatery rather than the restaurant portion, where tables with white tablecloths and fine glassware and an electric fan to cool patrons provided a superior experience on that hot Summer day. The two men sat in the finer portion but were asked to relocate "for no other reason than that Ferguson was a colored man." Indeed, he was a person of color—with both an interesting past and future. He had been born in Detroit on May 22, 1857, to Joseph and Martha Ferguson. His mother was born on October 18, 1832, to William and Agnes Jones Webb, and thus plaintiff Ferguson wore the name of his paternal grandfather—one of the most famous antebellum Black leaders in Southeast Michigan, as discussed in the text. William Webb had hosted the meeting of Frederick Douglass and John Brown on March 12, 1859.

---

477. David D. Anderson ed., *Lieutenant William E. Sleight and the 102nd Regiment, U.S. Colored Infantry, in the Civil War* (East Lansing: The Midwestern Press, 2003), 35-42 (typos corrected).

Ferguson was sworn in as a member of the Michigan House of Representatives on January 4, 1893. He was the first African American elected and to serve in the Legislature. In 2018, a portrait of Ferguson was unveiled in the State Capitol, where it continues to be viewed outside the historic chambers where the Court heard arguments and delivered the ruling in his case.

VIII. The Most Recent Black Civil War Soldier to be Awarded the Medal of Honor

Initially nominated for the Medal of Honor in 1916 by a White surgeon who served with him in the 55th Massachusetts, Andrew Jackson Smith was denied the honor in January 1917 after the War Department performed a meager two weeks of research. But Smith's daughter, Caruth Smith Washington, never forgot her father's legacy, which she shared with her nephew—Smith's grandson—Andrew Bowman.

After escaping slavery in Kentucky during the rise of the Civil War, Smith happened upon a military path—first as an unarmed body servant with the 41st Illinois at the Battle of Shiloh, where he was struck while trying to deliver a horse to the major he served. Upon healing—and President Lincoln's announcement of the preliminary emancipation proclamation—Smith was determined to travel to Boston to enlist in the 54th Massachusetts Volunteer Infantry Regiment, the first unit of Black soldiers to be raised in the North. While he didn't arrive in time for a place in the "Glory"-bound 54th, he joined up with its sister regiment, the 55th Massachusetts. And by the summer of 1864, Smith was in combat in South Carolina. But his bravery in battle met its peak during the November 30, 1864, Battle of Honey Hill:

> Forced into a narrow gorge crossing a swamp in the face of the enemy positions, the 55th's Color-Sergeant was killed by an exploding shell, and Corporal Smith took the Regimental Colors from his hand and carried them through heavy grape

and canister fire. Although half of the officers and a third of the enlisted men engaged in the fight were killed or wounded, Corporal Smith continued to expose himself to the enemy fire by carrying the colors throughout the battle. Through his actions, the Regimental Colors of the 55th Infantry Regiment were not lost to the enemy.

These details—text from Smith's Medal of Honor citation—were largely pieced together through the efforts of his grandson, Andrew Bowman. Traveling to battlefields, museums, courthouses and historical societies, Bowman spent years gathering a slew of testimonies to prove Smith's heroics—including two 1865 orders from Smith's commanding officers commending and promoting him because of his bravery at Honey Hill. So, with a military historian's help, Smith was again nominated for the Medal of Honor, with U.S. Rep. Thomas W. Ewing (R-IL) reviving the effort in Washington. In 2000, Congress passed a bill that allowed Smith to be awarded the honor, removing the statutory time limit in certain cases. On January 16, 2001, President Bill Clinton posthumously presented Smith's Medal of Honor to Andrew Bowman and Caruth Smith Washington, stating "sometimes it takes this country a while, but we nearly always get it right in the end."

Today, one can see Smith's Medal of Honor on display at the Abraham Lincoln Presidential Library and Museum in Springfield, Ill. The visitor can also find the 55th Massachusetts's regimental colors at the Concord Museum in Concord, Mass.[478]

Also connected to the 55th is the remarkable story of Africa-born Nicolas Said, who volunteered for service in the regiment and served alongside the 102nd after a period during which he lived in Detroit. He first arrived in December 1860 and boarded at 154 Beaubien. George Duffield, minister at First Presbyterian, found Said employment at a

---

478. Courtesy of American Battlefield Trust, https://www.battlefields.org/learn/articles/head-tilting-history/better-late-never

private school for children of color. The native of modern-day Nigeria endured the 1863 riot and, when Blacks were permitted to enlist, left Detroit in June for Massachusetts.[479]

IX. A Letter About "Greater Courage"

As mentioned in the text, a national memorial to the service of African American soldiers in the Civil War has existed since 1998. Both a monument and a museum serve this purpose. The dedication of the memorial came a lifetime after the following letter appeared in a Detroit newspaper:

> Why No Monument To Negroes Who Fell In The Civil War? Press Correspondent of Fairbanks Post Says It is Pleasing to Note That the Insane Prejudice Against the Black is Passing.
>
> To the Editor—So far as the writer is aware, there is no monument in all this country erected especially to the memory of the negro soldier, in honor of the important part he took in the Civil war. Thousands upon thousands of dollars have been expended for monuments—one-man monuments, town, city, county, state and battlefield monuments; but not a stone raised to show appreciation of the humble, yet heroic sacrifice made by a people who, of all others in this great land, are sadly in need of encouragement and uplift.
>
> In the beginning of the war, Union generals who were inclined to utilize the negro in war service were strictly forbidden to do so. The policy was not to interfere with the "peculiar institution." If the Confederates laid down their arms, or if the rebellion could be put down within a reasonable length of time, slavery would remain to be dealt with by

---

479. Dean Calbreath, *The Sergeant: The Incredible Life of Nicholas Said* (New York: Pegasus Books, 2023), 97-115; *The Autobiography of Nicholas Said; A Native of Bornou, Eastern Soudan, Central Africa* (Memphis: Shotwell & Co., 1873), 200-201; "A Native of Bornoo" in *The Atlantic Monthly*, Vol. XX (Boston: Ticknor & Fields, 1867), 485, 494.

some sort of gradual abolishment. In the second year of the war, congress authorized the enlistment of colored troops; but Lincoln found prejudice so strong against the idea that he did not deem it wise to avail himself of the benefits of the law. It was questionable as to whether the recruiting of negroes and putting them into service would have the effect of hastening the end of the bloody strife, or, through retarding enlistments of white volunteers in the Union army, prolong the struggle. It was necessary that long months of further desolation of the homes of south and north lands of appalling expenditure of blood and treasure, before the unworthy hostility to negro enlistments was so far removed as to make those enlistments practical.

First Colored Infantry.

The first colored Infantry was organized (895 strong) and mustered into the service in February, 1864, and from first to last about 186,000 served. The fact that in one year elapsing till the end of the war no less than 36,847 gave their lives, attest how well they fought, and made binding on the nation's honor and sense of gratitude, good will of every patriotic citizen toward the survivors as also the descendants of the dusky martyrs of the field.

It required greater courage for an intelligent negro to enlist than it did for a white man. This is explained by the fact that defeat and capture meant death in nearly every known instance; the massacre at Fort Pillow, near Memphis, Tennessee, in April, 1864, being as notable an instance of violation of the rules of war as ever disgraced annals of history.

Another instance of uncivilized feeling against colored troops: In the charge of a "forlorn hope" at Fort Wagner, there was a great slaughter (33 per cent) in a regiment led by Col. Shaw, a young man of wealth and culture, handsome and brave, who was among the slain. The response to a flag of truce calling for his body, was: "We have buried him with his n--s!" One writer upon the subject has stated that the body of the colonel was placed beneath those of the others. A movement to recover the body is said to have produced a letter from the loyal father to the general commanding, saying "We hold that a soldier's most appropriate burial place is on the field where he has fallen!" A poet, in the years long gone by, gave this tribute:

> "They buried him with his 'n--s!'
> Earth holds no prouder grave;
> There is not a mausoleum
> In the world beyond the wave
> That a nobler tale hath hallowed,
> Or purer glory crowned.
> Than the nameless trench where they buried
> The brave so faithful found!'"

Ill Treatment.

It was not alone in the south that the negro did then, and even now, in certain localities, receives ill treatment. When the Fifth Massachusetts regiment of collored [*sic*] troops went to the front, it was dispatched from Boston by water to South Carolina, because the chief of police of New York declared his inability to protect the negroes from mob violence while passing through. In the draft riots of July, 1863, in New York, the fury of the mob was especially turned against the negroes.

It is pleasing to every citizen who has the welfare of the country at heart to know that while insane prejudice still exists in many minds, north and south, against the negro, the instances of murder of prisoners awaiting trial, maltreatment of the inoffensive, and deprivation of the rights of citizenship are growing less yearly. A righteous public sentiment should firmly and continuously set its foot upon the curse of race hatred, and stamp it out at the polls and everywhere else. The peace, safety and welfare of our country demand that those who are so ignorant or vindictive as to cause them to war

against the rights of any class whatever to a full and free "pursuit of happiness," be not entrusted with the reins of power in government!
PRESS CORRESPONDENT.
Fairbanks Post,
Department of Michigan, G.A.R. Detroit, November 29, 1910.[480]

The Fairbanks Post of the Grand Army of the Republic, the national Union veterans' organization, was chartered on May 9, 1881, at Barnes Hall located at Woodward and Grand River Avenue in Detroit. It was one of several in the city, named in honor of Major John D. Fairbanks, who was wounded at Charles City Cross Roads, Virginia, in 1862 and died a month later. The Fairbanks Post continued until its last member, Augustus F. Chappell, died in January 1942.[481]

X. "Other Colored Troops"

The 46th volume of Michigan regimental rosters included soldiers from the Great Lakes State who served in "other colored" units. The 14 listed units: Third U.S. Colored Cavalry; Fifth and Ninth U.S. Colored Heavy Artillery; Thirteenth U.S. Colored Artillery; Thirty-First, Thirty-Eighth, Forty-Ninth, Fifty-Third, Fifty-Fourth, Fifty-Fifth, Fifty-Eighth, Sixty-First, and One Hundred Twenty-Third U.S. Colored Infantry; and Captain Powell's Regiment, Colored Infantry.[482] No history is given of the service of these units, and most of the individual entries provide only enlistment and mustering in dates, duration, and age, then stating "No further record." Several entries do mention the point of enlistment: Ann Arbor; Decatur; Detroit; Dover (no county given); Flint; Grand Rapids; Jackson; Kalamazoo; Kalamazoo County (Brady, Schoolcraft); Lockport (St.

480. *Detroit Free Press*, Dec. 4, 1910, A10.
481. See Stuart McConnell, *Glorious Contentment: The Grand Army of the Republic, 1865-1900* (Chapel Hill: University of North Carolina Press, 1992).
482. *Record of Service*, Vol. 46, 1, 115-120.

Joseph County); Manchester; Newark (Gratiot County); Pipestone Township; Pontiac; Sparta; Volinia (Cass County); Washington. Those without designation of rank very likely were of African American descent.

Others were not of such descent.

Zimri H. Howe of Manchester is given "as First Sergeant" in the 55th U.S.C.T. as of March 26, 1864, age 30. The 1880 Census records him in Beatrice, Nebraska, born in 1833 in Michigan and White.

Clark G. Russell is given as enlisting "as First Sergeant" in the 61st U.S.C.T. on March 21, 1864, age 18.[483] The same individual appears on the roster of the 3rd Michigan Cavalry as having enlisted from Van Buren County on September 17, 1861, age 18, and "discharged for promotion" with transfer "to U.S.C.T." in September 1863.[484] His gravestone in Lansing's Mount Hope Cemetery is inscribed "1845-1924 Co. C, 3 Mich. Cav." In the 1880 Census, he was living in Bangor, Van Buren County, recorded as "White."

One individual, Noyce Coats, is listed as entering service in the 58th U.S.C.T. "as Surgeon, age 43. Mustered Sept. 23, 1864. No further record." The 1860 U.S. Census lists Coats in Indiana and as White. He is recorded as having brought his family to Ann Arbor to attend "a full course of lectures," after which he obtained his appointment as surgeon. To be attributed to Michigan, it appears likely that his commissioning came while in Ann Arbor. Another, J.R. Taylor, entered service in the 123rd U.S.C.T. as Chaplain, age 46, in December 1864.[485] He is listed as J. Rice Taylor in another post-war resource.[486] A classmate of Rutherford B. Hayes at Kenyon College, he founded a congregation at Allegan in 1858. In 1864, "he entered upon the service of the Christian Commission, subsequently serving

---

483. Id. 119.
484. *Record of Service*, Vol. 33, 146.
485. *Record of Service*, Vol. 46, 119; https://www.findagrave.com/memorial/16281901/noyce-coats
486. U.S. War Department, Adjutant General's Office, *Official Army Register of the Volunteer Force of the United States Army for the Years 1861, '62, '63, '64, '65*, Part VIII (1867), 304.

as chaplain of the 123rd Colored Infantry." He made his home in Saugatuck in 1869 and died there in 1900, being "never satisfied in his latter years to be long away from the sight of its woods and waters and the sand dunes across the river."[487]

More information on U.S. Colored regiments can be found in an official post-war source.[488]

XI. Declaration of Sentiment and Resolves, Dec. 2, 1859

The meeting of the congregation of the Second Baptist Church in Detroit on this date produced, enthusiastically, the following bold statement regarding the execution of abolitionist John Brown:

> Whereas, We, the oppressed portion of this community, many of whom have worn the galling chains and felt the smarting lash of slavery, and know by sad experience its brutalizing effects upon both the body and the mind, and its damaging influence upon the soul of its victim, and
>
> Whereas, We, by the help of Almighty God and the secret abolition movements that are now beginning to develop themselves in the southern part of this country, have been enabled to escape from the prison-home of slavery, and partially to obtain our liberty; and having become personally acquainted with the life and character of our much beloved and highly esteemed friend, Old Capt. John Brown, and his band of valiant men, who, at Harper's Ferry, on the 16th day of October, 1859, demonstrated to the world this sympathy and fidelity to the cause of the suffering slaves of this country, by bearding the hydra headed monster, Tyranny, in his den, and by his bold, effective, timely blow is now causing the South to tremble with a moral earthquake as he totally and

---

487. Mary Frances Heath, *Early Memories of Saugatuck, Michigan, 1830-1930*, 4th Ed. (Grand Rapids: Wm. B. Eerdmans Pub. Co., 1953), 207-208 (typo corrected).
488. Part VIII of the *Official Army Register* beginning at 141.

freely delivered up his life to lay as a ransom for our enslaved race and thereby, "solitary and alone," he has put a liberty ball in motion which shall continue to roll and gather strength until the last vestige of human slavery within this nation shall have been crushed beneath the ponderous weight, Therefore,

Resolved, That we hold the name of Old Capt. John Brown the most sacred remembrance, now the first disinterested martyr for our liberty, whereupon the true Christian principle of his Divine Lord and Master, has freely delivered up his life for the liberty of our race in this country. Therefore will we ever vindicate his character through all coming time, as our temporal redeemer whose name shall never die,

Resolved, That, as the long lost rights and liberties of an oppressed people are only gained in proportion as they act in their own cause, therefore are we now loudly called upon to arouse our own interest, and to concentrate our efforts in keeping the Old Brown liberty-ball in motion and thereby continue to kindle the fires of liberty upon the altar of every determined heart among men and continue to fan the same until the proper time, when a revolutionary blast from liberty's trump shall summon them simultaneously to unite for victorious and triumphant battle.

Resolved, That we tender our deepest and most heart felt sympathy to the family of Capt. John Brown in their sad bereavement, and pledge to them that they shall ever be held by us as our special friends, in whose welfare we hope ever to manifest a special interest.

Following approval of the declaration, "able and eloquent speeches of the Revs. Messrs. Anderson, Green, Webb, and Mr. John D. Richards, who responded so ably and eloquently to the declaration that the fire of liberty was kindled in the hearts of the whole assembly, in whose remembrance the name of Old John Brown will never die." The gathering then resolved that "the proceedings of this meeting be presented to the city papers for publication, and that copies be sent to the several anti-slavery papers throughout the country, requesting them to publish the same."[489]

XII. Abolitionism and a Church in Nankin Township

The first church organized in this township (west of Dearborn, east of Canton, south of Livonia) was Methodist Episcopal, and the year was approximately 1828. A split occurred in 1841 with withdrawal of the majority of members on account of their anti-slavery views:

> This movement was inaugurated by Rev. Marcus Swift of Nankin, Rev. Samuel Bibbins of Plymouth, and Rev. Ebenezer Doolittle of Dearborn, and from this vicinity it spread to surrounding localities throughout the State, and has since been known as the great Wesleyan Methodist secession.
>
> The Wesleyan church which originated in this secession at once became aggressive in all its movements in opposition to slavery. The feeling between them and most other churches which they designated as pro slavery churches, became mutually uncharitable and intolerant. At their communion services the new church invited members of all orthodox churches to join them. Provided always, they were not slaveholders, and that they did not believe it right to hold slaves. Some of the ministers drew the lines in stronger terms. I remember the preaching of Rev. Jesse McBride in the Perrinville church in the summer of 1854. He had been preaching in North Carolina, and is the man represented by "Father Dickinson" in Mrs. Stowe's "Dred." He had been mobbed many times by slaveholders themselves. His earnestness was intense and his style fearless. He preached with power on this occasion, and invited nobody to the communion who would consent to commune with other churches not wholly anti-slavery. The

---

489. Quarles, *The Negro in the Civil War*, 20-23.

excitement became so intense that some of his congregation threatened to tear him from the pulpit. They "wouldn't stand it."

This circumstance was but an extreme manifestation of the habitual manners of that church in all its earlier years. The ministers treated slavery as a legitimate object of hatred, and they "loved to lie awake nights to hate it." No sermon, whatever its subject, was considered complete without some reference to "the sum of all villainies." They would buy no books of any publishing house that refused to publish anti-slavery literature.

While on this subject, I will say that the predominant influence of the neighborhood was in sympathy with this anti-slavery movement.[490]

XIII. Two Men of Marshall and Mass

In the spring of 1843, Noel Johnson liberated himself from enslavement in Missouri. With fellow escapee Thomas Smith, he came to Marshall, Michigan, where he found a home and a job. He was pursued by his former enslaver and left for more secure points north. By October 1846, mail awaited him in the post office at Fort Wilkins in Houghton County, the only one in the Copper Country. He is credited as the discoverer of the Mass Mine in Ontonagon County, in 1848. With help from abolitionist Cyrus Mendenhall and mine investor Horatio Bigelow, Johnson is reputed to have secured an "elaborate opinion" from then-Attorney General John J. Crittenden[491] allowing him to purchase his manumission and file claim to mineral and farming rights in the County in 1851. He died in 1853, leaving behind a widow and two children. Wife Mary Ann remarried; their son died in

---

490. Melvin D. Osband, "My Recollections of Pioneers and Pioneer Life in Nankin" in *Michigan Pioneer and Historical Collections*, Vol. XIV, 2d Ed. (Lansing: Wynkoop Hallenbeck Crawford Co., 1908), 431, 444-445.

491. Attorney General of the United States, 1850-1853.

his youth; daughter Louisa became Mendenhall's ward and inherited a significant sum from her father's estate.[492]

The original site of the town of Mass was abandoned when a developer platted Mass City in 1899.[493]

Marshall and the Upper Peninsula featured in the life of another self-liberator, John Brown, who had been enslaved in Georgia. He made his way to Michigan and later recounted his experiences:

> I set off one morning for Marshall, in Michigan.
>
> It would not interest my readers much to follow me on my journey, for nothing of any consequence occurred to me. I travelled chiefly by night, that being the safest time. Indeed, I made very light of any real privations I now experienced. The sense of present security, and the certainty of freedom awaiting me, more than compensated me for temporary inconveniences. I felt quite happy, knowing I should meet with none but friends on my road to Canada. My way seemed perfectly clear, and the only description I can give of my sensations, is, that I felt like a new man.
>
> I arrived in Marshall one morning, and was in search of a certain friend, when I was hailed, as I was going down the street, by a number of coloured people who were building a chapel, and who had been hired to do the work by Mr. Fitch. They asked me various questions, and I soon discovered that, like myself, they were fugitives from slavery. Their names were Samuel Patterson, Noel Johnson, Thomas Smith, a man named Samuel, Elias Earle, and Thomas Christopher. They told me I need not fear any thing, as I was now quite out of danger, and asked me whether I would join them, and work for my living. I readily consented, and accordingly I was set to carry bricks and mortar. On the third day I felt

---

492. National Park Service; http://tinyurl.com/5xc9ee4r
493. Romig, 357.

unaccountably dull, and something told me not to go to my work, so, instead, I went into the woods to cut timber for the same building, which occupation suited me better, I being a carpenter. I had been there about half the day, when some one came and told me that the props of the chapel had given way, and that the men had only escaped by a sort of miracle.

Another curious circumstance also happened whilst I was employed here. Two of my mates, Noel Johnson and Thomas Smith, had belonged to one John Shelby, of Lexington, in Kentucky. They had been willed to his son-in-law, one West, and he had removed them into Missouri, whence they had run off. West traced them to Marshall (where I fell in with them,) after they had been there quite two years, and one day made his appearance for the purpose of claiming and taking them back into slavery. When we heard of it, we determined to stand by them; and all rose, as one man, to defend them, and prevent them from being carried off. Finding us so resolute, West became very much alarmed, and actually appealed to his former slave, Johnson, for protection. Johnson at once extended it to him; took him home and gave him some dinner, and afterwards got him safely away.

But to return to myself. I remained in Marshall until the chapel was completed—that is, for about a twelvemonth—and then made straight for Detroit. Here I fell in with one Mr. Joseph Teague, captain of a party of Cornish miners, who were fitting out to explore the copper region on Lake Superior. I engaged myself to Captain Teague, believing that I should be safer with Englishmen in the mines than anywhere else. He was a native of Redruth, in Cornwall, where he resided when at home. He had come over under contract, to test the copper-mines belonging to Jones & Co., of Boston. We went from Detroit to Copper Harbour, by Mackinaw and Sault St. Mary, and thence to the mouth of the Ontonagon River, Michigan. From this place we went to Cyrus Mindenhall's location, and afterwards to the Porcupine Mountains. I remained working in the mines, as a miner's carpenter, for eighteen months, when Captain Teague started to return to England.[494]

XIV. 1864 National Convention of Colored Men

Michigan sent four delegates to this meeting in Syracuse, New York, in early October 1864, at which 144 individuals represented 18 States. Frederick Douglass served as convention President, and the gathering approved a Declaration of Wrongs and Rights and an Address to the people of the United States hoping that the future "may bring to us all the blessings of equal liberty" instead of "the woes of slavery and continued social degradation."[495] The list of attendees "would leave any student of African American culture star struck."[496]

The Michigan delegation included:[497]

- Henry F. Butler, Adrian
- H.P. Harris, Adrian; also served as a Vice-President and member of the Committee upon Permanent Organization
- George H. Parker, Detroit; also elected as a Vice-President of the National Equal-Rights League to be organized coming out of the Convention
- John D. Richards, Detroit; also served on the Business Committee, and was elected as a Member of the Executive Board for the National Equal-Rights League

---

494. L.A. Chamerovzow ed., *Slave Life in Georgia: A Narrative of the Life, Sufferings, and Escape of John Brown, a Fugitive Slave, Now in England* (London: W.M. Watts, 1855), 165-168.
495. *Proceedings of the National Convention of Colored Men, Held in the City of Syracuse, N.Y., October 4, 5, 6, and 7, 1864* (n.p., 1864), 8, 41, 44, 47.
496. Eric Gardner, "A Word Fitly Spoken: Edmonia Highgate, Frances Ellen Watkins Harper, and the 1864 Syracuse Convention" in P. Gabrielle Foreman et al. eds., *The Colored Conventions Movement: Black Organizing in the Nineteenth Century* (Chapel Hill: University of North Carolina Press, 2021), 72.
497. *Proceedings*, 6-8, 10-11, 29-30.

The Business Committee reported to the convention a resolution "in reference to colored soldiers." Richards "ably discussed" the proposal. Among other things, it petitioned Congress not to make "invidious distinctions, based upon color, as to pay, labor, and promotion" in military service and opposed a Reconstruction "with slavery."[498] More specifically, it stated:

> Resolutions.
> 1. *Resolved*, That a petition be sent to the Congress of the United States, in the name of this Convention, asking them respectfully, but most earnestly, to use every honorable endeavor that they may, to have the rights of the country's colored patriots now in the field respected, without regard to their complexion; and that our Goverment [*sic*] cease to set an example to rebels, in arms against it, by making invidious distinctions, based upon color, as to pay, labor, and promotion.
> 2. *Resolved*, That the unquestioned patriotism and loyalty of the colored men of the United States—as shown in the alacrity with which, shutting their eyes to the past, and looking steadfastly to the future, at the call of the country, without pay, without bounty, without prospect of promotion, without the protection of the Government, they have rallied to the defence of "Liberty and Union"—vindicate our manhood, command our respect, and claim the attention and admiration of the civilized world.
> 3. *Resolved*, That we hereby assert our full confidence in the fundamental principles of this Government, the force of acknowledged American ideas, the Christian spirit of the age, and the justice of our cause; and we believe that the generosity and sense of honor inherent in the great heart of this nation will ultimately concede us our just claims, accord us

---

498. Id. 12, 33-34.

our rights, and grant us our full measure of citizenship, under the broad shield of the Constitution.

4. *Resolved*, That, should an attempt be made to reconstruct the Union with slavery, we should regard such a course as a flagrant violation of good faith on the part of the Government, false to the brave colored men who have fallen in its defence, unjust to the living who are perilling their lives for its protection, and to be resisted by the whole moral power of the civilized world.

5. *Resolved*, That we extend the right hand of fellowship to the freedmen of the South, and express to them our warmest sympathy, and our deep concern for their welfare, prosperity, and happiness; and desire to exhort them to shape their course toward frugality, the accumulation of property, and, above all, to leave untried no amount of effort and self-denial to acquire knowledge, and to secure a vigorous moral and religious growth. We desire, further, to assure them of our co-operation and assistance; and that our efforts in their behalf shall be given without measure, and be limited only by our capacity to give, work, and act.

6. *Resolved*, That we recommend to colored men from all sections of the country to settle, as far as they can, on the public lands.

7. *Resolved*, That, as Congress has exclusive control over the elective franchise in the District of Columbia, we earnestly pray that body to extend the right of suffrage to the colored citizens of said District.

8. *Resolved*, That the President of the United States, his Cabinet, and the Thirty-seventh Congress, are hereby tendered our warmest and most grateful thanks,—

For revoking the prohibitory law in regard to colored people carrying the mails;

For abolishing slavery in the District of Columbia;

For recognizing the National Independence of Liberia and Hayti;

For Military Order 252, retaliating for the unmilitary and barbarous treatment of the colored soldiers of the Union army by the rebels.

The Convention further tenders its thanks to Senator Sumner, for his noble efforts to cleanse the statute-books of the nation from every stain of inequality against colored men.

And also to Gen. Butler, for the course he has taken in suggesting a way for lifting the slaves first to the condition of contrabands, and then to the position of freedmen.

And to all other noble workers, both in our legislative halls and elsewhere, who have contributed to bring about the improved state in which, as colored men, we find ourselves to-day.

9. *Resolved*, That we witness, with the most grateful emotions, the generous and very successful efforts that have been made, and are still in operation, by the "National Freedmen's Relief Association," the "American Missionary Society," the "African Civilization Society," and their auxiliary and kindred bodies, for the mental and moral instruction, and the domestic improvement, of the colored people in our Southern States, who have hitherto been the victims of that impious slave-holding oligarchy, that is now in open rebellion against our American Republic.

10. *Resolved*, That we view with pride, and heartily indorse, the efforts of the gentlemen composing the faculties and executive boards of the "Institute for Colored Youth" at Philadelphia; the "Avery College" at Alleghany City, Penn.; the "Wilberforce University" at Zenia, O.; and the "Albany Enterprise Academy" at Albany, O., to develop the intellectual powers of our youth, and for opening a field for the honorable employment of those powers.

11. *Resolved*, That we are indebted to the publishers of the "Anglo-African," "Christian Recorder," and "Colored Citizen," for the manifestation of intellectual energy and business tact which they have shown to the American people by the publication of those journals; the contents of which are complimentary to the heads and hearts of their conductors, and the people whom they represent.

12. *Resolved*, that a committee of three—consisting of John S. Rock and George L. Ruffin of Boston, and William H. Day of New Jersey—be appointed to revise, correct, and publish the proceedings of this National Convention for general distribution.

13. *Resolved*, That this Convention returns its sincere thanks to its officers for the manner in which they have conducted its business; to the Rev. J. W. Loguen, and those citizens of Syracuse who have composed and co-operated with the Reception Committee; also to such of the newspapers as have made a just report of our proceedings.[499]

Richards had been born on March 1, 1831, in Fredericksburg, Virginia. He died on April 13, 1882, at the age of 51, in Detroit. Burial was in Elmwood Cemetery, Section N, Lot 150, Grave 21. According to find-a-grave.com, he was a businessman and supporter of the Underground Railroad, as well as being instrumental in organizing the 1st Michigan Colored Infantry.

Among his siblings was Fannie Mae Richards. She is famous as the first African American school teacher in the Detroit public school system. Born in Fredericksburg in 1840, she did not marry and died on February 13, 1922, age 81. Burial was also in Elmwood, in the Richards's plot in Elmwood, Grave 31.[500] During the Civil War, she opened a private school for Black children.[501]

---

499. Id. 33-36.
500. Findagrave #20424864.
501. Robin S. Peebles, "Fannie Richards and the Integration of the Detroit

XV. Equal-Rights Leagues

As indicated in VIII, *supra*, the National Equal-Rights League had its origin in the Syracuse Convention of October 1864. The first annual meeting convened in Cleveland, Ohio, on September 19, 1865. John D. Richards served as acting secretary when it opened. He was one of five credentialed Michiganders present. The others: O.P. Anderson; George De Baptiste; James W. Johnson; and B.D. Paul.[502] In some quarters it is viewed as the oldest nationwide human rights organization in the United States.

In January 1865, a statewide convention met in Adrian and launched the Michigan State Equal Rights League of Colored People. It set up a bureau in Detroit, and the League sent a delegation to Lansing to press for enfranchisement. Among that group was John D. Richards.[503]

XVI. John D. Richards

This individual is mentioned on various occasions in the text and appendix. A late 20th Century history gave this as his biography:

> Born in Fredericksburg, Virginia, and educated in Washington, D.C., Richards came to Detroit in 1851 and quickly rose to prominence in the black community. During the Civil War he served as a sutler of the 102nd United States Colored Infantry, and he built a reputation among black and white

---

Public Schools" in *Michigan History*, Vol. 65 (Jan./Feb. 1981), 30ff; William W. Stephenson Jr., "For a True System of Free Schools Should Afford Equal Opportunities For All." Integration of the Detroit Public School System During the Period, 1839-1869" in *The Negro History Bulletin*, Vol. 26, No. 1, Oct. 1962, 23ff.

502. *Proceedings of the First Annual Meeting of the National Equal Rights League Held in Cleveland, Ohio, October 19, 20, and 21, 1865* (Philadelphia: E.C. Markley & Son, 1865), 3, 9.

503. Katzman, 49. An effort appears to have occurred to create an Equal Rights League of Michigan via a convention in Detroit in September 1865, but the Adrian-launched effort was "the more active." Id.

in the city "as a man of more than ordinary intelligence and culture" and as the most eloquent black orator in Detroit. Frequently mentioned as a candidate for Congress in the 1870s, and elected Wayne County coroner in 1880, Richards worked with William Lambert, Dr. Joseph Ferguson, and others to organize and sponsor many of the public meetings of the Detroit black community, and to make certain that the platform would be shared with Detroit's leading Republicans. Often a featured Negro orator at celebrations and meetings of the black community, Richards helped turn the affairs into Republican rallies. On March 31, 1870, for instance, Detroit Negroes held an informal assembly to commemorate President Grant's endorsement of the Fifteenth Amendment and to plan a more formal celebration. With Lambert in the chair and Richards dominating the proceedings, it readily became apparent that the celebration would be a Republican party event: marchers would carry banners with the portraits of prominent Republicans and the inscription, "The Republican Party Made Us Free."[504]

He was brother to "the famed Fannie Richards, a pioneer in Detroit and in African American education in Michigan." They joined to successfully litigate desegregation of Detroit public schools. A measure of his post-war standing was the honor of giving a keynote speech in the State's celebration of passage of the 15th Amendment to the U.S. Constitution in 1870.[505]

XVII. Michigan's "Famous USCT Officer"

According to a study of officer-enlisted relations that appeared soon after *Glory* did on the big screen, one of "two most famous officers in the USCT who remained in the army after the war" was William

---

504. Katzman, 176.
505. Richard F. Miller, *States at War: A Reference Guide for Michigan in the Civil War* (Ann Arbor: University of Michigan Press, 2020), 37-38.

Rufus Shafter of Michigan. After serving "brilliantly in Virginia," he took command of the 17th U.S.C.T. "and led it superbly." Major-General George H. Thomas extolled Shafter's capabilities for higher command:

> Colonel Shafter is one of the most successful Officers who has ever held position in the Colored Regiments. He has given his whole attention to the subject of their improvement and his command has attained to a degree of discipline and soldierly bearing which is not only creditable but very remarkable.[506]

From Galesburg, Shafter was commissioned in the 7th Michigan Infantry as 1st Lieutenant on June 28, 1861. He was wounded in action at the Battle of Seven Pines (Fair Oaks) on May 31, 1862. Rising to Lieutenant-Colonel, he received command of the 17th on April 19, 1864. He received a brevet promotion to Brigadier-General in May 1865.[507] His military career continued with command of the all-Black 24th U.S. Infantry and culminated with service in Cuba during the Spanish-American War. He received the Medal of Honor in 1895, died November 12, 1906, age 71, and was buried at the Presidio in the San Francisco National Cemetery. He appeared in two films made by the Edison Manufacturing Co. in 1898 relating to the war in Cuba: *Surrender of General Toral*, and a self-titled 30-second film that is viewable online.[508]

XVIII. Civil War Centennial Commissions

The Civil War Centennial, 1961-1965, posed a sharp question to the country: had the war to end slavery brought about equality of opportunity for all Americans, as promised in the Reconstruction Amendments to the U.S. Constitution?[509] The 1960s ushered in a

---

506. Glatthaar, 235-236.
507. *Michigan in the War*, 926.
508. https://www.youtube.com/watch?v=YKO6BQSdCms
509. The 13th, 14th, and 15th.

second great civil rights crusade as America confronted its failure to fashion a "more perfect union" where equal rights for citizens of all races and ethnicities were safeguarded.[510] The work of the national Centennial commission foundered when it focused on post-war reconciliation as the main theme, rather than a more comprehensive and inclusive remembrance. Michigan's Centennial commission charted a modest course but one that officially opposed racial segregation.[511]

This 9-member body was created by the Legislature thanks to action on the last day of session for which committees could tout bills for floor consideration. Among those at the signing ceremony on July 14, 1959, joining Governor G. Mennen Williams, was Representative Edgar C. Currie (D-Detroit), first elected in 1948, native of Newport, Arkansas, a World War I veteran, labor leader, and member of the House State Capitol and Buildings Committee.[512] Females Beulah Tyrell Whitby of Detroit and Juanita White of Highland Park, both African American, were members of the Commission.[513] Whitby was born in 1897 in Virginia, obtained her Master's degree from the

---

510. The quote is from the Preamble to the U.S. Constitution.
511. Jack Dempsey, "Centennial Legacy: The Michigan Civil War Centennial Observance Commission" in *Chronicle*, a publication of the Historical Society of Michigan, Vol. 31, No. 2 (2008), 28. Among its publications, one discussed how a Christian denomination during the War attended to: "the support of the war, the abolition of slavery, help to the emancipated Negro." Jessie Ethelyn Sexton, *Congregationalism, Slavery and The Civil War* (1966), 19.
512. *Report of the Michigan Civil War Centennial Observance Commission to the Governor, Legislature and the People of Michigan*, 9-11. Currie, born Sept. 1, 1893, during the Jim Crow era, served the 2d District of Wayne County. He attended Shorter College in Argenta (North Little Rock). *Michigan Manual, 1959-1960*, [59: image], 108, 193, 198. Founded in 1886 by the African Methodist Episcopal Church, Shorter College is one of the nation's Historically Black Colleges and Universities. His death on June 18, 1965, was mourned in House Concurrent Resolution 125, *Journal of the House of Representatives of the State of Michigan, 1965 Regular Session*, Vol. II (Lansing: Speaker-Hines & Thomas, 1965), 2515-2516. An interesting Jim Crow-era monograph is Christian A. Fleetwood, *The Negro as a Soldier* (Washington: Howard University, 1895).
513. *Report of the Michigan Civil War Centennial Observance Commission*, 4, 10-11.

University of Michigan, and served the southeast Michigan community in various capacities until her death in 1990.[514] White had B.A. and M.A. degrees, attended four colleges, had been employed by the NAACP, and had married Dr. Horace A. White, church minister, State legislator, and "spokesman for the rights of the Negro."[515]

One of the body's achievements, jointly with Wayne State University and the J.L. Hudson Company, was commemorating the first public announcement in Detroit of the signing of the Emancipation Proclamation on January 5, 1963. Vice-President Lyndon B. Johnson, Governor George Romney, and Commission Chairman Floyd Haight together with Pastor A.A. Banks spoke at the unveiling.[516]

In 1966, the museum that became the Charles H. Wright Museum of African American History opened in a house owned by its founder on West Grand Boulevard in Detroit. Groundbreaking for a new museum took place in May 1985, and then again in August 1993. The current facility in the city's cultural center on Warren Avenue is said to be the largest in the world focusing on African American history. A permanent exhibit, "And Still We Rise," offers a comprehensive look at the history of African Americans.

XIX. Honor During the Sesquicentennial

In 2007, Governor Jennifer M. Granholm issued an executive order directing the Michigan Historical Commission to lead Michigan's commemoration of the Civil War Sesquicentennial—the 150th anniversary of the war for Union and liberty.[517] Serving at that time was a distinguished member of the Detroit African American community, Samuel Logan Jr., publisher of the *Michigan Chronicle*. First

---

514. *Detroit Free Press*, Jan. 23, 1990, 12.
515. *Report of the Michigan Civil War Centennial Observance Commission*, 4; *Detroit Free Press*, Feb. 12, 1958, 15.
516. *Report of the Michigan Civil War Centennial Observance Commission*, 20-21; *Detroit Free Press*, Jan. 7, 1963, 3; Moon, 96.
517. Executive Order No. 2007-52, issued Dec. 27, 2007, *State of Michigan, Journal of the Senate, 94th Legislature, Regular Session of 2008*, Jan. 9, 2008, 8-10.

appointed in 1995, he had received reappointment several times.[518] With Commissioner Logan's support, the Commission created a committee to aid in its work of the commemoration and adopted a plan in November 2009 for implementation. Among the goals it approved was one addressing the salient issue of racial disharmony:

> To create a lasting legacy focused on increasing the public's understanding of Michigan's outstanding role in helping save the Union and eliminate American slavery, making the commemoration relevant to all ethnicities as part of a discussion on equal rights for all citizens.[519]

The very first undertaking of the Commission was to be a sponsor, along with the University of Michigan-Dearborn and others, of a conference at the Charles H. Wright Museum of African American History in Detroit in March 2009, entitled "His Soul Goes Marching On: John Brown, Frederick Douglass, Detroit, and the Path to Freedom." With presentations from diverse speakers, the all-day session pivoted on the meeting in March 1859 in Detroit among Black community leaders, the great Frederick Douglass, and abolitionist John Brown. This event was the very first Civil War Sesquicentennial event in the nation. That it centered on an event with a racial foundation deserved notice. Indeed, the *Detroit Free Press* carried two items about it; the Governor issued a Certificate of Tribute, the Mayor of Detroit issued a Proclamation, and the Detroit City Council issued a Testimonial Resolution.

The *Michigan Chronicle* published three articles in 2011 about the effort, the first issuing a clarion call:

> Michigan's Civil War Sesquicentennial should make us all proud by including the history of "self-liberation" within the

---

518. His death in December 2011 was widely mourned.
519. *The Michigan Historical Commission: A Centennial Review* (Lansing: Michigan Department of Natural Resources, May 2013), 21-22.

commemoration. It should not repeat the travesties and errors of the 1960's.[520]

In April 2011, a ceremony at Historic Fort Wayne saluted the service of the 102nd U.S.C.T. Part of the event involved a tribute to the original soldiers, part a salute to the living historians who were keeping the story alive and who had supported restoration of the regimental flag with their monetary donations.

In the Spring of 2013, representatives of the Michigan Civil War Sesquicentennial Committee paid a visit to the national cemetery in Beaufort, South Carolina. They were drawn there by the need, and the appropriateness, of honoring the final resting places of men of the 1st Michigan Colored. It was a brilliant afternoon, one well-suited to pay tribute to the sacrifice of Black Michiganders who never returned home from their Civil War service. To stand near their graves and contemplate the courage they exhibited in risking their lives in the Deep South was truly humbling. The modern-day Michiganders brought a memorial wreath, solemnly posted it upon the sacred ground, shared stories of sacrifice and strength, and paused for a time of remembrance.[521] The soil of Michigan lay hundreds of miles away, across many rivers and mountains. No one present on that sunny afternoon could fail to comprehend the sacrifice offered by these forebearers of a century-and-a-half prior.

Michigan's Sesquicentennial effort included advocacy for naming public roads to commemorate Civil War stories. One such recommendation was adopted by the Michigan Legislature in Public Act 494 of 2014, signed into law by Governor Rick Snyder. The bill was sponsored by African American Senator Coleman Young Jr., namesake

---

520. Edition of October 12-18, 2011, B-4.
521. The laurel wreath, adorned with a white banner labeled MICHIGAN and a red, white and blue ribbon, was placed where the Michigan soldiers, buried largely together, rest in Section 31. During the commemoration, a military jet appeared overhead on its departure from Parris Island, as if performing an honorary flyover. Overhead, far above the jet, the sliver of the moon shone in the sky, a fitting companion to the event.

of the first Black mayor of the city of Detroit, who was a veteran of the Tuskegee Airmen during World War II. The legislation provided: "The portion of highway I-375 that is within Wayne county shall be known as the '102nd United States Colored Troops (U.S.C.T.) Memorial Highway'."[522] On March 28, 2021, Lieutenant-Governor Garlin Gilchrist, other dignitaries, and members of the public, including those who had raised the required private funds, dedicated the highway sign on the east side of Detroit.[523] The duration of the designation remains an open question since the Michigan Department of Transportation is engaged in reconfiguring the roadway.[524]

XX. *Signal of Liberty*

Under the heading of "Beauties of the Peculiar Institution," this abolitionist newspaper published an article on August 18, 1848, summarizing a case in Mississippi decided in 1837. The *Signal's* synopsis stated:

> A father emancipates his own son, and his mother; he dies, having devised his property to his son; the Supreme Court of Mississippi declares the act of emancipation to be an offence against morality, &c.—declares the son and mother to be slaves—sets aside the father's will, and gives them and the property to distant relatives.

The paper told its readers that the case "illustrates in a very striking manner, the practical working of slavery." The report was not apocryphal or biased; the decision itself, Hinds *et al.*, *v.* Brazealle *et al.* is found in *Reports of Cases Argued and Determined in the High Court*

---

522. Michigan Compiled Laws § 250.1090, effective March 31, 2015.
523. https://www.fox2detroit.com/news/i-375-gets-new-name-honoring-detroit-regiment-that-fought-in-civil-war accessed April 29, 2022. The Michigan Memorial Highway Act requires private contributions for erection of the signage.
524. https://www.michigan.gov/mdot/projects-studies/studies/current-environmental-studies/i-375-environmental-assessment

of Errors and Appeals of the State of Mississippi, Vol. II (Philadelphia: T.K. & P.G. Collins, 1839), 837-844. The Chief Justice regarded the father's plan as "an offence against morality, pernicious and detestable." Id. 843.

XXI. Modern Monument

In 2022, a new memorial honoring Black Civil War soldiers was unveiled in Ypsilanti's Highland Cemetery on North River Street. The bronze and granite monument by retired Eastern Michigan University Professor of Sculpture John Nick Pappas features images of soldiers and eagles. Cemetery records document 19 marked gravesites of Black Civil War soldiers, and more may be located nearby.

XXII. First Day of Issue

This final item is to note the issuance by the United States Postal Service on March 9, 2024, at Church Creek, Maryland, of a stamp series commemorating the Underground Railroad. The pane of 20 stamps featured 10 sepia-toned portraits of men and women who escaped slavery or who helped others escape. The verso portrayed general routes that freedom seekers followed and a list of the 10 individuals, with a few words of biographical information about each. Below the portraits were lines of text that juxtaposed characteristics they shared: black/white cooperation; trust/danger; flight/faith; courage/risk; defiance/hope.

Of the 10 honored "heroes," two Michiganders are included: Laura Haviland and William Lambert. Information on both courageous individuals is contained within the text of this volume.

Bibliography

A Thrilling Narrative from the Lips of the Sufferers of the Late Detroit Riot, March 6, 1863, With the Hair Breadth Escapes of Men, Women and Children, and Destruction of Colored Men's Property, Not Less Than $15,000 (Detroit: n.p., 1863)

Abraham Lincoln Presidential Library and Museum

American Battlefield Trust

American Biographical History of Eminent and Self-Made Men, Michigan Volume (Cincinnati: Western Biographical Publishing Co., 1878)

An act for enrolling and calling out the national forces, and for other purposes, 12 Stat. 731

An Act respecting fugitives from justice, and persons escaping from the service of their masters, 1 Stat. 302

An Act to confiscate Property used for Insurrectionary Purposes, 37th Congress, 1st Session, Pub. L. 37–60, 12 Stat. 319

An act to prevent the further introduction of Slaves, and to limit the Term of contracts for Servitude within this Province, July 9, 1793

An Act to suppress Insurrection, to punish Treason and Rebellion, to seize and confiscate the Property of Rebels, and for other Purposes, Pub. L. 37–195, 12 Stat. 589

Anderson, David D. ed., *Lieutenant William E. Sleight and the 102d Regiment, U.S. Colored Infantry, in the Civil War* (East Lansing: The Midwestern Press, 2003)

Ann Arbor News

---

525. All works listed were consulted in research for this volume.

Aptheker, Herbert. *Negro Casualties in the Civil War* (Washington: Association for the Study of Negro Life & History, Inc., 1945)

_____. *The Negro in the Abolitionist Movement* (New York: International Publishers, 1941)

Armstrong, Nellie C. *Negro Troops in the Civil War* (Champaign: University of Illinois, 1919)

Ashlee, Laura. *Traveling Through Time: A Guide to Michigan's Historical Markers* (Ann Arbor: University of Michigan Press, 2005)

The Atlantic Monthly, Vol. XX (Boston: Ticknor & Fields, 1867)

The Autobiography of Nicholas Said; A Native of Bornou, Eastern Soudan, Central Africa (Memphis: Shotwell & Co., 1873)

Bak, Richard. *A Distant Thunder: Michigan in the Civil War* (Ann Arbor: Huron River Press, 2004)

Basker, James G. ed. *Black Writers of the Founding Era: A Library of America Anthology* (Library of America, 2023)

Beasecker, Robert ed. *This is a War for the Utter Extinction of Slavery: The Civil War Letters of James Benjamin Franklin Curtis, Hospital Steward, 1st Michigan Colored Infantry* (Grand Valley State University, 2020)

Berlin, Ira et al. eds. *Freedom: A Documentary History of Emancipation, 1861–1867*, Series I, Vol. II (New York: Cambridge University Press, 2012)

Black, Andrew K. "In the Service of the United States: Comparative Mortality among African American and White Troops in the Union Army" in *The Journal of Negro History*, Vol. 79, No. 4, Autumn 1994 (University of Chicago Press)

Blackett, R.J.M. *The Captive's Quest for Freedom: Fugitive Slaves, the 1850 Fugitive Slave Law, and the Politics of Slavery* (New York: Cambridge University Press, 2018)

Blight, David W. *A Slave No More: Two Men Who Escaped to Freedom, Including Their Own Narratives Of Emancipation* (Boston: Mariner Books, 2007)

_____. *Frederick Douglass: Prophet of Freedom* (New York: Simon & Schuster, 2018)

Boatner, Mark M. III. *The Civil War Dictionary* (New York: David Mackay Co., 1988)

Bordewich, Fergus M. *Bound for Canaan: The Underground Railroad and the War for the Soul of America* (New York: HarperCollins Publishers, 2005)

Boyd, Mark F. "The Federal Campaign of 1864 in East Florida" in *Florida Historical Quarterly*, Vol. 29, No. 1 (Jul. 1950)

Boyd, Melba Joyce. *Discarded Legacy: Politics and Poetics in the Life of Frances E.W. Harper, 1825-1911* (Detroit: Wayne State University Press, 1994)

_____ ed. *Roses and Revolutions: The Selected Writings of Dudley Randall* (Detroit: Wayne State University Press, 2009)

Bragg, William H. "Victory at Honey Hill: 'A Mere Flicker of Light'" in *Civil War Times Illustrated*, Vol. XXII, No. 9, Jan. 1984

Brock, R.A. *Virginia and Virginians* (Richmond: H.H. Hardesty, 1888)

Brown, Ida C. *Michigan Men in the Civil War* (Ann Arbor: University of Michigan, 1959)

Brown, William W. *The Negro in the American Rebellion: His Heroism and His Fidelity* (Boston: Lee & Shepard, 1867)

Burlingame, Michael. *The Black Man's President: Abraham Lincoln, African Americans, and the Pursuit of Racial Equality* (New York: Pegasus Books, 2012)

Burton, Clarence M. ed. *The City of Detroit, Michigan, 1701-1922*, Vol. I (Detroit: S.J. Clarke Pub. Co., 1922)

_____ & M. Agnes Burton eds., *History of Wayne County and the City of Detroit, Michigan*, Vol. II (Chicago: S.J. Clarke Pub. Co., 1930)

Calarco, Tom et. al. *Places of the Underground Railroad: A Geographical Guide* (Santa Barbara: Greenwood, 2011)

Calbreath, Dean. *The Sergeant: The Incredible Life of Nicholas Said* (New York: Pegasus Books, 2023)

Carse, Robert. *Department of the South: Hilton Head Island in the Civil War* (Hilton Head Island: Heritage Library Foundation, 2002)

Castel, Albert. "The Fort Pillow Massacre: A Fresh Examination of the Evidence," *Civil War History* 4 (Mar. 1958)

Cathcart, William ed. *The Baptist Encyclopedia* (Philadelphia: Louis H. Everts, 1881)

Catton, Bruce. *The Coming Fury, The Centennial History of the Civil War, Volume One* (Garden City: Doubleday & Co., 1961)

_____. *Never Call Retreat, The Centennial History of the Civil War, Volume Three* (Garden City: Doubleday & Co., 1965)

Cecelski, David S. *The Fire of Freedom: Abraham Galloway & the Slaves' Civil War* (Chapel Hill: University of North Carolina Press, 2012)

Chamerovzow, L.A. ed. *Slave Life in Georgia: A Narrative of the Life, Sufferings, and Escape of John Brown, a Fugitive Slave, Now in England* (London: W.M. Watts, 1855)

Chardavoyne, David G. "Michigan and the Fugitive Slave Acts" in *The Court Legacy*, Vol. XII, No. 3 (Detroit: Historical Society for the United States District Court for the Eastern District of Michigan, Nov. 2004)

Chipman, Bert L. *The Chipman Family, a Genealogy of the Chipmans in America, 1631-1920* (Winston-Salem: Bert L. Chipman, 1920)

Chipman, R. Manning. *The Chipman Lineage, Particularly as in Essex County, Mass.* (Salem: Salem Press, 1872)

Cimprich, John. "The Fort Pillow Massacre: Assessing the Evidence" in John D. Smith ed., *Black Soldiers in Blue: African American Troops in the Civil War Era* (Chapel Hill: University of North Carolina Press, 2002)

Claspy, Everett. *The Negro in Southwestern Michigan: Negroes in the North in a Rural Environment* (Dowagiac: n.p., 1967)

Cleveland, Henry. *Alexander H. Stephens in Public and Private with Letters and Speeches, Before, During, and Since the War* (Philadelphia: National Publishing Co., 1866)

Clowes, Walter F. *The Detroit Light Guard: A Complete Record of this Organization from its Foundation to the Present Day* (Detroit: John F. Eby & Co., 1900)

Collected Works of Abraham Lincoln (Springfield: Abraham Lincoln Association, 1953), Vol. VI, VII, VIII

Congressional Research Service, *American War and Military Operations Casualties: Lists and Statistics*, RL32492, version 32 (2020)

Constitution of 1835

Constitution of 1850

Constitution of the Confederate States of America (Montgomery: Shorter & Reid, 1861)

Cooper, Afua. "The *Voice of the Fugitive*: A Transnational Abolitionist Organ" in Karolyn S. Frost & Veta S. Tucker eds., *A Fluid Frontier: Slavery, Resistance, and the Underground Railroad in the Detroit River Borderland* (Detroit: Wayne State University Press, 2016)

Cornish, Dudley T. *The Sable Arm; Negro Troops in the Union Army, 1861-1865* (New York: Longmans Green, 1956)

Courtenay, William A. "Fragments of War History Relating to the Coast Defence of South Carolina, 1861-'65, and the Hasty Preparations for the Battle of Honey Hill, November 30, 1864" in *Southern Historical Society Papers*, Vol. 26 (1898)

Cozzens, Peter. "Smokescreen at Honey Hill" in *Civil War Times Illustrated*, Vol. XXXVIII, No. 7, Feb. 2000

Cullum, George W. *Biographical Register of the Officers and Graduates of the U.S. Military Academy* (New York: James Miller, 1879)

Cyclopedia of Michigan: Historical and Biographical Synopsis of General History of the State (New York: Western Pub. & Engraving Co., 1900)

Daily Journal of the Convention to Form a Constitution

Davis, Jefferson. *The Rise and Fall of the Confederate Government*, Vol. I (New York: D. Appleton & Co., 1881)

Dempsey, Jack. "Centennial Legacy: The Michigan Civil War Centennial Observance Commission" in *Chronicle*, a publication of the Historical Society of Michigan, Vol. 31, No. 2, 28 (2008)

_____. *Michigan and the Civil War: A Great and Bloody Sacrifice* (Charleston: The History Press, 2012)

_____. *Michigan's Civil War Citizen-General: Alpheus S. Williams* (Charleston: The History Press, 2019)

_____. "The Man with the Branded Hand" in *Michigan History*, Vol. 99, No. 1, Jan./Feb. 2015

_____ & Brian James Egen, *Michigan at Antietam: The Wolverine State's Sacrifice on America's Bloodiest Day* (Charleston: The History Press, 2015)

_____ ed. *When Slavery and Rebellion Are Destroyed: A Michigan Woman's Civil War Journal* (Athens: University of Georgia Press, 2023)

Detroit Advertiser and Tribune

Detroit *Evening News*

Detroit Free Press

Dew, Charles B. *Apostles of Disunion: Southern Secession Commissioners and the Causes of the Civil War* (Charlottesville: University Press of Virginia, 2001)

Dobak, William A. *Freedom by the Sword: The U.S. Colored Troops, 1862-1867* (Washington: Government Printing Office, 2011)

Douglass, Frederick. *Life and Times of Frederick Douglass, Written by Himself* (Hartford: Park Pub. Co., 1881)

Downs, Jim. *Sick from Freedom: African American Illness and Suffering During the Civil War and Reconstruction* (New York: Oxford University Press, 2015)

Du Bois, W.E. Burghardt ed. *Economic Co-operation among Negro Americans* (Atlanta: Atlanta University Press, 1907)

Dunbar, Willis F. *Michigan: A History of the Wolverine State* (Grand Rapids: William B. Eerdmans Pub. Co., 1970)

Duncan, Russell ed. *Blue-Eyed Child of Fortune: The Civil War Letters of Colonel Robert Gould Shaw* (Athens: University of Georgia Press, 1999)

Dunn, William. *A History of the First Michigan Colored Regiment*, M.A. Thesis, Central Michigan University, Jan. 1967

Dwyer, Dustin. "After more than 150 years, the legacy of a thriving Black community in Cass County continues on," Michigan Radio, Feb. 17, 2022

Dyer, Frederick H. *A Compendium of the War of the Rebellion* (Des Moines: Dyer Pub. Co., 1908)

Earle, Thomas. *The Life, Travels, and Opinions of Benjamin Lundy* (Philadelphia: William D. Parrish, 1847)

Egerton, Douglas R. *Thunder at the Gates: The Black Civil War Regiments That Redeemed America* (New York, 2016)

Eighth U.S. Decennial Census

Emilio, Luis F. *History of the Fifty-Fourth Regiment of Massachusetts Volunteer Infantry, 1863-1865*, 2d ed. (Boston: Boston Book Co., 1894)

Faber, Don. *The Boy Governor: Stevens T. Mason and the Birth of Michigan Politics* (Ann Arbor: University of Michigan Press, 2012)

Farmer, Silas. *The History of Detroit and Michigan: or, The Metropolis Illustrated* (Detroit: Silas Farmer & Co., 1884)

Fennimore, Jean Joy L. "Austin Blair: Civil War Governor, 1861-1862" in *Michigan History*, Vol. 49, No. 3, Sept. 1965

Fields, Harold B. "Free Negroes in Cass County Before the Civil War" in *Michigan History*, Vol. 44, No. 4, Dec. 1960

Finkelman, Paul ed. *Encyclopedia of African American History 1619-1895: From the Colonial Period to the Age of Frederick Douglass*, Vol. 2 (New York: Oxford University Press, 2006)

_____ & Martin J. Hershock eds., *The History of Michigan Law* (Athens: University of Ohio Press, 2006)

Finkenbine, Roy. "A Community Militant and Organized: The Colored Vigilant Committee of Detroit" in *A Fluid Frontier: Slavery, Resistance, and the Underground Railroad in the Detroit River Borderland* (Detroit: Wayne State University Press, 2016)

_____. "A Beacon of Liberty on the Great Lakes: Race, Slavery, and the Law in Antebellum Michigan" in Paul Finkelman & Martin J. Hershock eds., *The History of Michigan Law* (Athens: University of Ohio Press, 2006)

_____. *Sources of the African American Past: Primary Sources in American History* (New York: Longman Publishers, 1997)

First Annual Report of the Board of Managers of the Association of Friends for the Aid and Elevation of the Freedmen (Philadelphia: Merrihew & Sons, 1865)

Fleetwood, Christian A. *The Negro as a Soldier* (Washington: Howard University, 1895)

Foner, Eric. *Gateway to Freedom: The Hidden History of the Underground Railroad* (New York: W. W. Norton & Co., 2015)

Foote, Abram W. *Foote Family, Comprising the Genealogy and History of Nathaniel Foote, of Wethersfield, Conn., and His Descendants*, Vol. I (Rutland: Marble City Press, 1907)

Foreman, P. Gabrielle et al. eds. *The Colored Conventions Movement: Black Organizing in the Nineteenth Century* (Chapel Hill: University of North Carolina Press, 2021)

Fourth U.S. Decennial Census

Fox, Charles B. *Record of Service of 55th Regiment of Massachusetts Volunteer Infantry* (Cambridge: John Wilson & Son, 1868)

Franklin, John Hope. *From Slavery to Freedom: A History of Negro Americans*, 4th Ed. (New York: Alfred A. Knopf, 1974)

Freeman, Douglas S. *R.E. Lee*, Vol. I (New York: Charles Scribner's Sons, 1934)

Frost, Karolyn Smardz & Veta Smith Tucker eds., *A Fluid Frontier: Slavery, Resistance, and the Underground Railroad in the Detroit River Borderland* (Detroit: Wayne State University Press, 2016)

Fuller, George N. ed. *Messages of the Governors of Michigan*, Vol. II (Lansing: Michigan Historical Commission, 1926)

Gallagher, Gary W. *The Union War* (Cambridge: Harvard University Press, 2011)

Gardner, Eric. "A Word Fitly Spoken: Edmonia Highgate, Frances Ellen Watkins Harper, and the 1864 Syracuse Convention" in P. Gabrielle Foreman et al. eds., *The Colored Conventions Movement: Black Organizing in the Nineteenth Century* (Chapel Hill: University of North Carolina Press, 2021)

Gates, Henry Louis Jr. *Life Upon These Shores: Looking at African American History, 1513-2008* (New York: Alfred A. Knopf, 2011)

Gavins, Raymond. *The Cambridge Guide to African American History* (New York: Cambridge University Press, 2016)

Girardin, J.A. "Slavery in Detroit" in *Michigan Pioneer and Historical Collections*, Vol. I, 2d Ed. (Lansing: Robert Smith Printing Co., 1900)

Glatthaar, Joseph T. *Forged in Battle: The Civil War Alliance of Black Soldiers and White Officers* (New York: Meridian, 1991)

Glover, L.H. ed. *A Twentieth Century History of Cass County, Michigan* (Chicago: Lewis Pub. Co., 1906)

Greene, Robert E. *Black Defenders of America, 1775-1973: A Reference and Pictorial History* (Chicago: Johnson Pub. Co., 1974)

Hamilton, Lowell D. *The Battle of Honey Hill, South Carolina Wednesday, 30 November 1864*

Harbour, Jennifer R. *Organizing Freedom: Black Emancipation Activism in the Civil War Midwest* (Carbondale: Southern Illinois University Press, 2020)

Hargrove, Hondon B. *Black Union Soldiers in the Civil War* (Jefferson: McFarland & Co., 1988)

_____. "Their Greatest Battle Was Getting Into The Fight: The 1st Michigan Colored Infantry Goes to War" in *Michigan History*, Vol. 75, No. 1, Jan./Feb. 1991

Harris, Leslie M. & Daina Ramey Berry. "Researching Nineteenth-Century African American History" in *The Journal of the Civil War Era*, Vol. 12, No. 4, Dec. 2022

Hattaway, Herman & Archer Jones. *How the North Won: A Military History of the Civil War* (Urbana: University of Illinois Press, 1983)

Heath, Mary Frances. *Early Memories of Saugatuck, Michigan, 1830-1930*, 4th Ed. (Grand Rapids: Wm. B. Eerdmans Pub. Co., 1953)

Heitman, Francis B. *Historical Register and Dictionary of the United States Army*, Vol. 1 (Washington: Government Printing Office, 1903)

Hepburn, Sharon A. Roger ed. *Private No More: The Civil War Letters of John Lovejoy Murray, 102nd United States Colored Infantry* (Athens: University of Georgia Press, 2023)

Hershock, Martin J. *The Paradox of Progress: Economic Change, Individual Enterprise, and Political Culture in Michigan, 1837-1878* (Athens: Ohio University Press, 2003)

Hine, Darlene Clark & Earnestine Jenkins eds. *A Question of Manhood: A Reader in U.S. Black Men's History and Masculinity*, Vol. I (Bloomington: Indiana University Press, 1999)

http://capitol.michigan.gov/

http://www.fireandfury.com/

http://www.nationalregister.sc.gov/

http://www.stratfordhall.org

https://babel.hathitrust.org/

https://bioguide.congress.gov

https://detroithistorical.org/

https://d.lib.msu.edu/

https://emergingcivilwar.com/

https://nativeamericansofdelawarestate.com/

https://naucenter.as.virginia.edu/blog-page/936

https://omeka.coloredconventions.org/

https://scholarworks.gvsu.edu/

https://southadamstreet1900.wordpress.com

https://www.aoml.noaa.gov/

https://www.battlefields.org/

https://www.bethelamechurchdetroit.org/

https://www.civilwarmed.org/

https://www.elmwoodhistoriccemetery.org/

https://www.findagrave.com

https://www.fjc.gov/

https://www.fox2detroit.com/news/

https://www.hmdb.org

https://www.loc.gov/

https://www.michigan.gov/som

https://www.micourthistory.org/
https://www.nps.gov/
https://www2.census.gov/
In re Elizabeth Denison, 1 St Ct Terr Mich 63 (1807)
Jackson Weekly Citizen
Jeffrey, Julie Roy. *The Great Silent Army of Abolitionism: Ordinary Women in the Antislavery Movement* (Chapel Hill: University of North Carolina Press, 1998)
Johannsen, Robert W. *Stephen A. Douglas* (New York: Oxford University Press, 1973)
Joint Committee on the Conduct of the War, *Report No. 65*, 38th Congress, 1st Session, May 6, 1864
Joint Documents of the State of Michigan, for the Year 1860, No. 2, 1-24 (Lansing: Hosmer & Kerr, 1861)
Journal of the House of Representatives of the State of Michigan
Journal of the Senate of the United States of America
Journals of the Continental Congress, 1774-1789, Vol. XXXII (Washington: Government Printing Office, 1936)
Katzman, David M. *Before the Ghetto; Black Detroit in the Nineteenth Century* (Urbana: University of Illinois Press, 1973)
Klunder, Willard C. *Lewis Cass and the Politics of Moderation* (Kent: Kent State University Press, 1996)
Kundinger, Matthew. "Racial Rhetoric: The Detroit Free Press and Its Part in the Detroit Race Riot of 1863" in *Michigan Journal of History*, Winter 2006 (Ann Arbor: University of Michigan Press)
Larrie, Reginald R. *Black Experiences in Michigan History* (Lansing: Michigan History Division, 1976)
_____. *Corners of Black History* (Detroit: Olympian King Co., 1971)
_____. *Makin' free: African Americans in the Northwest Territory* (Detroit: Blaine Ethridge Books, 1981)
Lasorda, Jesse. "Orrin Edgar Wilson: The Life of an African American Civil War Veteran" in *Chronicle*, Vol. 35, No. 3, Fall 2012
Lauck, Jon K. *The Good Country: A History of the American Midwest, 1800-1900* (Norman: University of Oklahoma Press, 2022)

Leach, Nathaniel. *The Second Baptist Connection, Reaching Out to Freedom: History of Second Baptist Church of Detroit* (Detroit: 1988)

Levine, Bruce C. *Confederate Emancipation: Southern Plans to Free and Arm Slaves During the Civil War* (New York: Oxford University Press, 2006)

Lincoln, Abraham. *Message to Congress*, July 4, 1861, Abraham Lincoln Papers, Manuscript Division, Library of Congress

Littlejohn, Edward J. "Slaves, Judge Woodward, and the Supreme Court of the Michigan Territory" in *Michigan Bar Journal*, Vol. 94, July 2015

Litwack, Leon F. *North of Slavery: The Negro in the Free States, 1790-1860* (Chicago: University of Chicago Press, 1961)

Long, E.B. & Barbara Long. *The Civil War Day by Day: An Almanac 1861-1865* (Garden City: Doubleday & Co., 1971)

Lumpkin, Katherine DuPre. "'The General Plan Was Freedom': A Negro Secret Order on the Underground Railroad" in *Phylon*, Vol. 28, No. 1 (1st Qtr. 1967)

Mabee, Carleton & Susan Mabee Newhouse. *Sojourner Truth: Slave, Prophet, Legend* (New York: New York University Press, 1993)

MacRae, Cordella & Emma Ribbron compilers. *Civil War Veterans of the 102nd United States Colored Troops, the First Michigan Colored Regiment, Buried in Elmwood Cemetery, Detroit, Michigan* (Detroit: Fred Hart Williams Genealogical Society, 1990)

Manning, Chandra M. What This Cruel War Was Over: Soldiers, Slavery, and the Civil War (New York: Alfred A. Knopf, 2007)

Map of Virginia: Showing the Distribution of its Slave Population from the Census of 1860 (Washington: Henry S. Graham, 1861)

Mason, Philip P. & Paul J. Pentecost. *From Bull Run to Appomattox: Michigan's Role in the Civil War* (Detroit: Wayne State University Press, 1961)

May, George S. *Michigan and the Civil War Years, 1860-1866: A Wartime Chronicle*, 2d Ed. (Lansing: Michigan Civil War Centennial Observance Commission, 1966)

Mays, Joe H. *Black Americans and Their Contributions Toward Union Victory in the American Civil War, 1861-1865* (Lanham: University Press of America, 1984)

McCargo, Samuel E. "Taney's Negroes: Can the Court Un-Ring the Bell" in *Michigan Bar Journal*, Vol. 94, No. 5, May 2015

McConnell, Stuart. *Glorious Contentment: The Grand Army of the Republic, 1865-1900* (Chapel Hill: University of North Carolina Press, 1992)

McCormick, Jacob. "Reckoning With a Troubled Past: The John Taylor Lynching" in *Chronicle*, Vol. 44, No. 1 (Spring 2021)

McPherson, James M. *The Negro's Civil War: How American Blacks Felt and Acted During the War for the Union* (New York: Vintage Books, 2003)

McRae, Norman ed. *Negroes in Michigan in the Civil War* (Lansing: Michigan Civil War Centennial Observance Commission, 1966)

Meacham, Jon. *And There Was Light: Abraham Lincoln and the American Struggle* (New York: Random House, 2023)

Michigan Chronicle

Michigan Civil War Association, *His Sword a Scalpel: General Charles Stuart Tripler, MD, USA* (Traverse City: Mission Point Press, 2023)

Michigan Compiled Laws § 250.1090

Michigan Department of State, *Pathways to Michigan's Black Heritage* (Lansing: 1988)

The Michigan Historical Commission: A Centennial Review (Lansing: Michigan Department of Natural Resources, May 2013)

Michigan Historical Commission, *Michigan Biographies*, Vol. I (Lansing: 1924)

Michigan Manual

Michigan Pioneer and Historical Collections, Vols. XIII & XIV, 2d Ed. (Lansing: Wynkoop Hallenbeck Crawford Co., 1908)

Michigan Women in the Civil War (Lansing: Michigan Civil War Centennial Observance Commission, 1963)

Michna-Bales, Jeanine. *Through Darkness to Light: Photographs Along the Underground Railroad* (Princeton: Princeton Architectural Press, 2017)

Miles, Tiya. "'Shall Woman's Voice Be Hushed?': Laura Smith Haviland in Abolitionist Women's History" in *Michigan Historical Review*, Vol. 39, No. 2, Fall 2013

Miller, Richard F. *States at War: A Reference Guide for Michigan in the Civil War* (Ann Arbor: University of Michigan Press, 2020)

Minutes of the State Convention, of the Colored Citizens of the State of Michigan, Held in the City of Detroit on the 26th and 27th of October, 1843 for the Purpose of Considering Their Moral & Political Condition, as Citizens of the State

Mitchell, W.M. *The Under-Ground Railroad* (London: William Tweedie, 1860)

Moat, Louis S. ed. *Frank Leslie's Illustrated History of the Civil War* (New York: Mrs. Frank Leslie, 1895)

Moon, Elaine Latzman. *Untold Tales, Unsung Heroes: An Oral History of Detroit's African American Community, 1918-1967* (Detroit: Wayne State University Press, 1994)

Moore, Frank ed. *The Rebellion Record: A Diary of American Events*, First, Second, and Sixth Volumes (New York: G.P. Putnam, 1861, 1862, 1863)

Moss, Juanita Patience. *Forgotten Black Soldiers Who Served in White Regiments During the Civil War*, Vol. II (Berwyn Heights: Heritage Books, 2014)

Mossell, Gertrude Emily Hicks Bustill. *The Work of the Afro-American Woman* (Philadelphia: Geo. S. Ferguson Co., 1894)

Mull, Carol E. *The Underground Railroad in Michigan* (Jefferson: McFarland & Co., 2010)

Narrative of Sojourner Truth (Battle Creek: Review & Herald, 1884)

National Archives

National Park Service

The Negro History Bulletin

Wilbur Nelson Diary 1864, Michigan State University, Archives and Historical Collections

New York Times Magazine

Ninth U.S. Decennial Census

Northwest Territory Celebration Commission, *History of the Ordinance of 1787 and the Old Northwest Territory* (Marietta: 1937)

Nye, Russel B. *Fettered Freedom; Civil Liberties and the Slavery Controversy 1830-1860* (East Lansing: Michigan State University Press, 1963)

O'Den, Jeffrey. "Michigan's Soldiers of Color" in *Michigan History*, Vol. 95, No. 4, Jul./Aug. 2011

Oakes, James. *The Crooked Path to Abolition: Abraham Lincoln and the Antislavery Constitution* (New York: W.W. Norton & Co., 2021)

_____. *Freedom National: The Destruction of Slavery in the United States, 1861-1865* (New York: W.W. Norton & Co., 2013)

Osband, Melvin D. "My Recollections of Pioneers and Pioneer Life in Nankin" in *Michigan Pioneer and Historical Collections*, Vol. XIV, 2d Ed. (Lansing: Wynkoop Hallenbeck Crawford Co., 1908)

Palmer, Friend. *Early Days in Detroit* (Detroit: Hunt & June, 1906)

The Palmetto Herald

Pearson, Elizabeth Ware ed. *Letters from Port Royal Written at the Time of the Civil War* (Boston: W.B. Clarke Co., 1906)

Peebles, Robin S. "Fannie Richards and the Integration of the Detroit Public Schools" in *Michigan History*, Vol. 65 (Jan./Feb. 1981)

"Perry Sanford: In and Out of Slavery" in *Michigan History*, Vol. 95, No. 1, Jan./Feb. 2011

Personal Memoirs of U.S. Grant, Vol. II (New York: Charles L. Webster & Co., 1886)

Peterson, Carla L. *"Doers of the Word": African American Women Speakers and Writers in the North (1830-1880)* (New York: Oxford University Press, 1995)

Pinheiro, Holly A. Jr. "USCT Kin's Generational Battle for Equality" in *Journal of the Civil War Era*, Sept. 19, 2023

Pittman, Samuel E. *A Sketch of the Operations of General Alpheus S. Williams' Command Known as the Red Star Division of the 12th and 20th Corps of the Army of the Potomac and Army of the Cumberland, respectively, October 1861 to June 1862* (Michigan Commandery of the Loyal Legion, 1899)

_____. *Sketch of the Operations of the Red Star Division of the 12th Corps Army of the Potomac and 20th Corps Army of the Cumberland Commanded by Gen'l Alpheus S. Williams in the Pope Campaign June 1862 to Sept. 2nd 1862* (Michigan Commandery of the Loyal Legion, 1900)

Plessy v. Ferguson, 163 U.S. 537 (1896)

Polk's Detroit City Directory for 1857

Pollard, Edward A. *The Lost Cause; A New Southern History of the War of the Confederates* (New York: E.B. Treat & Co., 1867)

Pontiac Courier

Proceedings of the First Annual Meeting of the National Equal Rights League Held in Cleveland, Ohio, October 19, 20, and 21, 1865 (Philadelphia: E.C. Markley & Son, 1865)

Proceedings of the National Convention of Colored Men, Held in the City of Syracuse, N.Y., October 4, 5, 6, and 7, 1864 (n.p., 1864)

Public Act 147 of 1903

Public Law 9-22, 2 Stat. 426

Pub. L. 31–60, 9 Stat. 462

Quaife, Milo M. ed. *From the Cannon's Mouth: The Civil War Letters of General Alpheus S. Williams* (Detroit: Wayne State University Press, 1959)

Quarles, Benjamin A. *The Negro in the Civil War* (Boston: Little, Brown & Co., 1953)

_____ ed. *Blacks on John Brown* (Urbana: University of Illinois Press, 1972)

Quist, John W. ed. *Michigan's War: The Civil War in Documents* (Athens: Ohio University Press, 2019)

Ramold, Steven J. *Slaves, Sailors, Citizens: African Americans in the Union Navy* (DeKalb: Northern Illinois University Press, 2002)

Randall, Dudley. "Memorial Wreath" in Melba Joyce Boyd ed., *Roses and Revolutions: The Selected Writings of Dudley Randall* (Detroit: Wayne State University Press, 2009)

Record of Service of Michigan Volunteers in the Civil War 1861-1865 (Kalamazoo: Ihling Bros. & Everard, 1903)

Redkey, Edwin S. ed. *A Grand Army of Black Men: Letters from African American Soldiers in the Union Army, 1861-1865* (Cambridge: Cambridge University Press, 1992)

Reed, George I. ed. *Bench and Bar of Michigan: A Volume of History and Biography* (Chicago: Century Pub., 1897)

Reid, Richard M. ed. *Practicing Medicine in a Black Regiment: The Civil War Diary of Burt G. Wilder, 55th Massachusetts* (Amherst: University of Massachusetts Press, 2010)

Report of the Michigan Civil War Centennial Observance Commission to the Governor, Legislature and the People of Michigan

Reports of Cases Argued and Determined in the High Court of Errors and Appeals of the State of Mississippi, Vol. II (Philadelphia: T.K. & P.G. Collins, 1839)

The Revised Statutes of the State of Michigan, Passed at the Adjourned Session of 1837, and the Regular Session of 1838 (Detroit: John S. Bagg, 1838)

Robertson, John. *Michigan in the War* (Lansing: W.S. George & Co., 1882)

Robertson, Stacey M. *Hearts Beating for Liberty: Women Abolitionists in the Old Northwest* (Chapel Hill: University of North Carolina Press, 2010)

Romig, Walter. *Michigan Place Names* (Detroit: Wayne State University Press, 1986)

S. 1942, Pub. L. No. 117-339

Sander, George P. ed. *The Statutes at Large, Treaties, and Proclamations of the United States of America*, Vol. XII (Boston: Little, Brown & Co., 1863)

Sanderson, James M. *The Cook's Creed* (Washington: Government Printing Office, 1862)

Dred Scott v Sandford, 60 U.S. 393 (1857)

Scott, Robert Garth ed. *Forgotten Valor: The Memoirs, Journals, & Civil War Letters of Orlando B. Willcox* (Kent: Kent State University Press, 1999)

Sears, Stephen W. ed. *The Civil War Papers of George B. McClellan: Selected Correspondence, 1860-1865* (New York: Ticknor & Fields, 1989)

Seventh U.S. Decennial Census

Sexton, Jessie Ethelyn. *Congregationalism, Slavery and The Civil War* (Lansing: Michigan Civil War Centennial Observance Commission, 1966)

Shane, Scott. *Flee North: A Forgotten Hero and the Fight for Freedom in Slavery's Borderland* (New York: Celadon Books, 2023)

Siebert, Wilbur H. *The Underground Railroad from Slavery to Freedom* (New York: MacMillan & Co, 1898)

Simmons, William J. *Men of Mark: Eminent, Progressive and Rising* (Cleveland: Geo. M. Rewell & Co., 1887)

Slavery Abolition Act of 1833

Smith, John D. ed. *Black Soldiers in Blue: African American Troops in the Civil War Era* (Chapel Hill: University of North Carolina Press, 2002)

Smith, Michael O. "Raising a Black Regiment in Michigan: Adversity and Triumph" in Darlene Clark Hine & Earnestine Jenkins eds., *A Question of Manhood: A Reader in U.S. Black Men's History and Masculinity*, Vol. I (Bloomington: Indiana University Press, 1999)

_____. *The First Michigan Colored Infantry: A Black Regiment in the Civil War* (Wayne State University, M.A. Thesis, 1987)

Smythe, Mabel M. *The Black American Reference Book* (Englewood Cliffs: Prentice-Hall, 1976)

Snodgrass, Mary Ellen. *The Underground Railroad: An Encyclopedia of People, Places, And Operations*, Vol. One (Armonk: Sharpe Reference, 2008)

South Carolina Department of Archives and History

Souvenir Program, Marker Unveiling Ceremonies, Memorial to First Michigan Colored Regiment, 102nd United States Colored Troops, Army Infantry Volunteers, Duffield School Ground, Sunday, May 19, 1968—4:30 P.M.

Spencer, Edward. "Confederate Negro Enlistments" in *The Annals of the War* (Philadelphia: Times Pub. Co., 1879)

State of Michigan, Journal of the Senate, 94th Legislature, Regular Session of 2008

Statutes at Large, I

Stephenson, William W. Jr. "For a True System of Free Schools Should Afford Equal Opportunities For All." Integration of the Detroit Public School System During the Period, 1839-1869" in *The Negro History Bulletin*, Vol. 26, No. 1, Oct. 1962

Still, William. *The Underground Rail Road: A Record of Facts, Authentic Narratives, Letters, &c.* (Philadelphia: Porter & Coates, 1872)

Stocking, William. "Slavery and the Underground Railroad" in Clarence M. Burton ed., *The City of Detroit, Michigan, 1701-1922*, Vol. I (Detroit: S.J. Clarke Pub. Co., 1922)

Successful Men of Michigan: A Compilation of Useful Biographical Sketches of Prominent Men (Si. U. Collins, 1914)

Tanner, Robert G. *Stonewall in the Valley: Thomas J. "Stonewall" Jackson's Shenandoah Valley Campaign, Spring 1862* (Garden City: Doubleday & Co., 1976)

Taylor, Clarence. *The Black Churches of Brooklyn* (New York: Columbia University Press, 1994)

Taylor, Paul. *"Old Slow Town": Detroit During the Civil War* (Detroit: Wayne State University Press, 2013)

Third U.S. Decennial Census

Tripler, Charles S. & George Curtis Blackman. *Hand-Book of the Military Surgeon* (Cincinnati: Robert Clarke & Co., 1861)

Trudeau, Noah Andre. *Like Men of War: Black Troops in the Civil War, 1862-1865* (Boston: Little, Brown & Co., 1998)

Tucker, Veta Smith. *A Twenty First Century History of the 1847 Kentucky Raid* (Kalamazoo: Fortitude Graphic Design & Printing, 2010)

———. "Forging Transnational Networks for Freedom: From the War of 1812 to the Blackburn Riots of 1833" in *A Fluid Frontier: Slavery, Resistance, and the Underground Railroad in the Detroit River Borderland* (Detroit: Wayne State University Press, 2016)

Turlay, Karen. "Michigan's Soldiers' Aid Societies: Heroines of the Homefront" in *Michigan History*, Vol. 95, No. 5, Sep./Oct. 2011

U.S. Constitution

U.S. War Department, Adjutant General's Office, *Official Army Register of the Volunteer Force of the United States Army for the Years 1861, '62, '63, '64, '65*, Part VIII (1867)

———. *Atlas to Accompany the Official Records of the Union and Confederate Armies, 1861-1865* (Washington: Government Printing Office, 1891-1895)

———. *General Orders, Adjutant General's Office, for 1863* (Washington: Government Printing Office, 1864)

———. *Index of General Orders, Army of the Potomac, 1861* (Headquarters Printing Office, 1862)

Vanacker, Matthew J. *Lansing and the Civil War* (Charleston: The History Press, 2023)

Voegeli, V. Jacque. *Free but Not Equal: The Midwest and the Negro During the Civil War* (Chicago: University of Chicago Press, 1967)

Wallace, Matt H. "Bittersweet: Black Virginians in Blue at the Battle of Honey Hill and Beyond," John L. Nau Center for Civil War History, University of Virginia

The War of the Rebellion: A Compilation of the Official Records of the Union and Confederate Armies (Washington: Government Printing Office, 1881-1901)

Washington, Booker T. "Two Generations Under Freedom" in *The Outlook*, Vol. 73, No. 6, Feb. 7 (New York: Outlook Company, 1903)

Washington, Margaret. "'I Am Going Straight to Canada': Women Underground Railroad Activists in the Detroit River Border Zone" in Karolyn Smardz Frost & Veta Smith Tucker eds., *A Fluid Frontier: Slavery, Resistance, and the Underground Railroad in the Detroit River Borderland* (Detroit: Wayne State University Press, 2016)

Webster, Noah. *A Dictionary of the English Language* (New York: N. & J. White, 1833)

Webster, Rachel Jamison. *Benjamin Banneker and Us: Eleven Generations of an American Family* (New York: Henry Holt & Co., 2023)

Williams, Frederick D. *Michigan Soldiers in the Civil War* (Lansing: Michigan Historical Commission, 1960)

Williams, George W. *A History of the Negro Troops in the War of the Rebellion 1861-1865* (New York: Harper & Bros., 1888)

_____. *History of the Negro Race in America from 1619 to 1880: Negroes as Slaves, as Soldiers, and as Citizens* (New York: G.P. Putnam & Sons, 1885)

Willis, Deborah. *The Black Civil War Soldier: A Visual History of Conflict and Citizenship* (New York: New York University Press, 2021)

Wilson, Benjamin C. "Kentucky Kidnappers, Fugitives, and Abolitionists in Antebellum Cass County Michigan" in *Michigan History*, Vol. 60, No. 4 (1976)

Wilson, Joseph T. *The Black Phalanx: A History of the Negro Soldiers of the United States in the Wars of 1775-1812, 1861-'65* (Hartford: American Pub. Co., 1888)

Woodford, Frank B. *Father Abraham's Children: Michigan Episodes in the Civil War* (Detroit: Wayne State University Press, 1961)

Woodward, W.E. *Meet General Grant* (New York: Literary Guild of America, 1928)

Yacovone, Donald ed. *Freedom's Journey: African American Voices of the Civil War* (Chicago: Lawrence Hill Books, 2004)

Yee, Shirley J. *Black Women Abolitionists: A Study in Activism, 1828-1860* (Knoxville: University of Tennessee Press, 1992)

Yurgalite, Karren. "The Frances Harper Inn: A Home for Black Women" in *Chronicle*, Vol. 46, No. 2, Summer 2023

Index

1st Michigan Colored Regiment, 27, illustration 1, 108–165
1st Michigan Infantry, xxxi, 55, 75
1st Michigan Light Artillery, 38n
2nd Michigan Infantry, 75
8th Michigan Infantry, 76, 127, 127n
13th Amendment, xxii, 53, 168
14th Amendment, xxii, 170
54th Massachusetts Volunteer Infantry, illustration 6, 110, 201
102nd U.S. Colored Troops, xxvii, illustration 9, 185, 200
160th anniversary, xxxii
1863 Detroit riot, xxxii, 79–103

abolitionism, 7n, 8, 11, 18n, 160, 210–211
Adrian, 7, 23, 71, 120, 214, 219, 219n
Afric-American Female Intelligence Society, 160
African American Civil War Memorial, 178
African American POWs, 114
African Dorcas Society, 160
Alexander, Lucy, 32
Allen, Jacob, 173
Allen, Robert, 35
Alvord, Henry H., 142, 145, 186
Anderson, G.W., 10, 209
Anderson, O.P., 219

Ann Arbor, 7, 9, 33n, 115, 190, 206, 207
Annapolis, 122, 127–128, 130
Army of the Potomac, 56, 60, 64n, 66, 69, 121
Army of the Valley, 69
Army of Virginia, 69
Articles of Confederation, 16
Artis, Kinchen, 28, illustration 7
Association of Friends for the Aid and Elevation of Freedmen, 163
Augustus, Charles, 175

Baker, Edward, 58
Baldwin, 133–134, 183, 184
Baldwin, Henry, 167
Baltimore and Ohio Railroad, 58, 62
Banks, Elizabeth, 162
Banks, Nathaniel P., 56
Banks, Robert, 7
Banks, Samuel, 164n
Banneker, Benjamin, 173n
Barnes, Henry, 113, 122, 122n, 162
Battle Creek, 28, 73, illustration 7, 114, 162, 175, 187
Battle of Antietam, xxxvi, 75, 75n, 79, 79n
Battle of Ball's Bluff, 57
Battle of Boykins Mill, 149
Battle of Cedar Mountain, 69
Battle of Chancellorsville, 125

Battle of First Bull Run, xxxi, 65
Battle of Gettysburg, 70n, 71, 125
Battle of Honey Hill, illustration 10, 137–155, 183, 184–185, 185n, 186–189, 190, 201–202
Battle of Winchester, 65–70
Beaufort, illustration 14, 123, 133, 135, 137, 146, 169, 183, 184, 186, 187, 225
Bennett, O.W., 142
Bennette, Robert, 83, 83n
Bethel A.M.E. Church of Ann Arbor, 23n
Bethel A.M.E. Church of Detroit, 161, 161n
Bibb, Henry, 9, 17n, 35, 159
Bibb, Mary, 159
Biddle, Nick, 110
Bigelow, Isaac J., 9
Bingham, Kinsley, 44–45, 51
Birney, James G., 43
Blackburn Riot, 20, 20n
Blair, Austin, 45, 52–53, 55, 60, 80, 109, 109n, 113, 115–116, 125, 169
Bloss, Mr., 95
Bon, Parker C., xxix
Bonn, Mrs. Louisa, 84, 87, 91
Boyd, Joshua, 83, 85, 92
Boyd's Landing, 140, 145, 189
Broad River, 138, 140
Brooke, George Mercer, 32
Brooks, Paul W., xxxn
Brown, Henry A., 120
Brown, Horace, 101
Brown, John, xxxiii, 17–18, illustration 12, illustration 13, 200, 208–209, 224
Buchanan, James, 19, 45
Buck, John, 168
Buckner, Thomas, 87, 96
Buffalo, 23, 34
Burley, Robert, 101
Burnside, Ambrose E., 121, 129

Butler, Benjamin F., 74, 217
Butler, Henry F., 214

Cahill, Edward, 171
Caldwell, James, 111, 162
Calhoun, John C., 7
California, 15, 38
Caliman, Sarah Jane, 173
Cameron, Simon, 73–75
Camp Ward, xxvii, 115, 118, 162
Canal Lock No. 22, 60
Canandaigua, 34, 124
Capitol, xxxv, 3, 36, 37, 38, 40, 41, illustration 4, illustration 15, 169, 201
Capitol Park, 40–42
Carolinas Campaign, xxviii, 148
Carter, William H., xxix
Cass, Lewis, 15, 45
Cass County, 21, 110n, 118, 120, 157, 207
Cassopolis, 115, 117, 118, 120
Catoctin Mountain, 62
Chain Lake Baptist Church and Cemetery, 22
Chandler, Zachariah, 45, 52, 109
Charles H. Wright Museum of African American History, illustration 12, 223, 224
Charleston, xv, 43, 46, 54, illustration 9, 111, 125, 128n, 129, 139, 143, 148, 149, 151, 169, 172, 175, 184, 186, 187, 188, 190, 191, 198
Charris, Eugene, 120
Chase, S., 10
Chesapeake and Ohio Canal, 58
Chillicothe, 34
Chipman, Henry C., 123, 124
Chipman, Henry Laurens, illustration 8, 122–126, 129, 140, 147, 149, 150, 151, 153, 184, 191, 192
Chipman, Laura, 124, 125

Chipman, Martha, 123, 124
Christian Industrial Club, 161
Cincinnati, 34
Civil Rights Act, 170
Civil War Centennial, xvi–xviii, xxxiv, 178, 221–222
Civil War Sesquicentennial, xviii, 223–225
Clark, Ephraim, 85, 85n, 94
Clark, Newcom, 128n
Cleveland, 34, 56, 152, 219
Coats, Noyce, 207
coffee, 59, 68, 191
Colman, Lucy, 164n
Colored Ladies' Soldier's Aid Society, 119
Colored Masons, 167
Compromise of 1850, 15
Comstock, Darius, 41
Conant, Shubael, 8
Confederate States of America, 43, 48, 49, 51, 53, 114, 154
Constitution of 1835, 4, 7, 40, 52
Convention of the Colored Citizens of Michigan, 35, 35n, 46
Convention of Radical Political Abolitionists, 17
"The Cook's Creed," 60
Coosawatchie, 139, 146
Cowles, Edwin W., 8
Cuckwold's Creek Bridge, 183
Cumberland, 61, 64, 66
Currie, Edgar C., 222, 222n
Curtis, James, 148

Dale, Marcus, xxix, 83–85, 89
Dannals, Charles, 63
Darnestown, Md., viii, 56, 57, 64
Daughters of Union Veterans of the Civil War, 173, 174
Davis, Jefferson, 51, 80, 139, 199
Davis, S.H., 10
de Baptiste, George, 17, 170, 219

Declaration of Independence, xxxvi, 16, 45, 46, 49, 54n
Declaration of Sentiment and Resolves, 208–210
Democratic Party, 44, 46, 83
Department of the Potomac, 56
Derrick, Alford, 35
Detroit, xi, xix, xxii, xxiii, xxvii, xxviii, xxix, xxxii, xxxiii, xxxiv, 3, 4, 6, 7, 9, 15, 17, 17n, 18, 20–22, 27, 30, 31, 32n, 34–36, 38–40, 55, 56, 59, 62, 63, 69, 70, illustration 16, 82, 98, 101, 103, 112, 118, 120, 123–125, 135, 152, 153, 159–162, 167, 170, 171, 173, 174, 177–179, 186–188, 190, 198, 200, 202, 203, 206, 213, 214, 218–220, 222–224, 226
Detroit Advertiser and Tribune, 72, 108
Detroit Anti-Slavery Society, 7
Detroit Association of Colored Women's Clubs, 161n
Detroit Female Benevolent Association, 160
Detroit Free Press, 72, 76, 80, 82, 173, 224
Detroit Liberty Guards, 72
Detroit Light Guard, 56, 125
Detroit Public Library, 41
Detroit River, xxii, xxiii, xxix, 20, 31, 37, 40, 41, 157
Devaux Neck, 146, 183
Dolarson, George W., 39, 171
Dollarson, Maria (Fletcher), 29, 30, 39
Dollarson, William, x, xi, xix, xxii, xxx, xxxi, xxxii, 18, 27–39, 55–70, 79, 79n, 82, 103, 109, 170–172, 179
Douglas, Stephen A., 15, 46
Douglass, Frederick, 8, 17–19, 72, illustration 12, illustration 13, 111, 200, 214, 224

Dred Scott, 16, 23, 32
Drury, Ann Elizabeth, 38n
Dunbar, Alexander T., 33
Dwight, Edward Joseph Jr., 174n, 175n

Edwards Ferry, 57
Ellsworth, Elmer E., xxxi, 144
Elmwood Cemetery, xxii, 27, 28, illustration 3, 124, 126, 218
Emancipation Proclamation, 17n, 75, 79, 162, 201, 223
Enrollment Act of 1863, 80, 82, 108n, 120
equal rights, 114, 162, 170, 172, 222, 224
Evans, Richard, 94

Fairbanks Post, 203, 206
Faulkner, Thomas, 83, 83n, 94
Female Literary Association, 160
Ferguson, Joseph, 17, 220
Ferguson, William Webb, 200–201
Ferguson v Gies, 172, 200
Finney, Jared W., 171
Finney, Seymour, 37, 38, 41, 70
Finney Hotel barn, 37, 40, 41
First Confiscation Act, 74
First Michigan Infantry Brigade, 55
Fish, Elijah Staunton, 9
Fletcher, C., 101
food preparation, xxxii, 29, 59, 66
Foote, Charles C., 17, 17n
Forrest, Nathan Bedford, 131, 138
Fort Pillow, 131, 204
Fort Sumter, 43, 54, 55, 58, 71, 74, 79
Fort Wagner, 110, 111, 175, 204
Fort Wayne, xxix, 55, 225
Fort Welles, 132
Forth, Elizabeth Denison, 158–159
Forth, Scipio, 159
Fowler, William, 175
Frances Harper Inn, 161

Frederick, 58, 61, 62, 62n
Fredericksburg, 31, 32, 218, 219
Free Discussion and Anti-Slavery Society, 9
Free Soil, 43, 44, 46
Freedmen's Village, 164
Fremont, John C., 45
Front Royal, 67, 69
Fugitive Slave Clause, 47
Fugitive Slave Law of 1850, 14, 36

Garrison, William Lloyd, 9
"The Gateway to Freedom," 42, 174
General Orders No. 143, 113
General Orders No. 252, 114
Georgetown, 149, 150, 184
Gifford, Catharine, 30
Gillam, Andrew, 120
Gillmore, Quincy A., 134n
Gordon, Richard, 35
Gorton, Dr., 102
Grahamville, 140, 141, 143, 146
Grand Army of the Republic building, 173
Grant, Ulysses S., 129, 129n, 138, 220
Grosse Ile, 159
gunboats, 139, 143

Halleck, Henry W., 138
Hamilton, Edward Norton Jr., 178n
Hamtramck, 38
Hancock, 64
Harberd, E., 89
Harlan, John Marshall, 24n
Harmonia, 162
Harper, Frances Ellen Watkins, 161
Harpers Ferry, 18, 58, 208
Harris, H.P., 214
Harrison, William Henry, 175
Harrisonburg, 67
Hartwell, Alfred S., 141–144, 185
Hatch, John P., 133, 143, 184, 184n, 185n

Haviland, Laura Smith, 23, 160, 227
Hill, Bennett H., 118
Hillsdale, 170
Hilton Head Island, 123, 126, 129, 132, 139, 183
Hollings, Celestine, 173
Holton, Thomas, 97
Houston, Lewis, 83, 90, 92
Houston, Solomon, 83, 90, 92
Hover, Ellen, 83
Howard, Jacob M., xxii, 168
Howe, Zimri H., 207
Hoyt, Othello P., 35
hurricane season, 137n

Ingersoll, Mr./Mrs., 102
Ingham County, 168, 172

Jackson, Henry, 35
Jackson, John, 17
Jackson, Michigan, 35, 43, 45, 115, 117, 170, 186, 187, 206
Jackson, Thomas J., 65, 67, 68, 69
Jackson Weekly Citizen, 112n
Jacksonville, 133, 135, 184
Johnson, James W., 219
Johnson, Noel, 211–213
Johnson, William H., 111
Joint Committee on the Conduct of the War, 131
Jones, Mrs. Mary, 100
Jones, William, 101

Kalamazoo, 110n, 115, 117, 118, 140, 175, 187, 206
Kalamazoo Theological Seminary, 23
Kansas-Nebraska Act, 15
King George County, 31
King William County, 32

Lacey, Samuel, 31–32
Lady Elgin, 39
Lambert, William, 7, 17, 35, 220, 227

Larned, Jane, 39
Leatherman, John, 175
Lee, Robert E., 31, 69, 139
Lenawee County, 41, 110
Lett, Acquilla, 172–173
Lett, D.G., 10
Lett, Jemima (Banneker), 173
Lett, Samuel, 173
Lewis, Arnold C., 64
Lewis, John, 71
Liberty Party, 17n, 43
Lightfoot, Madison J., 8, 35
Lincoln, Abraham, xvi, xxii, xxxi, 45, 46, 53, 54, 55, 71, 73, 75, 76, 79, 80, 82, 114, 134, 148, 150, 151, 162, 164, 198, 201, 202, 204
Lindsay, A.E., 142, 145, 187
Logan, Samuel Jr., 223
"Lost Cause," 149n
Luce, Cyrus, 172

Mackinac Island, 38n
Madry, Jesse W., 142
"March to the Sea" campaign, xxviii, 137, 150
Marshall, 7, 35, 115, 117, 211–214
Martin, Betty, 119
Martin, Cyrus F., 120
Mason County, 44
Mason's Island, 163, 164
Mathews, Mary, 99
May, Charles S., 117
McClellan, George B., 56, 61, 66n, 67, 69
McLaughlin, Simon, 128
Medal of Honor, xxviii, 154, 185n, 201, 202, 221
Memorial Highway, illustration 11, 226, 226n
Mexican-American War, xxx, 32, 39, 55, 64, 108, 184n
Michigan, statehood, 3, 4, 13, 20, 22, 37, 40

Michigan Central depot, 153
Michigan Chronicle, 223, 224
Michigan Civil War Centennial Observance Commission, xvii, xxxiv
Michigan Historical Commission, xxviiin, xxxiii, 177, 223
"Michigan Outfit," 63
Michigan Progressive Friends, 162
Michigan Soldiers' Aid Society, 125
Michigan State Equal Rights League of Colored People, 219
Michigan Territorial Library, 40
"Michigan's Own Dred Scott Case," 158
military draft, 80
Militia Acts, 74
Miller, Debraire, 173
Miller, G.P., 73
Mississippi River, xxiii, 15, 34, 131
Missouri Compromise of 1820, 15
Mitchell, Robert A., 174
Monocacy River, 61, 62
Monroe, William C., 10, 17, 35
Montague, Calvin S., 140
monthly pay, 130
Morton, Mr., 97
Muddy Branch, Md., viii, x, xi, 57, 60
Munroe, James, 175
Muskegon, 175n

Nankin Township, 210
Natchez, 33
National Association of Colored Women's Clubs, 161n
National Convention of Colored Men, 214–219
National Equal-Rights League, 214, 219
National Underground Railroad Network to Freedom, 28, 64, 159, 175
Nelson, Wilbur, 126, 130, 133, 150, 151, 151n

New Orleans, 32, 33, 108, 173
Nichols, D.B., 163
Niles, 110n, 115, 117, 118
Northern Neck, 31
Northwest Ordinance of 1787, 4, 7, 40, 168
nurses, xxiv, 158

Oakland County, 9, 33n, 34, 169
Ohio River, 34, 178
"Old Glory," 54
Old Northwest, 6
Old State Capitol, 36
Olmsted, Frederick Law, 27
Ordinance of Secession, 46

Parker, George H., 214
Paul, B.D., 219
Pearce, Lewis, 95
Peninsula Campaign, xxx
Perry, Rufus Lewis, 23
personal liberty law, 20, 20n
Pittman, James, 56, 125
Pittman, Samuel Emlen, ix, 56, 62, 63, 69, 79
Pocotaligo, 138, 184
Pontiac, 9, 34, 159, 187, 207
Pope, John, 69
Porter, A.L., 8
Porter, George F., 8
Potter, Edward E., 143, 149, 184, 185, 185n, 192, 195–197
Power, Nathan, 9

racial stereotyping, 177
Ray, Asher, 37
Republican Party, 15, 38n, 44–47, 51, 112, 124, 220
Reynolds, Mrs. Whitney, 84–85, 90–91, 103
Richards, Fannie Mae, 218, 220
Richards, John D., 112, 114, 119, 167, 209, 214, 215, 218, 219–220

Richardson, Israel B., 125
Richmond, 19, 32, 32n, 67, 126
Robert Burns, 32
Roberts, Louisa J., 163
Robertson, John, 113, 125
Romney, George, 177, 223
Rose, Silas, 15
Royal Oak, 36, 179
Russell, Clark G., 207
Russell House, 63
Russell, John, 120

Said, Nicolas, 202
Savannah, xxviii, 50, illustration 9, 137–139, 141, 143, 146–149, 155, 184, 190
Savannah and Charleston Railroad, 138, 184
Second Baptist Church of Ann Arbor, 23
Second Baptist Church of Detroit, 10, 17, 34, 71, illustration 5, 108, 161, 177, 208
Second Confiscation Act, 75
Seven Days Battles, 69
Shafter, William Rufus, 221
Sharpsburg, 79
Shaw, Robert Gould, 110n, 122, 123, 204
Sheley, Alanson, 38, 38n
Sheley, George A., 38n
Shenandoah Valley, xxx, 65, 67
Sherman, Thomas W., 73, 74
Sherman, William T., 135, 137, 138, 143, 144, 146, 148–151, 155
Signal of Liberty, 9, 226–227
Sims, George R., 35
Singleton, Benjamin, 98
Singleton's Plantation, 183, 184
slavery, xviii, xix, xxi, xxii, xxiii, 4–8, 13, 15, 18, 21, 30, 36, 40–42, 43, 44, 47–51, 54, 56, 64, 66, 79, 107, 123, 154, 161, 168, 169, 170, 173, 174, 176, 178, 199, 201, 203, 208, 209, 210–211, 212, 213, 214–216, 221, 222n, 224, 226, 227
Slavery Abolition Act of 1833, 174n
slave-trade, 5, 15, 44, 54
Sleight, William E., 147, 189–200
Smith, Andrew Jackson, 201–203
Smith's Landing, Arkansas, 34
Sons of Union Veterans of the Civil War, 174
Special Orders No. 117, 121
Spring Hill, 183
Springwells, 38
St. Joseph County, 21n
St. Matthew's, 161
Stanton, Edwin M., 113
Starks, Daniel, 120
State Library, 40
State Military Board, 55
Stephens, Alexander H., 49–50
Sterling, William, 120
Steward, Robert, 8
Stuart, Charles E., 45
Sullivan, officer, 95, 99
Sumnerville Cemetery, 22
Sumterville, 183
Swift Creek, 183

Taney, Roger, 16, 32
Taylor, John, 168–170
Taylor, J.R., 207
Territory of Michigan, 3, 6, 13, 37, 124
Thairs, Mr., 91
Thanksgiving, 59, 61, 162
Thomas, George H., 221
Thompson, Charles W., 32n
Tillifinny, 146, 184
Titus, Frances, 162
Tripler, Charles Stuart, 118, 119n

Troy, William, 10
Truth, Sojourner, 8, 111, 114–115, 161–164
Tubman, Harriet, 8, 8n, 162

Ulrich, Victor, 63
Uncle Tom's Cabin, 15
Underground Railroad, xi, xxi, xxiii, xxxiii, 11, 13, 21, 28, 29, 32n, 37, 40–42, 56, 63, 159, 170, 174, 179, 218, 227
Union Church, 23n
Union League Club of New York City, 137
U.S. Constitution, xxii, xxxvi, 6, 14n, 16, 24, 47, 53, 167, 168, 220, 221, 222n
U.S. Navy, 75n, 124

Van Buren County, 172, 173, 207
Vandalia, 22

Walker, Jonathan, 174n
Waring, William, 110n, 119
Warrenton, xxx, 70
Washtenaw County, 21, 35, 37
Wayne County, 9n, 21, 63, 120, 124, 220, 222n, 226
weather, 60, 66, 70, 153
Webb, William, 17, 200, 209
Weekly Anglo-African, 158
Westmoreland County, 31
Whig Party, 43, 44, 124

Whitby, Tyrell, Beulah, 222
White, Juanita, 222–223
White Pigeon, 21n
Whittelsey, Henry M., 56
Wilkins, William D., ix, 56, 63, 65, 69, 125
Willcox, Orlando B., xxxi, 125
Williams, Alpheus Starkey, viii, ix, x, xi, xix, xxx, xxxi, xxxii, 31, 39, 55–70, 79, 125
Williams, Charles Larned, 56, 57, 59, 63
Williamsport, 58, 65
Wilson, Frederick, 96
Wilson, Willis R., 17, 35
Winchester, 65, 67–70
Windsor, 17, 20, 174
Wise, Henry A., 19–20
Wisner, George W., 9
Wisner, Moses, 19, 20, 20n, 45
Withington, William D., xxxi
W.K. Kellogg House, 175n
women, xvii, 18, 157–165
Wood, Obadiah C., 72
Woodward, Augustus, 159
Woodward Plan, 40
Wurtz, Alexander, 127, 127n
Wynn, Waltham G., xxx

York, George, 120
Ypsilanti, xxviiin, xxix, 72, 115, 120, 175, 186, 187, 227

Acknowledgments

Grateful appreciation is expressed by the editor to the following, among others: fellow Board members of the Michigan Civil War Association for their dedication to the cause and support of this publication series; Margaret O'Brien and Matt Vanacker for continuing their invaluable thematic guidance, research assistance, and manuscript reviews; Brian James Egen for his stalwart and inspirational leadership; historian Michael O. Smith and David Ingall for research assistance; Bryan Cheeseboro of the National Archives for his review and assistance; the excellent and earnest staff at the Plymouth District Library for "MeL" and other assistance; and Dr. Marty Hershock, whose guidance has been invaluable in this series and whose insights and judgment particularly improved this volume. And, as expressed in 1859 by the Second Baptist Church, for "the help of Almighty God."

www.ingramcontent.com/pod-product-compliance
Lightning Source LLC
Chambersburg PA
CBHW070325010526
44107CB00004B/413